# Letters of Ring Lardner

Caricature for *Vanity Fair* (1925) by Miguel Covarrubias

# LETTERS OF
# RING LARDNER

EDITED BY CLIFFORD M. CARUTHERS

WITH A FOREWORD BY RING LARDNER, JR.

ORCHISES

*WASHINGTON*

1995

Copyright © 1979 and 1995 Orchises Press

**Library of Congress Cataloging-in-Publication Data**

Lardner, Ring, 1885-1933
   [Correspondence. Selections]
   Letters of Ring Lardner / edited by Clifford M. Caruthers ; with a foreword by Ring Lardner, Jr.
     p. cm.
   ISBN 0-914061-52-6 : $29.95
   1. Lardner, Ring, 1885-1933—Correspondence. 2. Authors, American—20th century—Correspondence.  I. Caruthers, Clifford M., 1935-   . II. Title.
PS3523.A7Z48  1995
818'.5209—dc20
   [B]                                                                     94-42459
                                                                                        CIP

SOURCES OF PHOTOGRAPHS

Ring Lardner, Jr.: front wrap, 5, 10, 19, 26, 28, 29, 30; Roger Lathbury: 1, 2, 7, 9, 11, 13, 14, 15, 16, 17, 18, 19, 20, 23, 24, 25, 27; Fort St. Joseph Museum (Niles, Michigan): 3, 4; Donnelley Library of Lake Forest College: 6; Library of Congress: 12; The Newberry Library (Chicago) 8.

———

An earlier version of this book was published in 1979 by Walden Press under the title *Letters from Ring*.

———

*Manufactured in the United States of America*

Orchises Press
P. O. Box 20602
Alexandria
Virginia
22320-1602

G6E4C2A

# Contents

*Foreword by Ring Lardner, Jr.  iii*

*Introduction  v*

*Acknowledgements  xiv*

*Editorial Preface  xv*


The Courtship Years  *1*
*1907-1911*

Years of Fruition  *95*
*1911-1926*

Years of Adversity  *203*
*1926-33*


*Index  289*


*A section of photographs follows page 140*

# Foreword

My father was not a frugal man, and it was not to save money that he refrained from buying carbon paper in a time when that was the only means of retaining a copy of what you wrote. The story has been told many times of how the first collection of his short stories had to be assembled by copying them from old magazines in a library. It would have been even more out of character for him to keep copies of his own letters. Prudent people generally make carbons or photocopies nowadays, of at least their important business letters, filing them away against tax audits and other contingencies. There were no files in my father's workroom, and no place but a wastebasket for incoming letters once he had read them.

He received a good deal of mail every day, and he read it all except the junk mail. Some of it gave him material for his daily column in the Chicago *Tribune* and later his weekly nationally syndicated feature. He tried to answer most of the requests for advice from aspiring writers, even the most pathetic ones; only after illness made sitting at the typewriter an ordeal did he begin to delegate some of these chores to my brother John when John was around to perform them. Always a family man, he kept in close touch with his relatives in the Middle West, especially his sister Anne Tobin and her family. He wote separate letters to as many as three sons away at school at the same time; only in the last couple of years when he was addressing four of them plus a nephew did he resort to a "round robin" to cover us all with the same effort.

He also wrote letters to and in behalf of a number of comparatively obscure friends from his home town and the early Chicago years. And he carried on intermittent correspondence with some of the most famous names in literary and theatrical circles of his day. The mail from both these groups suffered the same fate. Letters from Mencken and Nathan, Kaufman and Woollcott, Laurette Taylor and Claudette Colbert, all went as inexorably into that wastebasket as those with no autograph value. Not one letter was saved from Scott Fitzgerald's side of the most prolific and sustained correspondence Ring Lardner ever conducted outside the family.

Most of the recipients of his letters, including his sons, were not much better than he was about keeping them. His publishers kept theirs, of course, in designated file folders, and so did a critic and literary historian, Burton Rascoe. Fitzgerald, who preserved report cards and prom programs, held on to all of his. My mother didn't quite match that percentage, especially during the first couple of years of their courtship, but she saved so many that in number and length they formed the overwhelming bulk of the material available to Dr. Caruthers.

Thus a comprehensive or even a truly representative collection of Lardner letters could not be achieved. On the other hand, that's a practical goal only with a man who made and kept copies of all his personal letters. When a writer does that, you have to suspect that he wrote them with posterity as well as the recipient in his mind. One thing you can be sure of in my father's case is that he didn't dream you or any other third party would ever read these words of his. It never even occurred to him, when he started selling short stories, that they would survive their issues of the *Saturday Evening Post*.

—RING LARDNER JR.

# Introduction

## I

In addition to the newspaper columns that established him nationally as a humorous, sometimes sardonic commentator on post-World War I values, Ring Lardner wrote a few plays, some popular song lyrics, and about a hundred short stories dealing with elemental human dreams and frailties. More than sixty years later, Lardner's fictional characters still reflect the struggles of Americans limited by circumstances, environment, inadequate education, or biological nature, who naively strive for success in an unsympathetic world where morality and kindness frequently go unrewarded.

These performers on Lardner's stage have remained as memorable as any of the characters created by Lardner's contemporaries—including Lewis, Wolfe, Fitzgerald, and Hemingway. Most of Lardner's characters believe as fervently as Fitzgerald's Gatsby in the Great Success Myth. In a post-war era enjoying the pleasures of liquor, the roadhouse, bridge, big money, stock market investments, rampant social climbing, and even more arrogant social snobbery, Lardner's fictional world reminded his contemporaries—as it reminds us—that it takes more than desire to succeed. In his "comic mirror of American illiteracy" (as Carl Van Doren once described the Lardner canon), people ignore their flaws with outrageous rationalizations. Jack Keefe is a prototype of babbitry who never learns, never profits from experience, never alters his approach to problems, never improves his grammar, and never fails to exhibit his egotism, but always assumes that his friend Al will remain sympathetic. Jack never loses a game himself; it is always because of a muffed play, a bad climate, a sore arm, or just an ill wind. Alibi Ike has long been an identifying label in our language: "'I had malaria most o' the season,' says Ike. 'I wound up with .356.'" Other athletes are at best easygoing drifters like songbug Art Graham in "Harmony"; at worst they are dishonest, insensate, brutish, and hopeless.

Significantly, Lardner's fiction features characters speaking the language of the common man. In 1919, H.L.

Mencken was the first to praise Lardner's ear, calling his dialogue "authentic American," and Carl Van Doren followed suit by labeling Lardner a "comic philologist." In an era in which fictional characters still spoke mostly as English teachers wished, Lardner's semi-literates stood out as comic reproducers of realistic American speech, as much as Mark Twain's Mississippi Valley provincials had half a century earlier. Since then, no other American writer—not even Hemingway—has been more widely imitated.

Lardner had developed his ear for realistic language early in his newspaper career, by listening closely to ballplayers, using the words and speech rhythms he heard them use, and spelling those words as the half-educated speakers imagined they might be spelled. The resulting ungrammaticisms of Jack Keefe and his brethren became gold mines of American semi-literacy, to the extent that every baseball novelist since then has been automatically compared with Ring Lardner. Later, it was simple for Lardner to broaden his settings while retaining the voices and character types of the diamond.

Scott Fitzgerald, one of Lardner's closest friends, lamented after Lardner's death that Lardner's fictional world had been limited to "the diameter of Frank Chance's diamond." In fact, Fitzgerald not only ignored the multitude of non-ballplayers about whom Lardner wrote but failed to recognize that the diamond can be a metaphor for life beyond the ballpark. These "players" outside the ballpark exhibit universal ambitions and limitations, and they are no less realistic than their baseball counterparts. The vacuous golden honeymooners are obsessed with railroad timetables. Any of the characters in "A Caddy's Diary" will unhesitatingly cheat rather than admit that someone else is a better golf player. Jim Kendall of "Haircut" escapes his ne'er-do-well existence through cruel practical jokes, while his naive small-town barber can perceive little reality beyond the range of his scissors. Lardner's Broadway producers are nasty-tempered, obsequious, philandering, hypocritical philistines and plagiarists. Mr. Shelton of "Contract" laments that bridge players all feel "God sent them into the world to teach." Lardner's heroines babble on as vacuously about "B.F.s" and "G.F.s." Mabelle Gillespie of "Some Like Them Cold" cannot admit that she has been jilted. She has a new "man friend" herself, who will not permit her to continue her correspondence with Chas. F. Lewis. Edith Dole of "There

Are Smiles" ignores the fact that fast driving can destroy her beauty and end her life.

These larger-than-life boneheads, buffoons, sharpers, gullibles, wise boobs, bickerers, homicidal maniacs, social climbers, and innocents are all entrapped in a tragi-comic, cruel game of life that they will never master. With Keefeian rationalizations, they ignore their incapacities and blunder on in pursuit of their unattainable dreams. Only in "The Maysville Minstrel" does a character realize fully that his own intellectual emptiness prohibits success. After Stephen Gale learns that a water-heater salesman has duped him into attempting to sell his amateurish poems for a dollar a line, he realizes despairingly that there is "nothing he can do about it."

In this quasi-Swiftian world, honesty, kindness, and human sympathy are perhaps implicit ideals, but they are rarely compensated. Even Julie Gregg, one of Lardner's few admirable fictional women (having sacrificed her ambitions to care for her invalid mother in a small midwestern town), ultimately becomes the object of Jim Kendall's most insensitive joke.

The humor with which Lardner often softens his satire has also survived, sometimes in joke tags such as "Shut up, he explained," "You know me, Al," and "Alibi Ike." They have become part of our heritage to the extent that even people who have never read Lardner know of their source. And the voice of Jack Keefe still echoes in radio and television sports commentaries and advertisements delivered earnestly by today's slightly more literate sports heroes. The inanities of popular music were another favorite target for Lardner humor. "My God, what's the difference who marries a lyric writer?" one of the characters in *June Moon* exclaims. And Lardner's parody of Cole Porter's "Night and Day" is nearly as well-known as the original lyrics.[1]

It is especially significant that Lardner's fiction appeals to broad segments of our society. The "slangy sportswriter" that Charles Scribner reluctantly accepted into his stable of authors (at the urging of Max Perkins and Scott Fitzgerald) is still liberally represented in today's anthologies by such short stories as "Haircut," "The Golden Honeymoon," " A Caddy's Diary," "Horseshoes," "Alibi Ike," "Some Like Them Cold," "The Maysville Minstrel," and "The Love Nest." A few years ago, the Public Broadcasting System

---

[1] See p. 264.

American Short Story Series included "The Golden Honeymoon" among its television dramatizations, along with stories by James, Crane, Fitzgerald, Hemingway, and others.

However, the metaphorical overtones of Lardner's baseball diamond are arguably his most significant legacy, for they establish a tradition in literature of the game as metaphor—a tradition within which Bernard Malamud, Mark Harris, Robert Coover, and William Kinsella have notably flourished. In *The Natural*, a homicidal huntress nearly destroys the innocent Roy Hobbs, but he recovers to pursue his dream ("I know I have the stuff and will get there"). Predictably, although glory seems within his reach, his nature dooms him to climactic failure ("I never did learn anything out of my past life, now I have to suffer again"). In *Bang the Drum Slowly*, Harris's "doomeded" semi-literate catcher faces his fatal illness by keeping a book on pitchers for the first time in his career and thereby playing up to his potential in his final season. This modern hero inspires sympathy and new loyalty from his teammates, who subsequently play together well enough to win a world championship. But the novel ends on a typically Lardnerian note, as "Arthur," the pitcher-narrator, deplores the fact that only he of all the teammates attended Bruce Pearson's funeral.

In *The Universal Baseball Association* and *Shoeless Joe*, the diamond metaphor evolves further, into fantasy. *The Universal Baseball Association* traces the imaginary baseball world of J. Henry Waugh (a Prufrockian figure) as it gradually usurps his "real" world and grows into historical, political, and even theological allegory. In this evolution, Damon Rutherford, the rookie phenom struck down by a roll of the dice in year LVI of Henry's game, emerges by year CLVII as a mythic figure whose ritual sacrifice reflects both the renewal of elemental conflicts and a reaffirmation of the "game." In *Shoeless Joe*, reaffirmation includes redemption. The farmer-dreamer-narrator, a more intelligent if no less impractical version of Henry Waugh, whose love of baseball symbolizes the love of all things beautiful and delightful, obeys the voice of "god" (a disembodied baseball announcer) to construct a baseball diamond in the middle of an Iowa cornfield. Obeying the same voice, he "eases the pain" of J.D. Salinger by persuading that writer to accompany him to Iowa, where eventually the outcast Shoeless Joe Jackson and other refugees of his era reappear nightly to play the game on

Kinsella's diamond. There, for believers, "the word of salvation is baseball."

While these novels are all highly original, they are nevertheless heavily indebted to Lardner's fictional world. No one writes in a vacuum, T.S. Eliot has reminded us, and these inheritors of Lardner's literary conventions are prime examples. Lardner remains a significant influence in American literature, in the areas of dialogue and character development, in his scathing yet sympathetic depiction of human despair and intellectual emptiness, and in his artful creation of the baseball setting as metaphor.

## II

Lardner's letters provide substantial insights into his own creative process. In them, we can observe Lardner's private self evolving into the mature personality whose values are implicit in his later fiction. As Lardner experiments "in character" in his early letters, new voices emerge—voices that become personae and narrators later on in his public writing. One must be cautious, however, in extracting Lardner's own values from those implied by what his characters do or say. Lardner's privately stated views sometimes differ from values implied by his fiction. While Clifton Fadiman in 1933 overzealously argued that the vacuousness of Lardner's golden honeymooners reflected the "burning misanthropy" of their creator, Lardner declared in one of his last letters that "I cannot remember ever having felt any bitterness or hatred toward the characters I have written about." The dramatic difference here between a respected critic's interpretation and the author's stated view suggests the validity of Wayne Booth's theory that an "implied author" may often stand between the narrator and the real author, providing value judgments that may or may not be in harmony with the real author's values.

Lardner's letters are also worthy of study for what they reveal about a man who contributed so significantly to American literature. In most of his public writing, Lardner hid behind the masks of his personae. In much of his private correspondence, that mask is nonexistent. We begin to know a man who shunned the public eye but was passionately involved with sports, music, drama, his family, and his friends—friends who included such diverse people as Frank

Schulte, Heinie Zimmerman, Claudette Colbert, Bert Williams, Jack Dempsey, Warren Harding, George S. Kaufman, Scott Fitzgerald, Grantland Rice, and Sherwood Anderson. As a whole, these letters become a kind of epistolary biography, depicting Lardner's sensibilities, his intimate struggles, his remarkable achievements, and his tragedy.

The letters, written over a period from 1907, when he was 22, until his death in 1933, reveal Lardner first as a devoted suitor for a woman he always felt was above him; then as a young sportswriter, covering primarily Chicago baseball; then as a columnist rising to the challenge of writing a daily article of sport-oriented humor for the Chicago *Tribune* (initially at a little less than $3,000 a year); after a move to New York, as a nationally syndicated columnist whose work appeared in over 150 newspapers across the country from 1919 through part of 1927 (during which time he earned up to $30,000 a year from the column alone); secondarily from 1914 on as a short story writer (he appears never to have considered himself primarily a writer of fiction); and finally as a playwright and lyricist of popular songs (always one of his first loves). Lardner's record is one of amazing versatility.

It is of course his relationships with other people, revealed in some depth in these letters, through which we learn more about Lardner's values. Nearly a third of the letters in this volume are courtship letters written to his future wife, Ellis Abbott, over a four-year period before they were married in 1911. Their correspondence provides a nostalgic insight into the manners and conventions of a time quite different from today. The courtship is nearly unique in the degree to which it is literary; only once during the entire four years were Lardner and Ellis in close proximity for any sustained length of time—and then only for a few weeks. But he did court her, with eloquence and wit much beyond that of ordinary love letters, while Ellis played the roles required of a beautiful, intelligent young woman of social and economic prominence in Goshen, Indiana, in the first decade of the twentieth century. These courtship letters also convey the beginning saga of a young man who in 1907 had already been dismissed from five of the thirteen positions he had held since high school, discovering himself by 1911 as a newspaper sportswriter who had begun to see the world with considerable distance and increasing clarity, while he remained morally and philosophically a person of his own time and place.

Relationships with publishers are also exhibited in a number of letters to Hewitt H. Howland of Bobbs-Merrill and, later, to Maxwell Perkins of Scribner's. These two relationships form an interesting contrast. While Lardner's connection with Howland was professional and moderately profitable, it was not particularly stimulating beyond the cordial drinking companionship, while Perkins' praise and continual urging probably did elicit more fiction from Lardner than he might otherwise have written. Lardner had a special respect for the judgment of the man who shepherded Scribner's coterie of such famous writers as Fitzgerald, Hemingway, Wolfe, Stark Young, Struthers Burt, James Boyd, S.S. Van Dine, Marjorie Rawlings, Conrad Aiken, Christine Weston, Will James, and Arthur Train. It was Perkins, at Fitzgerald's urging, who convinced Charles Scribner that a "slangy sports writer" merited inclusion among Scribner's authors. The correspondence with both editors also reveals the problems that frequently arose in a time when fiction customarily was published in magazines before it was collected in book form. Though Lardner did unquestionably set high standards of accuracy and technical perfection for whatever he wrote, he seems to have cared little about his material once it was sold to a publisher. He rarely kept copies of his manuscripts (Perkins had to obtain back copies or photostats of the magazines in which Lardner's stories had appeared before he could assemble *How to Write Short Stories*) or his books, though magazines paid him as much as $4500 a story, a top price in those days, and *Round Up* sold over 80,000 copies in 1929 alone. Clearly Lardner wrote primarily for money (and was highly successful at it), but he had high standards for both the fiction and the newspaper pieces that he wrote under the pressure of daily deadlines.

The most fascinating letters in this collection are to Scott and Zelda Fitzgerald, mostly written while the Fitzgeralds were in France. From October 1922, when the Fitzgeralds became the Lardners' neighbors in Great Neck, Long Island, the two writers were close friends and heavy drinking companions. It was Fitzgerald who brought Lardner to the attention of Scribner's, much as he later did Ernest Hemingway. Though he felt that Lardner limited his fiction unnecessarily by focusing on the American lowbrow, Fitzgerald was still probably Lardner's greatest admirer. Lardner's letters to Fitzgerald are fascinating not only because of the intimate glimpses they provide of famous literary people but also because Lardner provided Fitzgerald with current gossip, some of it rather sensational, about happenings in New York society. Other famous people to whom Lardner wrote were H.L. Mencken, Burton Rascoe, Theodore Dreiser, George S. Kaufman, and Grantland Rice. Unfortunately, all the letters to Kaufman, with whom Lardner collaborated so effectively on *June Moon*, are lost. But letters to the others have survived. Mencken was one of the first to praise Lardner's fiction, and the two thought alike on many issues. Rascoe was a good friend from Lardner's early days on the *Tribune*. On the other hand, Lardner did not have a high opinion of Dreiser's art because of the imprecision of Dreiser's diction. The brief exchange of letters in early 1932 between the two resulted from Lardner's reportedly having labeled Dreiser "the prince of bad writers," though Lardner vigorously denied having used the phrase. Grantland Rice, whom Lardner had known since his earliest days as a Chicago sports reporter, was probably Lardner's closest friend over a long period of time, though they were contrasts in temperament. Rice was ebullient and positive about the sports world, while Lardner was an analytical critic, but they shared the same interests, became next-door neighbors in East Hampton, and annually took family vacations together in the late 1920s. Lardner's letters to Rice are family letters, because he and Ellis were also devoted to Kate Rice, to her mother and sisters, and to the Rices' daughter, Florence.

The portrait we draw from these letters is neither that of a "half-educated midwestern sportswriter" nor of a bitter hater of mankind. Yet Lardner was to a significant degree a disillusioned man. Though he was always devoted to Ellis and his children, his marriage could not possibly have measured up to the idyllic proportions he imagined repeatedly in his love letters, and he must have blamed himself for the disparity. He had believed totally the myth that marriage to the right woman guaranteed complete reformation, but though he did marry her, he was never able to stop smoking or drinking, and those habits did eventually contribute heavily to his ill health after 1926 and to a relatively early death (at the age of 48). His later letters to Ellis and to his four sons are letters of absolute devotion; yet he must have felt—in the light of those irrational early ideals—that he was at least a partial failure as a husband and a father. Still, he loved his family and his work as a journalist, a fictionist, and a playwright. And he had always enjoyed writing popular song lyrics (even for Florenz Ziegfeld, whom he disliked), though he once wrote that membership in the Lyric Writers Union was "limited to boys and gals who graduated from school at the age of three." He had no faith that virtue and human sympathy in real life would be rewarded in kind, and in his fiction generally they are not. But Lardner never gave up. In the last weeks before he died, he wrote an act and a scene of a play on which be hoped to collaborate with Kaufman. He had spent time in the West on his doctors' advice, in attempts to regain his health, but he continued to grow weaker, and when he returned to East Hampton for the last summer, he must have known that he would never write the longer fictional work that Perkins had urged. Yet he faced death courageously, by going on with his life and his work as long as he could.

Ultimately, this collection of letters illuminates the development of Ring Lardner's creative process, and it reinforces what many have felt was true of Lardner—that in addition to being a great writer he was a man who deplored dishonesty and self-deception and who responded warmly to others who struggled to see clearly amid a world of hostile or indifferent values.

—CLIFFORD M. CARUTHERS

# Acknowledgements

I am grateful to Ring Lardner Jr. for allowing me to publish the Lardner letters and for sharing many documents and much information. Diana Haskell of the Newberry Library aided me by providing copies of the Newberry Lardner holdings. Linda Stoltz Caruthers provided scholarly assistance during the writing of the original book, as did Marydale Stewart Caruthers during this extensive revision. Frank Hamilton, editor of Walden Press, helped me format the original book, and Roger Lathbury, editor of Orchises Press, assisted similarly with the revision.

Other helpful sources include Mrs. Montgomery Ostrander; Richard Lardner Tobin; Mrs. Scottie Fitzgerald Smith; Matthew Bruccoli; the New York Public Library (H.L. Mencken Papers, R.H. Davis Papers, Manuscripts and Archives Division, Astor, Lenox and Tilden Foundations); the Lilly Library of Indiana University at Bloomington; Princeton University Library; the Enoch Pratt Free Library of Baltimore; the Historical Society of Pennsylvania; the William R. Perkins Library at Duke University; Charles Scribner's Sons; Bobbs-Merrill Company; Doubleday and Company; the Purdue University Libraries; the Academic Center Library of the University of Texas at Austin; the University of Washington Library at Seattle; the Charles Patterson Van Pelt Library at the University of Pennsylvania; Mrs. John N. Wheeler; Carol and Tammy Green at the University of Missouri; and the Chicago Historical Society.

In addition to Ring Lardner Jr.'s invaluable *The Lardners: My Family Remembered* (1976), I am indebted especially to three other books. Donald Elder's biography, *Ring Lardner* (1956), contains some otherwise unavailable information drawn from personal interviews with Ellis and John Lardner. Jonathan Yardley's more recent biography, *Ring* (1977), focuses on Lardner's talent as a humorist and re-emphasizes the role baseball played in Lardner's development as a writer. Matthew Bruccoli and Richard Layman's descriptive bibliography, *Ring W. Lardner* (1976), lists all of Lardner's published works, including his newspaper articles.

—C.M.C.

# Editorial Preface

In selecting and editing the major correspondence of Ring Lardner, primary objectives have been to include letters of informational value and to achieve as much continuity and balance in the correspondence as possible. Since the number of extant courtship letters is much greater (and the content more repetitious) than the number of surviving later letters, many more of the early letters have been omitted.

Faithful transcription of the letters has been a goal insofar as it was practicable, but in order to provide for greater readability, the author's directions have been silently followed by omitting words crossed out, by inserting without notation words marked for insertion, and by following superimposed corrections without note. Obviously omitted words or typographical errors have been corrected with a substituted word in brackets.

Punctuation and format have been reproduced with a few exceptions: Lardner's placing of commas and periods either inside or outside quotation marks has been rendered consistent to minimize distraction from content, and Lardner's irregular spacing between words (most of his letters, except for the courtship letters and other early letters to Ellis Abbott's family, are typed) has been altered to achieve regular page margins. Em dashes and en dashes, which were not available on Lardner's typewriter, have been substituted where appropriate in place of single or double hyphens. Words that Lardner or other writers underlined have been italicized. Lardner's signatures have been included (in type), because frequently they indicate the degree of intimacy with the recipient. Printed stationery headings, or portions of them, have also been included where they seemed to be significant. In instances where letters were not fully dated, postmark dates on envelopes or dates derived from the content have been provided in brackets.

Substantial interstitial commentary has been provided for needed transitions or to amplify the subjects at hand. Footnotes further elucidate the text.

—C.M.C.

# The Courtship Years 1907–1911

Most of the surviving letters Ring Lardner wrote before July 1911 are courtship letters to his future wife, Ellis Abbott. The two met in July, 1907, during a marshmallow roast at the home of Lardner's friend Billy Beeson on the St. Joseph River in Niles, Michigan, Lardner's home town. They were probably introduced by Wilma Johnson, a friend of Ellis's, whom Ellis was visiting (and Lardner was dating) at the time. Lardner was immediately attracted to Ellis and pursued her during the following few weekends until she returned to Smith College that fall for her junior year. He then initiated a marathon correspondence that culminated in marriage nearly four years later.

At the time of this first meeting, Lardner was working on his first newspaper job as a reporter for the South Bend *Times*.[1] Ellis, the daughter of a wealthy lumber merchant in nearby Goshen, Indiana, was on her summer vacation from Smith College, located in Northampton, Massachusetts, before beginning her junior year that fall. From the first she obviously enjoyed Lardner's attention and found him a witty if somewhat daunting correspondent. In 1907 Lardner was twenty-two, six feet two inches tall (an exceptional height for that time) and somewhat self-consciously stoop-shouldered, lean, and rather dark-complexioned, with black

---

[1] Lardner's newspaper career would consist of the following associations: Fall 1905–November 1907 with the South Bend *Times*; December 1907–December 1908 with the Chicago *Inter-Ocean*; February 1908–November 1908 with the Chicago *Examiner*; November 1908–November 1910 with the Chicago *Tribune*; December 1910–February 1911 with *The Sporting News*; February 1911–October 1911 with the Boston *American*; December 1911–January 1912 with the Chicago *American* (as copyreader only); February 1912–May 1913 with the Chicago *Examiner*; June 1913–June 1919 with the Chicago *Tribune*; November 1919–March 1927 for the Bell Syndicate; December 1928–February 1929 with the New York *Morning Telegraph*; and February–April 1931 for the Bell Syndicate. See Matthew J. Bruccoli and Richard Layman, *Ring W. Lardner: A Descriptive Bibliography* (University of Pittsburgh Press, 1976) for listings of Lardner's newspaper pieces.

hair and brown eyes. Noting the prominence of his eyes, some of his baseball friends later nicknamed him "Old Owl Eyes." In *The Lardners: My Family Remembered*, Ring Lardner Jr. (Lardner's only surviving son) describes his father's eyes as "gentle and unusually large, with heavy dark brows, his nose so impressively aquiline that when Bob Davis, a well-known columnist and photographer of the twenties did a portrait of him, he captioned it 'the look of eagles.' Most descriptions of him emphasize that he was never seen to laugh; what is literally true is that he never laughed at his own jokes and applied high standards to other people's comedy. But he did laugh at people who amused him."

Ring Lardner Jr. describes Ellis as "a full foot shorter, small-waisted, wide-hipped, medium-breasted. Her hair was brown, her eyes blue, her complexion light. She had a small, straight nose and a full mouth . . . . She laughed easily and her voice had a vibrant quality that added interest to whatever she said. Intended or not, she had a smile and a way of walking that men found provocative."[1]

The following courtship correspondence provides insights into the couple's concerns and values and reflects many conventions of a departed era. Lardner was attracted to Ellis at first sight and wrote to her frequently thereafter (nearly every day for the last year and a half, usually managing some element of wit that makes many of these courtship letters memorable and charming. Ellis responded with considerable wit of her own, though she obviously strained to match Lardner's effusions. These letters exhibit the restrictive and demanding roles that young lovers felt compelled to play in the first decade of the twentieth century.

After indulging in humorous puns on two postcards to Ellis earlier that fall, Lardner initiated the correspondence with the following letter to her in Northampton, recalling in poetry their meetings during the previous July and August. Significantly, Lardner refers to her in this very first letter as "my affinity." The nickname "Rabbits" by which he addresses her is of course a pun upon her name, as his frequent signature "Ringling" or "Ringlets" is a pun upon his own. Ring Lardner Jr. suggests that "Ringlets" may also be ironic,

---

[1] Ring Lardner Jr., *The Lardners: My Family Remembered* (New York: Harper and Row, 1976), pp. 38–39.

because Lardner had begun to lose his hair early—to a considerable extent by his marriage at twenty-six."[1]

South Bend, Third Thursday
[3 October 1907]

Dear Rabbits, listen carefully to what I say to you:
Now, postal cards are all too brief from Ringling's point
    of view;
I met young Ellis Abbott on a warm night in July,
'Twas at a fine marshmallow roast, the St. Joe river by,
The first time that I cast my eyes upon young Ellis fair,
I thought: "It's my affinity who's seated over there
But she and I exchanged few words 'til the next Saturday
When she arrived in old South Bend, to see Grand Rapids
    play.
Next evening, it was Sunday, Sabbath calm was over all
My brother Rex and I at Johnson's paid a friendly call,
But Billy B., right there was he, and I regret to tell
I didn't get a chance to know young Ellis very well
A few weeks passed and then, at last, at the M. C. day-poe
I saw her jump from off a train, which Eastward then
    would go.
On my way home I purposely walked slowly and with ease
In hopes that I might get a chance to chat with Eloise.
The chance, it came, and that same eve I bore her gripsack
    down
Until we reached the Ginseng house—they live quite close
    to town.
At Beeson's house again that night, we had a quiet chat;
Her manner dazzled me 'til I knew not where I was at
And then, next night, Sunday again, we took a quiet roam
And on our way, we burglarized the Trammel Tremble
    home.
A few days later, years it seemed, to Goshen traveled I,
A picnic fair to witness there a pretty dam site by,
And Ellis once again I saw and said goodbye, alas,
For she was just about to go to that Northampton, Mass.,
And now I pray that she'll address a letter long to me
To 225 Piquette Av-nue, care M. Y. Bertole,
Detroit, for on next Sunday night, vacation does begin,
And I am going to the largest town in Michigin.

During his vacation from the South Bend *Times*, Lardner had attended the World Series in Chicago, between the Cubs

---

[1] Ring Lardner Jr., p. 37.

and the Detroit Tigers, where he had met Hugh Fullerton, the popular sportswriter of the Chicago *Examiner*. The meeting was arranged at Lardner's urging by a mutual friend, Arthur Jacks. During the same summer in which he met Ellis, Lardner had ended a first romance with Ethel Witkowsky (Pick),[1] a Jewish girl from Chicago whose family vacationed during the summers at Barron Lake, east of Niles, as did the Lardner family. While his break-up with Ethel and his desire to escape the restrictions of a small town were probably factors in his desire to move to Chicago, it is more likely that his need to advance professionally as a journalist was the main factor. The meeting developed into a test by Fullerton of Lardner's drinking capabilities as well as his baseball expertise, after which Lardner was recommended to and hired by Duke Hutchinson, sports editor of the Chicago *Inter-Ocean*.[2]

In addition to Ethel Witkowsky and Ellis, Lardner was popular with other women. His most significant involvement other than with Ellis appears to have been with Wilma Johnson ("Ginnie," "the ginseng girl," or "Johnny"), the Niles friend who had introduced Lardner and Ellis. The following verse epistle is one of approximately forty existing letters to Ginnie, who had known Ellis when the Johnsons earlier lived in Goshen and had become acquainted with Lardner after the Johnsons moved to Niles. It is probable that Lardner was attracted romantically to Ginnie, as he must also have been to Helen Hawks of Goshen (to whom he also apparently wrote letters during his period, though none has survived). Helen was a close friend of Ruby Abbott, Ellis's older sister, who knew them all well and who testified, many years later, to Ring Lardner Jr., that "each of the others, Ginnie and Helen, privately hoped Lardner's affections would turn to her."[3]

In any case, the friendship between Lardner and Ginnie involved at least a close camaraderie at the time, causing occasional jealousy on Ellis's part.

---

[1] See letter of 11 February 1931 to H. L. Mencken.

[2] Lardner described the meeting with Fullerton in "Caught in the Draft," in the 9 January 1932 *Saturday Evening Post*; the piece has recently been reprinted in Matthew J. Bruccoli and Richard Layman, eds., *Some Champions* (New York: Charles Scribner's Sons, 1976).

[3] Ring Lardner Jr., p. 33.

Lardner often wrote poetry as well as prose to Ginnie, of which the following, in the style of Longfellow's "Hiawatha," is an example. This and much other imitative verse by Lardner demonstrate both his knowledge of poems popular in this period and his sensitivity to poetic forms.

Saturday.
[30 November 1907]

Dear Ginnie,—
To continue in the same strain:

Walter tells me he has written
To my friend, Miss Wilma Ginseng,
Asking said Miss Wilma Ginseng
If her friends at old Lake Forest,
Who attend the Ferry Hall school,
Uttered compliments about us
After we had left the chapel
Where dramatic reads were given
By our old pal, Kuntzey-Baker;
Let me say to Wilma Ginseng:
Nought care I for those unknowns
Or for their opinions of us
Which my friend so boldly asks for—
Only care I what our hostess,
Gracious Peter Wilma Ginseng,
Thinks of me, who all unworthy,
Profited by her great kindness
And was entertained so highly,
Not by sight of unknown maidens,
But by her own gracious presence—
Therefore do not bother, Ginnie,
To inform Old Boy Ringlets
Whether they have cursed or blessed us;
Walter, as is usual with him,
Has to Miss Maud Rogers written
What he wrote he will not tell me,
But I'm betting him the seegars
That she will not deign to answer.
Not a word I've had from Rabbits;
P'rhaps she's angered at what we thought
Was the best one ever dreamed of;
Probably the very best one
That a human ever thought of.
Lonely is the old Boy Ringlets,
Now deprived of daily journeys
To and from the place Lake Forest

5

And the pleasant moments spent there
'Mong the Indians and Miss Ginseng.
Indians made me heap big happy
When they lifted Midway's scale
And rolled little Walter Steffen
All around the grassy meadow,
Till he got himself mixed up with
Loaves of bread, still in their childhood.
Answer Walter if you care to.
Answer me whate'er befalls you.
I'm important—he is nothing.
Anyway, you now are owing
Me two large and full-grown missives.
They will reach their destination
At 4–3–8 North State street, or
At the Inter Ocean office.
I will eagerly await them.
—Yours, half-wittedly, Old Ringlets.

Unfortunately, Lardner's propensity for poetry resulted in the first crisis in his courtship of Ellis. During an evening with Ginnie at Ferry Hall (a girls preparatory school affiliated with Lake Forest College, located about twenty miles north of Chicago), which Ginnie was then attending, the two composed a piece of humorous doggerel, referred to above as "the best one ever dreamed of," and each sent a copy to Ellis in Northampton. Here is an excerpt:

In the wildness of Lac Forest
Far from Knolls and far from kindred
Far from Goshen, Indiana,
But yet not so far from South Bend—
Mid the millionaires and Indians,
Savage Indians from Carlisle,
Training here for bitter warfare,
Warfare with the Midway army;
'Mid the millionaires and Indians
'Biding here along the North shore
Of Lac Michigan's wet waters;
Here I met fair Wilma Ginseng,
Wilma Ginseng, late of Goshen,
Goshen where the wild young rabbits
Chase about in mad carousal
Where the rabbits and the wild hawks
Chase about in mad carousal,
Where the warlike, mammoth rockwells
Cast young rocks down in the oil wells,

Where young R. B. Kelly[1] hailed from,
Who, while fighting for the South Bends,
Tried in vain to boost them upward
From the downward depths of baseball;
. . . . . . . . . . . . . . . . . . . . . . . . . . .
There met I fair Wilma Ginseng,
And we sobbed our very hearts out
That the Rabbits could not be there;
Absolutely, positively,
Sobbed our hearts and sobbed our souls out,
Till police gents hollered to us:
"Sobber up, you rascal Knollsites."

Not surprisingly, Ellis was annoyed at receiving two copies of a poem celebrating an evening with Ginnie. She responded:

> When I received on the same mail twin epistulas I was tempted to wire two telegrams of congratulations, but refrained. Don't do it again and if you write me any more poetry I am going to rebel and never answer your letters as long as I live. So the very next poetry I receive from you I shall understand as a tactful suggestion to whoa Elizabeth— in other words stop.

Some of Ellis's earlier comments suggest that she was also uneasy at responding suitably to Lardner's witty poetry—e.g., "You may have a fertile enough brain to think of a wonderful new poem each time but believe me mine is not fertile enough to coin a new adjective to fit each new one so don't expect it." In a January 1908 letter, she observed: "I think you suffer from Chronic Imagination." But in October 1907, she wrote:

> Your poem, as usual, was the best ever—and the sentiment beautiful. Do you do them extemporaneously or are they studied productions?
> Did you meet your fate on Hallow'een? Perhaps you did not know that Halloween had been but it has

---

[1] Robert Brown "Speed" Kelly was a resident of Goshen and, for the 1909 season only, a major league infielder-outfielder with the Washington Senators. He played in seventeen games. See also Lardner's letters of 29 July 1909.

and I would advise you to examine your past of the last few days.

My fair sister and the Miss Hawks have gone away on a visit so Goshen sees their beaming faces no more—Also Miss Ginseng has gone to Lake Forest, so Niles is doubly bereaved—Perhaps you will meet her in the busy Metropolis, even, it might happen, on Halloween.

Lardner seems to have been genuinely, if somewhat naively, puzzled. He responded by promising: "If you should ask me on bended knee to ship you more of my inimitable verse, I will refuse you with a curse in my throat and sneer in my ear." But he did ask for a picture of Ellis as a Christmas present. She replied:

I am sorry. I did not mean to hurt your poor abused feelings. I won't *ask* you to write any more poetry, but if you *should* I will read it—really I will and gladly, if I did say I wouldn't . . . .

Wilma wrote me about your gay and happy meeting in Lake Forest. I envy you both and was that not prettily said?

A letter to Ellis shortly thereafter refers to an after-Christmas dance in Goshen, at which Ellis was one of several hostesses. Lardner did not attend. It is unclear whether his work prevented attendance, or whether he declined because he did not like to dance. He had been born with a deformed foot and had undergone a corrective operation, after which he had worn a brace on his leg until he was eleven. Though he did not limp, this medical history may have contributed to a distaste for dancing. The "request" that Ellis had ignored was for a photograph. Though Ellis had responded to the earlier queries about the offensiveness of the "Lake Forest piece" with "words of comfort," Lardner cannot quite forget the matter:

[15 December 1907]
Sunday afternoon

Dear Rabbits,—
I have just received an invitation from you to attend a dance in Goshen the 28th. Perhaps you didn't know you sent me one, but you did. You have me very much fussed

over the Christmas surprise, but you paid absolutely not a bit of heed to my request.

I would certainly like to be in Northampton these dismal days, that I might see and hear you perform in your plays; also that I might hear your laugh, which I enjoy even more than Evan Harter's.[1] Which reminds me that I have a trade for you—Wilma Ginseng said you were the best screamer she ever knew. You owe me one. You have blighted my poetic hopes and your kind, but false words of comfort came too late. I have eschewed poetry. Never again will my peculiar pen burst into verse for your or others' eyes. You may have positively, usually done the world a service.

I would like to meet your Evanston room-mate. I will see her on the corner the day after Christmas. Mystery—why do all Goshen girls have Evanston room-mates at college? For the same reason that all the half-witted members of the Lardner family have moved to Chicago.

It staggers me to think that our days of Summer frolic are at an end. All of my vacations in this job will come in the Winter time. While you are roasting marshmallows and others, or are rapping on Tremble's door, or are watching the others cook supper at the dam Goshen, I will be pining away at the near desk, the sweat of my brow mingling with my rapid, vapid tears. Some day, though, you will be in our midst—perhaps even at Evanston. Then I will come and serenade you until you scream as Miss Ginseng says you alone can scream. And the sound of your voice will keep me afloat for another year.

I went to Church this morning, hoping I would see an Abbott. The collection plate cost a dime and I saw nothing.

When do you come home?
R W.L.

Lardner obviously hoped to see Ellis on Christmas day, but his plans were thwarted by an assignment to cover a Yale University basketball game and by uncooperative train timetables. He had to depart from Chicago only fifteen minutes before Ellis arrived from Northampton. Apparently he and Ellis saw each other over the Christmas holidays only long enough for him to give her a Christmas present (in addition to a box of candy he had sent her earlier), after which she departed to Northampton and he returned to his boarding house in Chicago.

---

[1] A member of the Niles circle of friends.

Shortly thereafter, Ellis wrote "admonishing" Lardner for having written a bad story and commenting: "I like to say very mean things to you because I know they don't make the slightest bit of difference." He answered soberly:

Sunday, January 19th

Dear Bunny,—

I realized that my story was bad. You were right about that; but you were wrong about something else—you said you knew it didn't make the slightest bit of difference to me if you said mean things. It does, and you really should know it if you do not. This and another, or two other, reasons prevent me from burdening you with more of my luscious poetry. One reason is that I am not at all sure that you would go back on your threat, but would refuse to answer. The other reason is that I have sworn and hate to break my oath. On one condition will I do so—namely, that you tell me why the Lake Forest effusion failed to please. Both Wilma Ginseng and I thought it was probably the most perfect epic we ever saw. I have never been able to figure what was wrong with it and I am very curious to know.

I think The Chicago American is going to want me soon, strange as it may seem. And if the opportunity comes, I am going to take it, because the reasons why I should outnumber and outweigh the reasons why I should not. This latter class consists almost entirely of my innate aversion to the sheet.

One of my reasons for accepting if I have a chance and do accept, is that it will give me one or two journeys through the East during the coming Spring and Summer. I should consider it extremely fortunate if I were sent to Boston for two or three days— How far is Northampton from Boston? And are Smith girls as much imprisoned as Ferry Hall students?

I am to dine today at a house on Ellis avenue. If it were on any other avenue, I would decline. Is there a Ringlets alley in your old town?

Do you realize that you write grievously short letters? To prove whether or not you like to read mine, I am going to count the words in yours hereafter and then answer with the same number.

Didn't you wish, just a little, that I had written more awful poetry when you told me not to, so that you really could carry out your threat?

Please don't be thoroughly disgusted with this missive. It is caused by my hunch that one Ellis Rabbit is weary of her bargain. If not, my real address is 438 North State street.
>Always,
>Ringlets

This foray into "truth" evoked assurances from Ellis that she wished to continue the correspondence, along with further explanation of her "wrath" at the Lake Forest poem:

> If the only condition to your writing poetry is to explain my apparent wrath I will do so gladly. I did appreciate it—really thought it wonderful—but you see I thought I was getting two, perfectly, good, nice, letters and when I found they were just the same—well you see I just got raging—nasty little spitfire that I am and there was the result. I apoligize. Am I sufficiently humbled?

Though Lardner had been negotiating with the Chicago *American*, he would move on February 1, 1908, to the *Examiner*, where he would become the next in a series of reporters to write under the by-line pseudonym of James Clarkson. He had been recommended for the position by his friend Hugh Fullerton. At a salary of twenty-five dollars a week, he was also one of several reporters struggling at the sports desk with the proofreading or rearranging of stories coming off the wire.[1]

In March, Lardner was assigned to travel with the White Sox; he sent the following "guide" both to Ellis and to Ginnie, and probably to other friends and relatives:

THE ROUTE OF RINGLETS.
Published as a Guide for his genial
Correspondents.
(With carbon copies)

On March 18, young Lardner'll go
Down to the city of N.O.,
New Orleans is the city's name,
A city not unknown to fame.

---

[1] "Eckie," in the 20 February 1932 *Saturday Evening Post* (reprinted in *Some Champions*), describes one of Lardner's experiences with the wire service at this time.

From March 19 to March 2-2,
He'll tarry in New Orleans, Lou.
And then, on March the 23,
He'll sojourn in Montgomery.
From this cute town in Alabam
He'll travel up to Birmingham
And there remain the 24th,
Before proceeding farther north,
To Nashville up in Tennessee,
And there the next three days he'll be.
On 28 and 29,
In burg of Evansville so fine,
On 30th and 31st
In Terre Haute, of towns the worst.
And on fair April's first two days,
In Indianapolis he stays;
In Cincinnati 4 and 5,
And then, my goodness, sakes alive,
To old South Bend he'll go once more
Renew acquaintance made of yore,
The 6th day of the month he'll spend
Among the ruins of old South Bend.
The next three days in cute Champaign,
Eleventh, twelfth in cute Fort Wayne,
And then back to Chicago go,
To stay about ten days or so.
And through this era, do not fail
As follows to address his mail:
"For Mr. Lardner, in the care
Of the White Sox," and b'lieve me, fair
Young correspondents, large and small,
I'm glad to hear from one and all.

 That spring, having heard a rumor that Ginnie had become engaged, Lardner wrote in verse to ask:

Heard some most distressing news
From an old time friend of youse,
Told me Ginnie was engaged
To be married—much enraged
I did shout aloud: "To whom?"
And was answered: "You big Broom,
"What's the difference who he is
"Really, its none of your biz"
. . . . . . . . . . . . . . . . . . . . . .
I, of course, am somewhat peeved
That I was so grossly leaved

Out of your sweet confidence
Please explain, explain at wence.

    Lardner may have been relieved to hear that this rumor was false, but he was about to face a crisis in his pursuit of Ellis. In the spring of 1908, Ellis was enjoying his attention, but she also had other suitors, and she was clearly occupied with her life at Smith College. One of her other admirers was Loring Hoover, whom she invited to her junior prom at Smith. Hoover recently had made a special impression on Ellis, for she wrote to her mother that he was "so much older and more self-possessed and nicer all around than he used to be that I was very pleased with him." The news of Loring Hoover and the junior prom made a lasting impression upon Lardner also, for thirteen years later, on Ellis's birthday in 1921, he amused Ellis with a play he had written reenacting the prom and featuring Hoover as Ellis's date.
    At the time of the prom, Lardner, in his new job with the *Examiner*, was covering the White Sox through spring training on the West Coast, during the preseason exhibitions through the Southeast, and on through the regular season, which began in mid-April. Thus, he had few chances to see Ellis, and he may not have written to her as regularly. If he did, she apparently took less care to save these letters of the spring of 1908. What is clear is that she wrote to him less often during these months, and that it worried him. The extant letters from her to him run about three to four a month early in 1908, but there is only one letter in April, wishing him a happy Easter. The beginning of this letter, postmarked April 19, 1908, suggests tonally that Ellis is more preoccupied with other matters:

>     As you are next on my Sunday afternoon communication list I guess you'll just have to sit still and take all that's a'coming to you. You don't deserve any kind of a letter at all but as I have not a postal card to my name and as I suppose you have been more or less busy, I will just make this a little note to wish you a "Happy Easter."
>     The dreadful thought has just occurred to me that I haven't the least idea where you may be. Why don't you stay in one place? It would be more convenient for your friends and save you a lot of trouble.

The courtship was clearly declining. Five weeks later, Ellis wrote:

> Last week we had our wonderful Junior Prom. And we are all still in the process of recovering. One of the most exciting events of the weeks festivities is to take the man (or men) out to a tea in the orchard and eat ice cream and have a dozen people take your picture at the same time. You see men are such a rarity here the girls want to keep them as long as possible even if only in a picture.

Meanwhile, Lardner described an exciting eleven-inning Sox victory to Ginnie. It seems clear from the tone and content of his letters that Lardner did not regard Ginnie as romantically as he viewed Ellis, but he wrote with ease to Ginnie of baseball dramas and other favorite subjects, while in letters to Ellis he was more self-conscious:

Friday [Chicago, 5 June 1908]

Dear Ginnie,—
Arrived on the home lot this morn, minus baggage and sleep.
Glad to hear that you are coming to our immediate vicinity, but regret to say that there are no Indians at Lake Forest now. However, if you will do some date setting, it would bring me delight to welcome you at our ball yard for the afternoon on your way hither or thither.
I would have been in Kneels yesterday and today, but for an accursed rain in blessed St. Looie on Wednesday, which caused us to spend our off-day at hard labor. But I think I would rather have missed Kneels than that second battle yesterday afternoon, which was probably and absolutely the most passionate I ever saw. Bitterly opposed, as a usual thing, to the talking of shop, yet I must needs give you a brief outline of the amazing happenings. Eleventh inning—score 1 to 1—pitchers, Rube Waddell, demon, for St. Louis; Frank Smith, hoodoo, for Sox. Hahn opened with single; Jones forced him. Davis singled, Jones taking second. Anderson flied to Stone. Two out. Donohue stung to left and Jones scored. Parent out, Waddell to first. St Looie's inning—Ferris singled; Spencer and Criss beat out bunts. Score 2 to 1, bases full of Looies, none out. Cold blast of air blows into press box, striking Ringlets in feet. Manager Jones hastens into infield for consultation. (Wilma Ginseng should know that left-handed batters are usually weak

against left-handed pitchers) Situation—Stone, good left hand hitter, and Hoffman, ditto, coming up. Smith, right hand pitcher in box. Consultation ends. Exit Smith and enter White, good left hand pitcher. Stone, whiff, whiff, whiff. One out—bases still full. Foolish (like a fox) St. Looie manager withdraws Hoffman, left hander, and sends Stephens (not Plowden) right hand hitter to bat. Another consultation. Exit White and enter Walsh—right-handed spitballist. Stephens—whiff, whiff, whiff—Two out—bases still full. But here is James Williams; he who had scored the only St. Looie run with reefo over right field wall. Williams—whiff, whiff—no whiff, no whiff, no whiff. Three balls, two strikes, bases full, two out, one run needed to tie. Zowie—ah, but the ball is reposing in the sumptuous mitt of Jagger Donohue and the chill blains disappear. But believe me, Ginnie, they never got my goat that way in South Bend, Ind.

I realize that this letter is intensely interesting and I don't want to carry it too far.

In regard to your reported betrothal, if I had believed it true, I would have maintained a dignified silence. I know you would consult me before taking so rash a step. I will tell you of the origin of said rumor when we meet.

New route list will be published soon.
In Chicago until 21st of June.*
Ringlets.

*A couplet.

The managerial strategy exhibited in the game described above reflects the kind of baseball that Lardner enjoyed most, rather than the long-ball style that emerged in the 1920s with Babe Ruth and the "TNT" ball.[1] As early as 1911, in some of his Boston *American* pieces, Lardner was deploring the use of what he suspected was a livelier baseball.[2]

By this time he had heard of Loring Hoover and Ellis's junior prom. Uneasily, he wrote the following verse letter to Ellis in mid-July, just after she had returned home from Smith for the summer vacation.

---

[1] See letter to John McGraw of 4 June 1932.

[2] See also letter to Ellis of 15 May 1911.

What, Rabbits have come home to roost?
Is this what you would tell us?
A full-fledged senior now is she,
But still heart-whole and fancy free,
This girl entitled Ellis?

Why no, she brought her trunk back home,
Its each and every part,
Then what was it she left behind?
Her fertile brain, her brilliant mind?
No, just her Goshen heart.

Far East of here she left her heart;
Is that what you would tell us?
Ah, rather had she left her shoes.
Her powder rag, the gum she chews,
This most forgetful Ellis.

What will she do without her heart?
Why that no one can tell us,
And least of all young Ringlets tall,
Why, no, he cannot tell at all,
So peeved is he and jealous.

We've lived full twenty years and more
And nothing e'er befell us
That stung so much as this same news
That she her Goshen heart did lose;
Is't true? Come, tell us, Ellis.

Distressed over the decline of Ellis's interest in him, Lardner tried unsuccessfully to call Ellis from the Goshen train depot during the team's return trip from New York. From Detroit the following Tuesday, he wrote this "pensive note":

Hotel Cadillac
Detroit, Michigan
Tuesday

Dear Rabbit,—
 Realizing that you wont write until I do, and desiring greatly to hear from you once more, I now take advantage of a brief season of rest to tickle you to death with the following pensive note.
 I was in Kneels over Sunday. Wilma Ginseng informed me that you were at Wawasee (if that is close to the way it is spelled). This statement disappointed me beyond expression,

because I had counted on seeing you next Sunday morn. On that day, we (the league leaders and myself) are going through Goshen on the way "home" from Cleveland. I think we pass by about 4:30 A.M. and it would be an easy matter for you to be at the daypo. But, of course, you had to go wandering off in the woods and just because you knew I was coming.

Oh, yes, I was told by a small bug that you came home from Northampton minus a vital organ towit, your heart. So I will know what's the matter if you haven't the heart to write to me any more. But I wish you would relate every detail of the romance to me. Talk to me as you would to your attorney. I can advise you.

You have evidently forgotten that I requested some more poetry from you. I enclose a special telegram. Please answer so I will hear the worst before leaving for the East again. At 438 North State street all next week.

Ringlets

Pardon both brands of stationery.

Clearly enjoying Lardner's attention and his jealousy, Ellis wrote the following letter, which both reassures and withdraws from definite commitment:

Dear Ringer—

I just think you must live in a dreadfully buggy place but you hurt those bugs—they are not safe. You see my heart is a much traveled organ and I think it is now in Chicago . . . .

I cant write you a poem today because it is raining and I *just cant* write rainy poetry. Do you know I think you and I are doomed to just miss each other through the rest of life. When I visit Johnny this summer you will come home the day I leave and when I am in Chicago you will leave the day I come. Isn't it tragic—and I long to see you so! I have a vision that when you are on your honeymoon I will dash past you in an automobile and toot my horn. Will you watch for me?

That letter was sufficient encouragement for Lardner to renew the courtship that summer with vigor. Early in August and on the road again with the White Sox, he also wrote to Ginnie, lamenting in detail his sufferings with the team:

Thursday.
[Philadelphia, Pa.
20 August 1908]

Dear Ginnie,—

    This stationary[1] is used, not because I am an employe of the Hearst papers, but because it is lemon color, my national shade. Being well aware of your ready sympathy and standing in need of it, I append a diary of my wretched existence in Washington, preceding it with the assertion that I will never go there again, except in the event that I am elected to the president's chair.

    Thursday, August 13—Arrived this afternoon, finding the thermometer at 105 in the shade, so sat out in the sun until supper time. Ate supper and became sick immediately afterward. Didn't sleep at all during the night.

    Friday, August 14—The Sox were beaten twice, and by Washington at that; watched the games.

    Saturday, August 15—Game was started at 3:30 o'clock, an hour earlier than usual at Washington. Scribes were all glad, as Saturday is a day when their first story has to be in the office before 6 o'clock. Game went fifteen innings. My story all right up to time and apparently being sent along by operator. Game ended and was informed that not a line had been sent. Tempest followed and usually sweet temper all shot to pieces. Too late for supper, which was a lucky thing, as it would have made me sick again.

    Sunday, August 16—Wrote masterpiece for paper at 6:30 P.M. Called Western Union boy and boy came, bearing away with him the masterpiece. Midnight, wire came from paper, asking where my story was. Failing to find it, wrote joke story in ten minutes, sent it and went to W.U. office to see what had happened. W.U. officials disclaimed all knowledge of ever having seen masterpiece; had sent a boy to hostelry, but he had returned masterpieceless, having been told by clerk that he was too late. Said clerk's vacation was to begin next morning and he had gone away for the night. No satisfaction.

    Monday, August 15—Sox lost all kinds of chances to win game and it was finally stopped in the eighth inning with score tied. Fearful storm broke. Athletes and scribes in hurry to catch train. Refused to ride in athletes' bus to hotel, thinking I could beat it on a car. Cars stopped in storm on account of trouble in the trolley wires. C. Dryden and I held up so we couldn't make 8 o'clock train. Asked ticket office

---

[1] One of Lardner's rare misspellings.

(Getting shock in the ear while telephoning) what time next train left. Was told that an express went at 10 o'clock. Boarded train with C. Dryden to find that it was called express because there were so many express cars on it. Had received your letter at hotel and settled in train to read it. Looked in pocket for it and there found score of game which should have gone with story. Hysterics. Laughter from C. Dryden. Got off train at Baltimore and ordered Washington W. U. to send C. Dryden's score also to Examiner. Colored lady got on at Elkerton and came in smoking car which C.D. and I had had to ourselves. Thinking we were near Phila., I remarked the same to C.D. namely, that we must be near Phila. Colored lady butted in and said: "The next stop is Wilmington." C.D.— "Thought you got on at Wilmington." C.L.— "No, I got on at Elkerton. I have lived in Baltimore two months." C. D.— "Thank you." C.L.— "Are you traveling men?" C. D.— "Yes, woman." Arrived at Philly at 2:35, covering the 115 miles in four hours and thirty-five minutes.
    Answer
R.W.L.

Eight months had passed since Lardner and Ellis had actually been together. On 4 September, after he had returned from an eastern road trip with the White Sox, he finally met Ellis by prearrangement at Marshall Field's downtown; they attended a White Sox game and saw a show. As usual, when he and Ellis were able to be together, the courtship advanced considerably. The evening was a great success, and Ellis wrote afterward: "Even if you are a bold wicked man you were very, very nice to me in Chicago."

The Chicago Daily Examiner
146 Franklin Street
Chicago, Ill.
[13 October 1908]
Wednesday.

Dear Rabbit,—
    Instead of enclosing my usual cute little poetical work, I am this time sending you, u.s.c. (under separate cover) "The Sentimental Song Book" by the Michigan song-bird. Mrs. Moore, who is the authoress, has long been my ideal and I have emulated her style repeatedly, as you, who have

seen so much of my work, can easily discern.[1] I have added explanatory notes in the early pages for the purpose of helping you to get into the spirit of the poems. I want you to read every one and to write me your honest opinion of them and their composer.

Thank you very much for admitting that you are afraid of me. You haven't much to fear from your sister, though, for I will subsidize her when we meet again.

My poor ball team lost out on the last day of the season, when most of us expected it to cop. I am almost over the shock, but have resolved to quit the national pastime, i.e. baseball, forever.

Let me know how you get along in your political studies and remember me kindly to the Smiths.

Rodently,<br>Ringlets.

The following letter was written shortly after 21 October 1908, when Lardner's sister Anna married Richard G. Tobin, Lardner's colleague on the *Inter-Ocean*. Lardner was best man. Along with his brother Rex, Lardner would share a southside Chicago apartment with the newlyweds for the next two years.

The section entitled "The Tribune" relates to the fact that Lardner after the World Series had left the *Examiner* to replace his friend Charles Dryden on the *Tribune*. Dryden, who retired, had recommended him. In those days the *Tribune*'s talented staff included Burton Rascoe as literary editor, Walter Eckersall as sports commentator, H. E. Keogh as Lardner's predecessor writing "In the Wake of the News," Finley Peter Dunne as author of the Mr. Dooley pieces, Harriet Monroe as a commentator on art, Lillian Russell as commentator on beauty hints, and John T. McCutcheon as a topical cartoonist. It was a great newspaper at that time.

---

[1] Julia A. Moore was a poet of the late nineteenth and early twentieth centuries whose first book, *The Sweet Singer of Michigan Salutes the Public* (1876; later reissued as *The Sentimental Songbook*) exhibited such banality and pedestrian detail that she became the object of parody and ridicule. In *Huckleberry Finn*, for example, the morbid poetry of Emmeline Grangerford, which gives Huck the "fantods," is Mark Twain's parody of Julia Moore.

The Chicago Examiner
146 Franklin Street
Chicago
Friday.

Dear Rabbit,—
    Here is a bunch of short ones:
        Going South.
The winter blasts are coming on, and Ringlets is a' cold,
No more he stands them as he did before he grew so old.
To warmer clime he must depart, to sunny, sunny South,
Before icicles close his eyes and freeze up tight his mouth.
Next Monday, he will Southward fly, 'bout sixty blocks or
    more,
To stay at least until the winter's worstest chills are o'er.
Therefore, when you do write him next, his address it will be
At 468 West Forty-eighth street, care of R.G.T.,
In care of Mr. R.G. Tobin, his young sister's spouse;
0, yes, please write him after this at Mr. Tobin's house.

    The Tribune.
And what is it, pray, this Chicago Tribune?
Which Ringlets is gone to work on so soon?
'Tis a paper that's gen'rally rated the best
In North, or in South, or in East, or in West.
And better than best it is quite sure to be
When it has the services of Bright young Me.
I can't just yet tell you what I am to write,
Whether checkers, or football, or racing or fight.
The chances are, Rabbit, I'll write not a thing
Till winter has yielded once more to the spring.
There'll be headlines, of course, and I'll send you a sheet
With each little task marked in pencil so neat;
I know this will please you, my innocent dove,
In return for which act, as a proof of your love
Devoted and grand, you must send out to me
Whatever that day's lesson happens to be,
And thus I can judge which is working the harder,
Miss Ellis, the Rabbit, or Ringlets, the Larder.

    Consolation.
I used to come to this large town
Thanksgiving day of ev'ry year,
When Michigan's great football team
    Played over here.

I was a football bug for fair,
But now I honestly don't care
What happens, since Chicago can
    No more play Michigan.[1]

It's really an outrageous shame
That I must go to ev'ry game
When I would rather be in bed
    Pounding my head.

And still, a game I would not miss,
And the reason's, Rabbit, this:
(But, p'rhaps, quite probably you may
    Not know where they play)

Well, then, they play on Marshall field
A field which Marshall Field did yield
For just that purpose: well, and where
    Is this field, fair?

Now to the reason we have got:
This Marshall field's a favored spot
With me; because it does remind
    Me of you, Rabbit, kind

At Marshall Field's one time we met;
That meeting I will not forget,
Nor joyous time that followed, at
    The ball combat.

And furthermore, I must tell you
The field's on *Ellis* avenue
So can't you see there are two things
That serve to counteract young Ring's
Dislike to going thither? Yes,
    I guess.
             Write.
             B.W.L.[2]

    The salutation of the following letter communicates a further advancement of the courtship. It is also clear from

---

[1] Because of intense crowd reaction at previous games, the Universities of Chicago and Michigan had discontinued their annual football game.

[2] Probably an imitation of Bert Leston Taylor, who signed his *Tribune* column ("A Line o' Type or Two") "B.L.T."

the content of the letter that Lardner was thinking seriously about marriage.

[18 November 1908]
Wednesday

Love of my Life,—
   No sooner had I mailed you the note regarding the peculiarities of addresses than your missive reached me in a dazed condition. The envelope told of visits to all parts of Chicago. I can't imagine what led me to say 468 West 48th street when the real one is 868 East 48th. Please remember the latter—868 East 48th. You are now at liberty to omit the "c/o R. G. Tobin," for I have already become notorious on the south side. (Since joining the Tribune forces, I have learned to spell south with a small s.
   Helena Hawks of Goshen, Ind., came over to our city a week ago Sabbath. Her and Me went slumming. In the course of a pretty nice conversation, Helen said: "Ellis is really the Brightest Girl. She writes the cutest and most interesting letters. You would enjoy hearing from her."
   R— "Yes, indeed I would; continuing, to myself, "and I does."
   Sister Anne wrote home to my mother, Mrs. H. Lardner of Niles, Mich., and a very merry soul, telling her, for lack of something more interesting, of the aforesaid slumming expedition. Mrs. Lardner told Sister Fatima, sometimes called Lena, of the awful affair. Said Fatima, the only member of the family for whom you ever admitted your love, then wrote to Ringlets, saying she was very jealous of Helena Hawks, as she herself had always wanted to go slumming, but had been afraid to ask Brother to take her— knowing his rude habit of  laughing at girls' ridiculous notions. All of which is relevant and appealed to me at the time as a strange coincidence, as follows: Ellis Rabbit likes Fatima and is jealous of Ringlets because he is her brother; Fatima likes Ringlets because he is her brother and is jealous of Helena Hawks because Ringlets didn't laugh at her when she wanted to go slumming; Helena Hawks likes slumming and is jealous of Ringlets because he can go every day if he wants to: Ringlets likes Fatima and is jealous of her because Ellis R. likes her too; he likes Helena and is jealous of her because she lives in Goshen, where Ellis R. sometimes lives; he likes Ellis R. and is jealous of slumming because she has never slummed with he.
   This is the most funniest farce comedy plot I ever will hear of and if I had the time, the space and the inclination, I would write the most Comical Farce Comedy you ever read.

In your letter, you said nothing about my offer to exchange a page of the Tribune for a list of the tasks given you by Mrs. Smith for a day. Unless I hear from you at once on this subject, I will consider the proposition declined.

Having nothing to do last night, I happened to pick up a Girls' Basketball guide. Therein I discovered several views of games at Mr. Smith's house, but I looked in vain for a long time, among the athletes and spectators for a sight of thy dear face.

Finding it not, I said to myself: "What's this old guide good for anyway?" And I cast it into the debris. (Debris being a French word derived from de Brie, or Fromage de Brie, meaning Cream of Wheat Cheese. De Brie means, or suggests, Cheese. Debris means rubbish, the equivalent—rather, a synonym for all kinds of cheese.)

Example— "He ate a debris last night."

This means, "He ate a heap of rubbish, or cheese."

We (used editorially) are hoping that your mother, yourself, the weather and Ginnie Ginseng will act harmoniously in bringing you to Niles Christmas week. Better still, your mother, yourself and the weather will bring you to Chicago. See that they do.

And remember, Rabbit, leap year is drawing to a close. Remember, I am as shy as a kitten, but ready and eager to jump at an opportunity when it is presented in the right spirit.

Here is a trade Last, as my father says:

Sister Anne (looking at pictures of Rabbit) "Who is this?"

Ring, with funny lights; "Ellis Abbott."

S. A.—Well, these don't flatter her at all. I think She is an Awfully Pretty Girl."

In giving Me a Trade in Return, please don't say Anything about My Hand-writing. A new picture will be gladly accepted in payment.

Write.          R.W. Tobin, née Lardner
868 East 48th

Ginnie had now returned to Niles and taken a job as bookkeeper with the gas company. Lardner, who had worked at the same gas company in 1904 and 1905, counseled her in light of his own experience:

[Chicago, Ill.]
Saturday
[6 December 1908]

Dear Ginnie,—
The beauty of this ink more than makes up for the rather faded condition of the paper.
I knew of your promotion long before you told me of it. I want to congratulate you, also to make a few suggestions. If you desire instruction in keeping books, I refer you to Harry Walker, who has kept a book of mine for six years.

*Don'ts*

Don't argue with Mrs. Steinman about the post office bill. She will talk a long time tearfully—then she will pay.

When W. H. Bullard comes in, smile pleasantly and say: "Well, Mr. Bullard, this weather is just about like (or very different from) the kind you brave men had to endure in '63." This will make him forget all about the 12 cents increase over last month. *Don't* sneer and say: "Hello, Billy."

3—Mr. K. W. Nobles will want discount on the 11th., because he, she or it was sick on the 10th and couldn't strut across the street. *Don't* give her to it, or he will want it on the 12th of next month.

4—When Charley (alias Tod) Montague comes in, pretend you *Don't* recognize him, else he will pretend he doesn't recognize you. Beat him to it.

5—Stay back of the cage when Miss C. Southworth wants to look at lamps. Supply yourself with a magazine and make believe she isn't there. *Don't* try to answer any questions.

6—Always *joke* pleasantly with Fred Eisner, and Dr. Toefry. *Don't* joke with W. E. Platt.

7—Don't trifle with Clayton Seely. He lost his sense of humor when he married Mrs. Clayton Seely.

8—Tommy Freeze will say: "You ought to make it pretty cheap to me. Look at the mail I bring you." This is a good joke—laugh. Don't ignore him.

You may be able to struggle along with the help I have given you.

The Daily Sun didn't give you much space, did it? When I have more time—I mean it—I will write you up, send you the stuff and you can submit it either of the papers.

Sorry you got Genevieve's letter instead of your own. You couldn't expect her to admit it was her'n, as our love is a secret (from both of us, too).

Your father goes to New York and other points in the East tomorrow, and will be gone two weeks.

I have become almost *acclimated*. Bet you $.15 you don't pronounce that word correctly. Even I didn't until yesterday.

Write.

L.F. Brown

When Lardner wrote "The Maysville Minstrel" in 1928, he obviously drew on the same experiences to which he alludes in this letter. One of his sadder and more moving stories, it depicts Stephen Gale's entrapment as a small town gas company bookkeeper.

Christmas 1908 came and went with Lardner in Niles and Ellis in Goshen. Because of lost letters and rescheduled parties, they did not see each other over that holiday, although he did mail her an illustrated booklet of his poetry, and she apparently sent him a new picture of herself. The following letter two weeks later describes another thwarted effort to meet Ellis, this time at Goshen during a trip to a baseball meeting in Cincinnati.

[10 January 1909]
868 East Forty-eighth street
Sunday

Dear Rabbit,—

Your letter wasn't awaiting me when I came back nor has it appeared yet. I'm afraid the wrong address got on again.

You must have thought I had gone crazy the other night. The history of the affair follows:

You remember I was expecting to see you in Niles last Monday. During all the week previous I had no word from you or from Miss Ginseng regarding her "party." On Saturday, it was decided to send me to Cincinnati for a baseball meeting. As I had to see some South Bend people and wanted to see one Goshen person, I decided to go early Sunday morning by way of Niles. I called up Miss W.J. about 11 o'clock to ascertain when you were coming. She said the "party" had come off the night before and that you had started home half an hour before I phoned. My intention had been to go to Goshen Sunday night to see you and then to leave there for Indianapolis early Monday morning. But on receiving Miss W.J's. information, I thought to myself thus: "She "(meaning you)" didn't care whether or not she saw me, for she didn't tell me the new arrangement, and I might have gone to Niles Monday night and have seen nothing but dogs, horses and cows before she would have stopped me."

Thus thought I and it was rather discouraging thinking. Then when I reached South Bend my wishes overcame my pardonable pride and I called you up. About an hour afterward I found out I would have to be in Cincinnati before noon Monday. I couldn't make it if I went to Goshen first, so back I had to go to Chicago and thence to Cincinnati. The before noon business is the practical and most conven-[1] reason for my not coming to Goshen. There was another, less practical but just as important, which I'll tell you when I know you better, if the Lord ever relents and allows me to. Not that you want to know any reason at all, but that I want to try to convince you I'm not entirely insane. The attendant disappointment and other uninteresting features need not be touched on in this extremely serious missive.

When you write, which you soon will do unless you care to be morally guilty of manslaughter, tell me what you said in the letter that I longed for,—and some more.

Ringlets
868 East Street

This epistle evoked the following answer:

Dear Ring—

I *did* send my letter to the right address! Your postman must walk in his sleep. Please wake him up in time to get this letter. Besides Johnny has never told me why she changed the party. Your explanation is complicated but lucid and I have everything carefully assorted and put in its proper place in my mind. I was, *really* and *truly*, *very* sorry not to see you and please dont say you dont know whether I mean it or not because I *always* mean what I say.

I suppose you think you are dreadfully mysterious with your "other less practical reason" but you neednt because I know what it was. This was it: You didnt come because you didnt want to and the reason you wouldnt tell me was because you thought it would hurt my feelings. Therefore you wait till you know

---

[1] The word is obviously "convenient," but it appears at the end of a line, and though Lardner uses a hyphen, he does not complete the word on the next line.

me better to tell me. You neednt deny it because I intend to beleive it unless you tell me some other reason.

I cant tell you what I said in the missing letter because I didn't say anything, as usual. You might have known that without asking.

I could tell you about the bridge party I went to and the prize I *didn't* win or the coasting party I went to and the spill we did get or many other equally exciting events. I think, however, on deliberation, that I wont tell you about anything but will write to my mother instead.

This is a very long letter and I am a very busy person. Moreover I know that you are busy too. That has a familiar sound, has'nt it? Anyway I am going to stop before I forget to.

Ever
the Rabbit

I forgot to tell you that I put on my very prettiest new dress Sunday after you telephoned. And *then*—I had to take it off again.

[16 January 1909]
Saturday

Dear Rabbit,—

Your logic is great. A person is working in Chicago. He is told to go to Cincinnati on a certain date. In order to do this, he might start from Chicago the evening before after having enjoyed his full quota of sleep the night before that. Instead of acting in this normal manner however, he sets out in the middle of said night before that, sleeps not at all, goes a roundabout way in order that he may stop at Goshen, gets almost there, calls up a Rabbit to apprise her of his advent, then, later, finding he can't come after all his well-laid plans, he calls up again—*Because He Doesn't Want To See Her.* Then he prepares to tell her this reason when he is better acquainted with her, because he would prefer hurting the feelings of his oldest acquaintances to those of persons he has not known as long. That "hurting the feelings" part was kind of you, but you don't believe it.

No, small Rabbit of the Indiana prairie, I wasn't trying to be mysterious and you are hereby forbidden to do any more guessing unless you admit the folly of your former attempt. Your mention of the new dress (or gown) only added to my misery—not that I would like you in said new dress (or gown) any better than in a purple calico ulster.

In the last year or two, after resolving to use my head, think twice etc., I have done the wrong thing nine times out of nine chances. If there had been ten chances, my average of mistakes undoubtedly would have remained 100.

Now we have talked long enough about the tragedy of Ringlet's existence. One of his New Years resolutions is: Next time he thinks he has a chance of seeing certain desirable people, he is going to say to himself, "You will not see them, you really haven't a chance, something will butt in and break it up." Then he is going on his way without making any preparations and, perchance, things may break in his favor for once.

Where did the coasting party come off? On Sycamore street hill, Niles, Mich?

Your old friend, Duffy Cornell,[1] is to wed a week from Sunday. Peculiar day to select, but you and I can't help that. This is a secret, so please don't tell anyone in Massachusetts, Indiana or Michigan.

As soon as I can get to it, I will write a long epic for your private eyes. I mention this to keep you on the qui vive.

Your letter came two hours ago. Remember that when you get this one. Also remember you are to admit you see several flaws in your reasoning.

      Lithely,
       R—ts.

That might mean three things—Ringlets, Rats or Rabbit's.

 868 East 48th Street

When Lardner's travels, this time with the Cubs, prevented his seeing Ellis during her college spring vacation, which she spent at Goshen, Ellis penned a warning to him: "You know, you cant expect one to keep up a very exciting correspondence on one conversation a year—and that over the telephone." He reacted early in May during the Cubs' road trip by taking a side trip to Northampton to see Ellis at Smith College during the team's transition from Boston to Brooklyn.

It was apparently during this hard-won Sunday afternoon together that Lardner first asked Ellis to marry him. She may have protested that they did not know each other well enough. The parlance about ballplayer-type contracts in the following letter alludes to the proposal:

---

[1] Duffy Cornell was a colleague of Lardner's on the Chicago *Examiner*. His home hown was Goshen.

[26 May 1909]

Dear Ellis,
You see I know you well enough now to call you by your first name.
I enclose the contracts, both copies, which you are to fix up to suit yourself. You are to sign and date them both and the one I have not signed you are to return to me to keep. You may add anything I have overlooked. Please be lenient.
Your F. and F.
R.
Route — May 29 — Fort Pitt hotel, Pittsburg
May 30 — Home, Chicago
May 31 to June 2 — Havlin hotel, Cincinnati
June 3+ Home, Chicago.
Please excuse the alleged Pome.[1] I think it will be the last inasmuch as they get worse *all the time*.

Saturday.
[29 May 1909]

Dear Ellis,—
Your letters pursue me even if you do not. The last one greeted me in Pittsburg this morning, so you see there has been no delay in this case either.
I'm afraid you don't understand the contract business. I quote you the following, which is part of Rule 33 of the National Commission:
"Each manager must send each player a contract before May 27. Said player must sign said contract or agree to the terms thereof on or before June 1. If said player refuses to sign said contract or to agree on terms thereof, his (or her) case shall be brought before the Commission for a trial. Said player, for failure to sign or to agree on terms, may be assessed a fine or suspended and blacklisted for five years."
You know very well I will not ask for your suspension or blacklisting, but I *will* fine you and you have no idea how heavy the fine will be. You still have time to fix up before June 1. Think it over carefully.
Why do the collegians so furiously chase me around? Arriving here this morning, the Yale club greeted me at the hotel mentioned above. Later, President Taft puffed in and the collegians had to quit me to entertain him. He is going to the ball game this afternoon and, afterward, we are to be

---

[1] Accompanying this letter was an undistinguished 83-line doggerel poem narrating the events of that Northampton Sunday afternoon — a day of "rabbit hunting / In the valleys of Mass'chusetts."

presented to him at the clubhouse. Glad to know you, Judge. Oh, Mr. Lardner? From Niles? That's near Goshen, isn't it? How do you do?

Tomorrow morning we shall pass through Goshen on the way home. I shall wake up. I shall be sorry not to see you, but I shall be properly grateful you are not there, as it might cause me to leave the train ("it" meaning your presence in Goshen) and leaving the train might be synonymous with losing the job, which, by the way, is still with me despite my flight to Northampton.

Something you thought (you didn't say it) when we were in Mrs. W. H's.[1] reception room (?) just before Mrs. W. H. introduced me to my rhyme, has been cutting ever since. At the next meeting, an explanation will be asked and the matter discussed thoroughly, for I want to know why. In order that you may prepare the explanation, I'll state the case:

I said, "I'm going to be a promoter next fall."

You *thought* I said, "I'm going to be promoted."

My own limitations, not those of the subject, made the pome bad. As for the term "chatter," it had no double significance. Once, years ago, we agreed to talk seriously for an entire conversation, at least, I did. But I forgot it before I saw you, which, I think, was some years later. But I've remembered it again now and propose to go through with it at the next meeting. Quotation from your letter: (1) "I am very humiliated to think what you must think of me." Further quotation (2) "Please, this is not fishing." Remark (1) What I think probably won't do me any good, but I can't help it. Remark (2) The fish already has been hooked. It never can swim again, so why don't you take it home or else put it out of its misery? Remark (2) is rather deep, but there is no double significance about Remark (1). I thought I knew exactly what (2) meant when I was writing it, but I know only vaguely now.

\**Good Poem*

>Them pictures that I have of you,
>Them pictures, miss, is mine.
>I'll send them to you, will I not?
>Yes, I will not. Behüt Dich Gott!
>Es hat nicht sollen sein.

\*Good because short

Havlin hotel, Cincinnati—Monday, Tuesday and Wednesday. After that, home.

>R.W.L.

---

[1] Washburn House, Ellis's residence in Northampton.

In June, Ellis graduated with honors from Smith College. At a time when it was unusual for women to obtain college educations, it is notable that she and two of her sisters attended Smith College.

By the time Ellis returned from Northampton to Goshen for the summer, Lardner had embarked on a road trip with the Cubs that would send him to Pittsburg, Philadelphia, Boston, New York, Washington, and Detroit before he would finally return to Chicago on August 21. His letters to her during this period reveal his frustration over his inability to see her and his tension over the fact that she had not yet given him a definite answer to his proposal.

While in Washington at the end of July, he wrote the letter below to Ginnie:

The Arlington
Washington, D.C.
[29 July 1909]

Dear Ginnie,—

    I haven't written to you for quite a spell. I'm telling you this because the chances are you haven't noticed it.

    I was astonished to see R.B. Kelly[1] sitting on the Washington bench today. I had noticed the name in the paper while I was with the Cubs, but I didn't know what Kelly it was. They say he was throwing them around a little whimsically while they were trying him out. All they did today for him was to let him carry a sponge up to the plate when the catcher was injured.

    After this city had been enjoying a period of comparative coolness, we ran into it just as the change came. No one can eat or sleep. The thought of the St. Joe river drives me wild, for between the heat and the athletes, I want either to swim or drown. Never travel with a ball team, Ginnie, for it means suicide if you stick at it long enough.

    The Niles Daily Star told me you had moved from north to south. I don't know whether I am glad or sorry. You are nearer Lardner's, but you are fu'ther from the station. You are nearer church, but you are fu'ther from Montague's. You are next to Carmi, but you are no longer next to Harriet and Jean and Ed and Jennie.

---

[1] See p. 7.

I presume you did your share toward marrying off Miss Rogers. I sent you an S.P.C.[1] while you were out in Linoleum, Kas, but no answering S.P.C. came to me.

On Saturday night last, the Cubs tearfully left me at New York and Mr. and Mrs. Tribune said I could do whatever I pleased until today. I pleased to go swimming, so I asked New Yorkers to point out a quiet spot. They evidently never heard of one so I had to go to Atlantic City. After swimming there all through Sunday, I met some one I didn't want to meet and as said some one was going to stick around, I had to get out. In the meantime, Mrs. Carroll Hamill, nee Pauline Micks, invited me to come to Parkesburg, Pa., so thither I hastened. It is a town of 3,000 inhabitants and I had one grand time there. If ever you hear of a town of that size that wants me, let me know please.

Helena Hawks dropped a line off the Cretis[2] the other day. According to her account, the travelers divide their time between sleeping and reading. It will not be thus when you and I go abroad.

The fact that I lapsed a little as regards my correspondence does not excuse you from writing as soon as you are in receipt of this. Moreover, if you had been as true a friend of mine as I had been led to believe, you would have written without waiting for an answer. There is an opening for a quarrel, a thing which you refused to start in your last, after promising you would.

You will find me as follows:
    Aug. 2–5, Aldine hotel, Philadelphia
    Aug. 6–10 , Copley Square hotel, Boston
    Aug. 11–13, Somerset hotel, New York
    Aug. 15–18, Cadillac hotel, Detroit.
                R.W.L.
Thursday

Lardner's allusion above to travelling abroad with Ginnie is of course a joke, but it is still surprising, because of his pending proposal and because he rarely indulged in jokes with sexual implications.

From Washington he also wrote to Ellis urging her to accept his proposal and suggesting that she visit him in Chicago when he returned at the end of August:

---

[1] "Special Post Card."

[2] The ship on which Helen Hawks traveled to Europe.

Thursday
29 July 1909]

Dear Ellis,—

I certainly was glad to hear that one of my rivals had become ineligible. Why should you say I ought to be careful or you will accept me? Don't you know I have been waiting years for your yes? I'm afraid you don't appreciate the value of my offer even yet. To make it stronger, I will add some special inducements:

1. If you tire of my companionship, I will leave home and stay away until you recall me.

2. If you don't want to hear me talk, I'll remain absolutely silent for days at a time.

3. If you cease to care for me as you do now, I will leave the premises, not to return until the old fire is kindled anew.

I wish you were here in Washington, taking your share of the heat. Among the impossibilities are sleeping, eating and walking. If I were the Senate and Mr. Taft, I would pass any tariff measures they offered and go home.

I was vacationing from Saturday night until yesterday. One day was spent in the ocean and the rest at Parkesburg, Pa. Mrs. A.C. Hamill, nee Pauline Micks of Elkhart, who lives there, said she would find me a soul mate among her new friends. She did, but I am holding out pending word from you. The S.M. is six feet, two inches tall, has a nose as long as the baseball season, is as pretty as the Carnegie library in Niles and a Roman Catholic. Please save me from this fate.

R.B. Kelly was seen on the Washington bench at the ball yard today. I shut my eyes, pretended I was at South Bend and that you were nearby, but the heat beat down just the same.

Regarding the pictures referred to, I don't think you are crazy and I only know that I still have some of my wits about me. But you evidently misunderstood some remark of mine. I *never* promised to send them back to you and I *never* will send them unless I receive something of equal value in exchange—equal value meaning more pictures. Why do you persist in talking about them?—you can't have them. And why should you want pictures of yourself when you have yourself? If I were as blessed, I'd never look at a picture.

Did you make the weekend visit to Chicago? You know right well it is possible and plausible to visit that city more than once in a season and there is lots of time after the twenty-first of old Augie. I don't blame you, though, for staying away when you have a lake.

Oh, yes, another thing—Do you mind telling me where you are going to be this fall?

There is one switch in the schedule I sent you. We are going to stay at the Aldine instead of the Majestic in Philadelphia.

Write.              R. W. L.

Thursday

At the end of August, Ellis did visit Lardner in Chicago. They attended a ballgame, and she stayed overnight at the Tobin apartment. Though Ellis was "considering seriously the offer of hand and heart," she was reluctant to marry immediately. With the intention of teaching after graduation for awhile, she had decided to attend normal school in Goshen briefly to obtain a teaching certificate.

Since the proposal, Lardner had begun his letters with "Dear Ellis." When she chided him, probably during her visit, for his formality, he responded with the following:

Hotel Euclid
Cleveland, Ohio
[6 September 1909]

Dear E____e,—

You can't tell what I am calling you now. The fear that you would hurt those B. Eyes looking so hard for the postman is one of the reasons I have answered promptly. The other is that I wanted another letter *right away*.

Two gents from South Bend came that far on our train last night and the result was I didn't retire until we had passed Goshen. I looked for you, hoping you had broken your other engagement, but evidently you had not. Why?

I thought for just a minute I would be in Goshen. The team is going back to Chicago tonight and tomorrow is an off day, them Sox going to St. Louis late in the evening. Said I to me: "I'll get off at 5 A.M. at Goshen and remain till 6 P.M." Then again said I: "I can't see E____s, for she thinks more of her certificate than she does of me." So I'm going right on through to St. Louis, wishing it were October and vacation time.

We were trimmed again this morning. Why didn't you stay with us? Because of your certificate?

My boon companion and old familiar friend is impatient. He wants me to start immediately for the ball orchard, but I won't until I want to.

Important query: "Do prospective brothers-in-law have the kissing privilege, too?" I thought of that the other day and it's been worrying me, for what privileges do I have, who am neither b. in l. or h. Please appoint me to some office—I'm tired of being in the ranks.

I'm glad you are considering seriously the offer of hand and heart. The family is after me, which fact would cause me to balk under other circumstances. Don't let them persecute me.

We will be at the Planters hotel in St. Louis until Saturday night and I will expect a letter there.

Yours,
Ringlets

Lardner did visit Ellis at Goshen on a weekend in October. A week after that visit, Ellis went at his invitation to the Lardner home in Niles. While there, she apparently accepted his proposal, but the engagement was to be secret, and they set no wedding date. On 17 October, Ellis wrote to her sister Florence about her visit:

> Their house is a *great big* tumbled down old fashioned one. Mr. & Mrs. Lardner, Anna & Dick—that is Mr. Tobin—and Lena and Ring were the only ones there. We really had a *good* dinner. I am crazy about the whole family. Mrs. Lardner is enormous and queer but very bright & a great talker. Mr. Lardner is an old *dear*. We spent the evening playing and singing. Ring plays awfully well and played an hour or more. We tried to play authors but he cheated so that we had to stop. I am *crazy* about Anna. She is *great* and was too nice to me for words.

After Lardner had returned to Chicago from having accompanied Ellis back to Goshen, he wrote the following letter:

[Chicago, 27 October 1909]

Dear Ellis,—

I was accompanied from Goshen to Elkhart by Jud Micks, who teaches in your very good college Tuesday and Friday mornings. Being greatly interested in my large affairs, he wanted to know what I was doing in Goshen, but was afraid to ask. He hinted around, and I led him to believe there was a great deal of mystery surrounding my visit. The chances are he thinks I am trying to buy the News-Times. I wish I could. I would engage you at once as a copy reader, regardless of Grace Schwendler's judgment.

Mr. Boss relieved my mind last night by assigning me to the Wisconsin-Northwestern game at Evanston next Saturday. The best thing about Evanston is that you don't have to use a sleeping car to get there. Brother Rex has agreed to go along to keep me company.

Part of last evening was spent in figuring up how much vacation was coming to me. Answer—thirty-three days. I was told it was possible, but not probable that I would get it all at once right after the football season's close. Some of it is coming then anyway. Don't you dare to leave Goshen, that is, unless you leave it for Niles.

Also, don't forget you have a diamond ring coming. I would send it at once if I knew where to get it, but such a thing and at such a price is hard to find even here in Chicago. I also must find a bank in which to plant my safety razor savings. Remember, at the end of ten months you will have not only a fortune of thirty dollars, but also a better looking husband. This isn't a hint. I already have an unsafety razor, which serves its purpose fairly well although it fails to improve the husband's looks. Nevertheless, your investment would be a profitable one, paying you sixty per cent interest a month on your money, whether or not the looks were improved.

I am writing a letter I don't owe. But that is only one of the hardships I am willing to endure rather than be cast off entirely by you. I am hoping you will be kind enough to let me win just one argument from you some time. I mean I hope you will be gracious enough to acknowledge defeat, for I already have some victories to my credit which you will not admit.

Heres a new bargain offer, another of the kind by which I alone profit. You are to write me twice a week as long as I write you that many times. Answer.

On the train yesterday were two alumni of Dartmouth. They never had seen Chicago and they took pains to knock it all the way over. Although neither was much bigger than B. Rockwell, I never opened my clam, knowing full well that both of them would be run over and killed by real street cars in a real city before they had been here long.

Will you write immediately, partner? I prithee, do.
                        Gaffer
P. S. How many people came to take you to the ball?
Wednesday.

Soon after, Lardner sent Ellis the previously-mentioned engagement ring, though it was by agreement not to be publicly acknowledged as such. Ellis responded:

The ring fits, thank you, and I wear it constantly to the unlimited amazement of my family who are all unsatisfied curiosity. Your savings bank will be shipped this evening. Just what sort of a quitter do you think I am? Also—the ring still continues to sparkle. It seems to be a characteristic of Rings.

Late in November Ellis, in response to Anne's invitation, visited Lardner and the Tobins again at the Chicago apartment. Afterward, she wrote:

In the first place I have so many things to thank you for that I dont know where to begin so I'll begin at the wrong end and go backwards. I certainly was glad to see Blanch Ring and like De*Wolf* Hopper I am "delightfully grateful" for the music. When I attempted to pay for my seat in the Pullman the gentleman said "Arent you the young lady the man brought down to the train? Well that's all right mam." Once more I am grateful. That I enjoyed my *visit* in Chicago goes without saying and for the third time I am grateful.

The next letter, to Ginnie (and his last to her—at least the last that Ginnie saved), illustrates again the marked contrast in personalities that Lardner exhibited in his correspondence with these two young women. Ginnie would marry Walter Ostrander of Niles on 7 July 1912.

Chicago, Ill.
[29 November 1909]

Dear Ginnie,—
This is called local stationery and can be procured at almost any downtown store.
Sister Anne has deserted us again. Rex, not knowing whence his next meal is coming, refuses to get up. Ringgold wouldn't be up either if he had not remembered to procure the local stationery last night.
I hope Mrs Miley hasn't sold all the pie. I'm coming, but no one knows when.
Did you read in the Chicago or Niles papers about the marital troubles of Attorney Louis J. Fletcher, former coach of my high school football team? I ran into him while I was buying stationery. He has lost fifty pounds of flesh and a wife since last I saw (or seen) him. But the point of the story

is this—Before we got through talking, he began to cry. You can't imagine my feelings unless you have been standing at some time in the midst of a Buck and Rayner drug store and the gentleman with you has started to cry—not just to sniffle, but to sob with loud sobs. I won't tell you what I did prior to my hasty exit.

Just when football season was over and vacation was due, a large and perfectly senseless baseball war[1] had to break out. So the dandy little war correspondent had to stick around awhile regardless of his desire to hurry to Niles and to the M.C. dining hall.

Mother hasn't been very regular about sending the papers lately, so I don't know what is going on in society. When you write, tell me all about your club life and affairs of the heart—I would have used the French term for that if I had knew it.

Rex is stirring about, so I may be asked out to breakfast—lunch—dinner.

Did you ever see such fall weather? Be sure to answer "Yes" or "No."

                          Ringgold.

*Sabbath.*

The following letter to Ellis is particularly interesting because it exhibits the athlete's dialect with which Lardner had been experimenting for several years. He would continue to develop this dialect in "In the Wake of the News" and other *Tribune* pieces in 1913 and perfect it in the *Saturday Evening Post* "busher" stories of 1914.

Thursday
[Chicago, 16 December 1909]

Friend Ellis,—

Well, Ellis, I was glad to hear from you. How have you been?

---

[1] The baseball war had developed as a result of American League President Ban Johnson's opposition to John Ward, a New York lawyer who was then a leading candidate for the vacant National League presidency. Johnson had accused Ward of unethical contract negotiations as a player's attorney and had threatened to pull the American League out of its partnership with the National League if Ward were chosen. The war was averted when Thomas J. Lynch, chief umpire of the National League, was elected as a compromise move.

I have been so busy making Exmas presents that I haven't had time to write to you before now. Well, Ellis, you know how it is. I don't have much time to get out let alone write letters any time of the year, but of course this time of the year, just before the holidays is the busiest time of the year for me, as I suppose it is the busiest time of the year for you, in fact for all.

Say Ellis, I must insist that you come to Niles before Jan. 6. I know Ellis you must be busy at this time of year, so near the holidays, but say Ellis you certunly will have one evening to spare before then. Why, Ellis, I intended to show you a good time some evening before then; we could go to South Bend to some show. I don't suppose we could see anything there as fine as we seen in Chicago.

Ellis, I wish you lived in Chicago. Sometimes on my nights off I could take you out and we could have great times. I don't know many people here, that is girls, none that I care anything about and of course you can't really enjoy yourself with someone who you don't care for, at least I can't. I never was one of those pretenders. I always show my feelings and I can't pretend to not care for anyone when I don't. I don't suppose it's a very good way to be, but Ellis, you know it's my Nature and I can't help that, can I? If people don't like me for what I am they don't half to like me, that's all.

Well, Ellis, I suppose I am tireing you with all this talk about myself. But, Ellis, you have knew me a long time and if you hadn't of liked me you would of told me so a long time ago. You see I know you got a frank disposin, to.

My married sister and myself are going home to Niles next Friday morning that is a week from tomorrow (Friday) morning. My sister isn't going to stay but till the following Wednesday morning. So you see you must come over to Niles before then.

I hope you'll anser real soon, dear, (you don't mind if I call you dear, do you dear?)
                        Yours with love,
                        Ringgold Lardner
P. S. I don't think none of us can come to your party. My married sister and her husband will be back from Niles and so will Rex.

Lardner wrote fewer letters to Ellis from mid-December through mid-February, because she was in Goshen during most of that time and he, having finally obtained some vacation time, was in Niles from Christmas Eve to 8 January. After returning to work for approximately three weeks, he took more time off early in February.

This was the only extended period during the entire courtship when the two were together.

Ellis's admission of love and acceptance of Lardner's proposal had taken place back on 26 January, when he and Ellis were together at the Tobin apartment. That moment is recalled by Lardner in his letter of 26 January 1911, on the anniversary of the event. But Ring Lardner Jr. says that during this later three-week period, his father "renewed his proposal impressively enough so that in my mother's recollection this was the real one. The event took place on a sleigh ride—one of the few means at their disposal to achieve the necessary privacy. The problem at the Abbott house, especially during vacations, was that they had five daughters and only three parlors."[1]

However, no date was then set for the wedding, because Ellis wished to teach for awhile and because her father was dubious about the respectability of Lardner's position as a sports reporter and about his ability to support Ellis adequately.

From this point to the marriage, Lardner's letters are even more frequent, they are more intense expressions of love, loneliness, and fear of losing Ellis, and they contain less Lardnerian wit. Clearly he was trying to handle the frustration of what promised to be a very lengthy engagement. One letter from Ellis at this time appeared to confirm his fear:

> But, honestly Ring, you know there is something the matter with us. I wouldnt have the courage to say it at all but I know that you know it, too. You know that neither of us feels very much at ease when we are together and I know that I always have a feeling of restraint. I never can say any thing I want to or be the least bit natural. I dont know whether it is because you dont really love me or because I dont love you. Sometimes I think it is one and sometimes the other. You spoke of that evening in the 'piano-room'. Do you know its queer but I was thinking just then that perhaps I didnt love you after all and I was trying to make up my mind. And yet with my head on your shoulder and your arms around me I was perfectly sure the next minute that I did. But listen,

---

[1] Ring Lardner Jr., p. 49.

dear, I'll never marry you until I am absolutely sure. I have wanted to say all this before but couldnt, and it is awfully hard to say it now but I just cant go on this way. If you will only tell me the real truth, if you really do care for me enough to want me forever and ever—it is a long time you know and I am a foolish thing. I have always loved to go and to have lots of attention and just have a good time. I dont know how to do any useful or sensible things. But the real me you dont know at all and I want you to. I want you to help me to be that and I cant be true to you or myself until I chase all these doubts out of my mind. I think perhaps half the trouble is that I am not sure of you and that I am makeing a great deal out of nothing. I have given you so much, Ring, I have let you kiss me so often and I have given myself to you so much that I have got to be sure that I am giving you my whole self. You wont misunderstand me, dear, will you and you will try to understand as much of this wandering as you can, and see that I am trying to be true to both of us. It is all so new to me for, though, I have had more or less attention and people have said they cared for me—it was always in just a childish foolish sort of a way.

Lardner received this letter on the morning of his arrival with the Cubs at West Baden Springs, Indiana, for spring training. The lover's agony in his response is painfully obvious:

Sunday.
[West Baden Springs
 27 February 1910]

Dear,—
No one had enough sleep on the train and almost everyone went to bed after breakfast this morning. I was going too, but your letter came and changed my schedule. Do you know, before I opened the envelope, I began to feel blue, for I knew, somehow, that there would be "bad news."
I have been thinking about the letter and you for two hours and wondering how to answer. I feel as if I were writing my own death sentence and that's not a pleasant task. I feel as if you were slipping away from me. I don't know how to prevent it and I don't think I ought to try. You ought to know just what I believe and feel about both of us

and I'm going to try to tell you. In the first place, there is no doubt at all in my mind about my love for you. You have all of it—to keep and keep forever. I'm simply sick when I'm away from you and I have no real interest in anything but you. You are just everything to me. Please don't think this is an appeal for sympathy—I'm just trying to let you know the truth. When you consider my "circumstances," the fact that I told you I wanted you may seem strange proof of love, but I offer it in evidence anyway. I would be less worthy than I am now if I had told you without meaning it and had asked you to share a lot anything but enviable if I hadn't cared so much that I couldn't help it. I don't believe I made that very clear, but I hope you'll understand it. What I think is the "matter with us" is just this—I don't honestly believe you care as much about me as you sometimes think you do—and you don't know all the time whether you do or not. And in that connection, I have another truth—I think it's a truth—in my mind that it's just impossible to tell you, because you wouldn't understand it, and wouldn't believe it if you did. You can't know how it hurts me to look at these things squarely and to come to the summing up. If I were a "good catch" instead of a bad muff, I could talk differently. As it is, I can say just this—If you don't *know* that you love me, you don't love me enough. I'm not fishing. Ever since that night at Anne's I have felt that it was only a question of time before hell would follow heaven. I believe people get out of life just what they earn. I have not earned such happiness as life with you would be. I don't deserve you. I don't think you want to be bound to me now, and I know you don't want to say so, so I am saying it for you. You are to consider yourself free unless you are *sure* and until you are sure. And if, as I think, you realize it was a mistake and that you never can care, please tell me so. And never reproach yourself for anything, dear. There is no one to blame except me. And you have given me a taste of more happiness than I ever thought of. I'm not trying to pose as a martyr. This all seems, natural, as if it couldn't have happened any other way.

But if I am wrong—I know I ought not to hope I am, but I do—or if you ever do love me truly, so that you feel you can't get along without me—that sounds funny and impossible, I know—don't hesitate about telling me, if it's tomorrow or five years from now, because there'll never be "another girl." I think I do know you as you are, Ellis, but anyway I know I love you as you are.

You can pretend you are keeping that ring for me, if you want to. But please don't hurt my feelings by giving it back to me. That's a favor I'm asking you.

I know this must be tiring you. Write to me—once at least. I still know enough to realize I mustn't ask too much of you. Dear, the very fact that you didn't want to write every other day hurt me and made me see you didn't feel as I did. This has been an awfully hard letter to write and it sounds like a funeral. I know you'll think it is an appeal for sympathy and all I can do is ask you not to think so.

I will try to wind up cheerfully. I don't know whether or not you saw this cartoon. It was a delicate way of telling me I was supposed to "buy." I couldn't see why I should, but I fixed up something for them. The waiter pretended to be taking their orders, which were very elaborate. Then he brought them a ham sandwich, a cup of coffee and a cigar apiece. My guests were very much put out. The paragraph about the feed was written by the boss for their benefit and not for the paper.

Mr. Schulte[1] is with us. Last night, he and I made an agreement to speak to each other only once a week and to try to be "decent" all season.

Ring.

The next day Ellis responded:

Cant the judge reconsider the death sentence and make it a life sentence or make the punishment just to take me back and keep me forever. I do know now, dear, and I will tell you how I know—it is just because I cant give you up. If you want me you can have me and I will be just the best kind of a wife I can to you my big boy—but you know I haven't had much experience and I may not succeed—just at first because I cant cook anything but cake and salad dressing. And will you please forgive me for all the dreadful time I must have caused you and try to love me more than ever. But Ring, I have been worried nearly frantic. Now I am never going to think of it again and I am just going to keep on learning to love

---

[1] In the letters of this period there are several references to Frank "Wildfire" Schulte, the Cub rightfielder from 1905 through 1915, who compiled a batting average of .270 over fifteen major league seasons. One of Lardner's preferred companions on the club, he was noted for his intelligence and wit and for a variety of interests, of which baseball was only one. His nickname had developed from the fact that he owned trotting horses, one of which he named "Wildfire" after the popular play in which Lillian Russell, a personal friend, had starred.

you more and trying to be more worthy of your love. It is always hard for me to keep from adding—"if you really love me." But I am not going to say it but try to belive that you do love me just as you say you do. You will tell me it often, though, wont you so that I'll know it every minute and I'll try never to doubt you again, *never*.

Do you know I cried and cried when I got your letter and I dont know why because it made me feel so sure. But, oh, I *am* glad I wrote you that letter because I couldnt have stood it any longer and now I am so much happier.

You know that I have never thought once in all this time of what you call your circumstances. I dont care and never will. I dont even know what father has or whether he can ever do anything for me when there are all the rest of the children, but I dont care and I know you dont.

And now, dear, will you write to me and tell me that you forgive me and love me. I want you to tell me everything you think and do always. *If* I could see you now I would kiss you and say I love you and you would put your arms around me and say that everything was all right now, wouldnt you?

       Ellis

P.S. I will write to you every other day and is it still hell?

Friday night.
[West Baden Springs
1 March 1910]

Dear Girl,

It's heaven again now and it makes up for the two long days of hell, which was hell in its worst form and all its branches. I don't think you are at all sensible, but you have no idea how glad I am that you aren't. I am selfish now and I refuse to think of giving you up, but before I forget to say it, remember you always have the privilege of telling me when you don't want me any more. Only, please want me.

Besides, you make the best salad dressing I ever tasted, although I don't love you for your cooking and absolutely don't care what you can or can't do as long as you are you.

Now I'm going to tell you about hell, admitting that it is a play for your sympathy to do so. Sunday night, after I had mailed the letter to you, I went out on the porch and ran into

Mr. Schulte. He said: "How do you feel by this time?" and when I asked him about what, he said "about our agreement." I told him I thought we had better call it off awhile and he acted as if the suggestion pleased him. He was lonesome and I was worse than that. I think if he had proposed that we fight a duel, I would have done it. It wouldn't have been any more foolish than, or half as unpleasantly expensive as what we did do. I'm afraid he is one athlete who hasn't profited much by his "training trip" to West Baden. After your dear letter came this afternoon, I told him the agreement was on again. He said "all right" without a question.

Poor girl, I didn't mean to make her cry and honestly thought my letter would relieve her from a lot of worry. I won't forgive you, though, because I don't know why I should.

The world looks different tonight, sweetheart, even brighter than it did before, when I was so horribly uncertain about your feeling for me. It's hard to believe you do care when I was so sure I was right and that you didn't. If you want me, there's nothing on earth that can prevent your having me to keep. I would give anything to have you with me tonight, so I could kiss you and tell you again that I love you and want you forever. When I thought I had lost you, I didn't care what happened. I have been just crazy for two days, dear, and I guess I'm even crazier now, but this form of insanity is pleasant to suffer, while the other was like dying.

I don't suppose I ought to, but I can't help wishing you had been used to nothing and that marrying me would be a sensible thing for you to do. I hate to think I can't give you anything and that you will almost be throwing yourself away. You are such a prize, dear, that it seems unbelievable I should have won you.

But you are foolish and you can't deny it.

I love you.

      Ring.

We are going away from here Thursday afternoon. Will there be a letter awaiting me at New Orleans Friday night?

In another letter to Ellis before he left with the Cubs for New Orleans, Lardner reflected on their past:

This is a peach of a day and if you were here, we'd go for a long walk. You think I don't like to walk and I don't—except with you. Every time you and I walk together after this—if we ever get a chance—I will be reminded of our seeing Northampton trip. I woke up on that walk, or just before it. I think it was when you first came into the room at "Hotel Washburn" that I fell. Then, all the rest of that afternoon and evening, I was just thinking about "it" and about what a fine chance I had. Do you know you always seemed unattainable—like a million dollars—I thought of you then as something I would give anything for, but something I couldn't have. I'm afraid you weren't very good for me then, because you seemed so far away that I was discouraged and discouragement always had a bad effect on me. I know you will think I can't be "much" to let things run away with me as they do, but, in self defense I will say that it's only the big things that bother me and you are one of the big ones—in fact the biggest one—despite the fact that you are really just a little bit of a thing.

Every change of season—since last May—has reminded me of you in different surroundings and at different places. In the fall I thought of you as you were at the dam Goshen—I don't know why, because that was almost summer, wasn't it?—and in the summer, as you were the first night I saw you. Now, just because it's like spring, I guess, I can't put you anywhere but at Northampton.

Lardner's next letter, from New Orleans, chatted about his ballplayer friends. Obviously, he enjoyed excellent rapport with many of the Cub ballplayers and with their playing manager, Frank Chance:

Monday.
[New Orleans, 7 March 1910]

Dearest,—
But I'm not enjoying the trip. I'm lonesome and I wish we were training in Goshen.

Last night I told Manager Chance it was my birthday and when he asked me what one and I answered him truthfully, he said: "Do you expect anyone to believe that? You are the oldest looking guy for twenty five that I ever saw." I wish I were about nineteen once more—I mean if you cared for me just the same, for I was very beautiful at that age and I'm not no more. Also, I'm getting to be a worse hand-writer the older I grow.

You know I would go walking with you if I were there and I wouldn't care about wet feet. I'm afraid, Miss Abbott, that you don't take enough precautions about your health. I know I wouldn't make much of a hit lecturing on the subject, but I don't want you to take any chances. If you should be sick, I would be too, so you see you have two people to take care of.

You ought to hear the athletes discuss the relative merits of their babies. There was an argument in my room last night that was the funniest I ever heard. Mr. Hofman's Mary Jane has two teeth and two others just breaking through. She weighs twenty-five pounds. Mr. Reulbach's Edward has four whole teeth and weighs twenty-six. But Mary Jane can pound her fist on the arm of a chair and laugh at the noise. Yes, but Edward is a boy. Whereupon I told them that my four months old nephew—there isn't any such—could dive from a tower ninety feet high into a dishpan full of salt water without making a splash. I wanted to get out of the room so I could go to sleep. One of them left a five o'clock call for my room by way of revenge. Whenever they start their debates in Schulte's presence, he quiets them by saying: "Wait till you hear what *my* dog can do." They don't want to hear so they disperse.

I'm glad you do think of me once in awhile. I think of you all the time and spend my "spare" moments reading your letters. You may tell your grandmother that I don't care whether or not you can keep house. It will be enough to have you there. I know I'll get along all right and I'll be perfectly happy and *contented* as long as I have you. It's awfully hard to wait for the time, though, especially when I don't know just when the time will be. I'm horribly afraid of losing you, dear, and I won't be really "at peace" until I have you all for my own. Did you ever consider the foolishness of quarrels between husbands and wives over practical things and details? There isn't a chance of our quarreling, because I love you too much and because you are too nice.

Isn't it too much to ask you to write every day?
      Yours.
      Ring

The closing comments above demonstrate the unrealistic way in which Lardner idealized his future marriage. He naively believed that afterwards he would be able immediately to eliminate all bad habits, such as drinking and smoking. No man or woman, however gifted, could have lived up to Lardner's ideals. This fact may explain why his marriage, though loving, does not appear to have provided him with the solace he needed in those last years when he saw himself at least partially as a failure as a husband and father and looked out on a world he depicted in his fiction as bleak, mostly insensitive, and largely unsatisfying.

The following letter is most notable for its reference to Frank Schulte's poetry, which Lardner was "quoting" in his

*Tribune* column. Frank Schulte frequently entertained his teammates with deadpan humor and satire similar to Lardner's own, and Lardner by this time had begun to draw upon Schulte's extemporaneous "monologues" and "poetry" for some of the realistic dugout dialogue that had begun to appear in his columns. It is impossible at this time to discern how much Lardner embellished them, but it seems likely that Schulte was a significant influence on the baseball dialogue that Lardner used a few years later in many of his short stories, and that Schulte's satiric representations especially of the dumb ballplayer type contributed to Lardner's delineation of Jack Keefe in the "busher" stories.

The reference toward the end of the letter to the quartet practice by Lardner and some of the Cub ballplayers anticipates the short story "Harmony" (1915), in which the protagonist is a ballplayer who loves to harmonize more than he values holding his starting position on the field; this story was undoubtedly inspired by such experiences.

The opening of the letter responds to a letter from Ellis saying she sometimes felt she should not be teaching Sunday School, because she was "such a little heathen." This admission prompted Lardner to assert his own liberal interpretation of the scriptures:

Wednesday
[New Orleans, 16 March 1910]

Dear Girl,
    Even if you are a heathen, I think you would be shocked by some of my beliefs, or unbeliefs, so I won't tell you what they are. I do think, though, the people that wrote the bible never intended to be taken as literally as they have been. If I were in your Sunday school class, I would shock everyone still more by getting up and kissing you every little while.
    My twin brother, Napoleon Lajoie,[1] is here now with the Cleveland team. His mouth is wider than mine and his nose longer and he isn't quite so good-looking. Do you remember him?
    They are making such awful mistakes with Mr. Schulte's poetry up in The Tribune office that I am almost

---

[1] Napoleon Lajoie was inducted into the Baseball Hall of Fame in 1937 as one of the great second basemen in the game. From 1896 to 1916, mostly with the Cleveland Indians, he achieved a career batting average of .339. In 1901, with the Philadelphia Athletics, his season batting average was .422.

discouraged by it, or with it, and will pass it up entirely unless they leave it alone. It is bad enough to start with, without their ruining it.

My mutter tells me that Anne has a new piano. That's good news, but the old one sometimes served as an excuse for not playing well. You must come over and try it.

We had quartet practice up in my room last night. "The Old Gray Bonnet" and "Roses Bring Dreams of You" were sung more effectively than any others. The Cleveland quartet will rehearse with us tonight and I feel sorry for the guests at this hotel.

And here is one for you:
    Miss Ellis Abbott? She knows that I do;
    That's only her name, but it's awfully true.
    I miss Ellis Abbott, I miss Ellis Abbott;
    Addressing her "Miss" is not merely a habit,
    It's true what I write on the envelope, dear,
    Miss Ellis Abbott"—I wish she were here.

But she owes me five pictures of herself. You wouldn't believe she was the kind of a girl that would forget her promises or refuse to pay her debts.

                But I love her.
                Ring

Hotel Havlin
Cincinnati
Wednesday night.
[13 April 1910]

Dear,—

There is time for a note after all. My loving friends all have deserted me and there is nothing to do until the manager comes back.

I fully intended to write you a long letter this afternoon and was just getting ready to do it when five people came into my room and started a poker game. I was ordered to play and I lost. After the game had broken up, Mr. Tinker, Mr. Evers[1] and I made an agreement not to play poker again this season. Any one of us violating the agreement must give fifty dollars to each of the other two. There's not much danger of my playing under those conditions, but I sincerely hope the other two are unable to resist temptation.

---

[1] Shortstop Joe Tinker and second baseman John Evers, of the famous Cubs' Tinker-to-Evers-to-Chance double play combination.

Manager Chance bought a pipe for Mr. Hofman[1] and one for me, to make our anti-cigarette resolution easier to keep. Oh, yes, the reform movement is strong in our midst.

Tobe finally has consented to tell me where I live. The address is 5002 Washington Park Place, and I think you owe Anne a letter, but please don't neglect me to write to her, for she has a husband and I have not.

It's good to be back in the real circuit, where decent hotels abound. But I never will get over my rage at Mr. Holmes[2] for making us play at Toledo yesterday. I could have seen you, honey, but for his obstinacy.—Maybe, if I have lots of luck, I'll see you sometime, anyway, and I'm just living for the time.

And here comes the manager.

Yours always,
Ring

The letter below responds to a query about Lardner's interest in Ginnie. A day earlier, Ellis had written:

I had such a funny letter from Wilma today. I hadnt heard from her since sometime in January or February and was getting worried. She said she had been hearing gossip and thought I might have told her about it also that Tom Swain (is that his name?) said that he thought you were going to marry that girl in Goshen. Are you? I dont know what to tell her because I'll get found out if I tell her a lie and I wouldn't tell Johnny a very big lie anyway. But I'll fix it some way or other. I have before. You dont like Johnny very well, do you dear? You never said so but I just know it. Johnny has lots of faults but she is wonderfully clever and we have been together all our lives. She is the kind of person you like to know even if you dont like every thing she does. She is what I

---

[1] Lardner had the day before resolved with Artie Hofman, the Cub centerfielder, to stop smoking until New Year's Day. Whoever resumed smoking first before New Year's was to pay the other one hundred dollars (who subsequently won or lost the bet is unknown).

[2] Howard Elbert "Ducky" Holmes was briefly, in 1906, a major league catcher with the St. Louis Cardinals. In 1909 he was manager of the Toledo Mudhens. Lardner's news reports from Toledo include numerous plays on Holmes's nickname because Holmes insisted on playing the game in the rain.

call 'live' and always braces me up like a nice fresh breeze. This is quite a dissertation but I do want to know whether you like her and why not?

Did you catch that?

Hotel Havlin
Cincinnati
Friday night
[15 April 1910]

Dear,—

This is the second one today, but I'm afraid there won't be much time tomorrow and Sunday, and this is to tell you that you're awfully wrong about the Wilma Johnson–Ring Lardner affair. My love for Wilma always has been unrequited. Really, I always enjoyed her thoroughly and liked her very much, but I began steering wide of her because she started acting as if I bored her to death. I dont know where Tom Swain got his tip. I guess Sister Anne, who is one of his sister Bessie's bosom friends, has been doing some guessing herself. The Great American Tongue again. But perhaps it's just as well that the awful truth has been hinted to her, for a sudden shock might kill her.

If you will tell me what paper your cruel and unusual was from, I'll send it to Mr. Taylor, for I think he ought to have it. My mother wrote some verses and sent them in for Hek's column and signed them L.B.L. When Hek used them he said they were sent in by a talented young lady at Niles.

Speaking of the Great American Tongue (you know we were) I have a stunt for you and me to do some day before long. It is a good one, but I won't tell you till I see you, so hurry and come.

You haven't much faith in my swearing off ability, have you, honey? I will fool you and the rest of them who think it will be up to me to pay the fines. No, dear, the cigarette question was not one of health. A pipe or a cigar is just as bad the way I smoke it. It was entirely a question of money. So you were wrong twice in the same letter, but I love you just the same.

We lost another game today and the manager is a little sore on the world tonight. If we don't win tomorrow and Sunday, we'll be afraid to travel to St. Louis with him. I only wish we were going back to Chicago tonight and that you were going to be there.

Remember, you must come.

Ring

On 21 April, Ellis visited Lardner again in Chicago, where they attended the ball game and she stayed overnight at the Tobin apartment.

Hotel Schenley
Pittsburgh, Pa.
Saturday
[30 April 1910]

Dearest,—

I haven't written to you for so long that I've almost forgotten your address. But I remember your name perfectly.

Four of us are to spend Sunday here—Brown, Dryden, Carson and Lardner. Carson and Dryden will stay in their rooms and read, so Brown and Lardner will have to plan an excursion.

I have nine or ten trades for you from persons who saw Thursday's game. I won't give you many of them without pay. Claire Briggs, eminent cartoonist, said, "I'll have to hand it to you; there certainly was some class to her." John DeLong, yachting expert, "She didn't look it, but there must have been something wrong with her mind or she never would have stood for you." H.E. Keough, (Hek): "I don't know how you get away with it, but she surely was a peach."

None of which was news to me even if they are newspaper men. But honestly, honey, I'm awfully proud of you and everything about you. I guess my reputation for unluckiness is all shot to pieces. If I am lucky enough to have you care for me, I surely will be lucky enough to have you for keeps some day.

It was great of you to stay over Thursday night and I wouldn't have missed those few extra minutes for anything. I hope you weren't sorry afterward that you stayed.

If it doesn't rain here Monday, Tuesday or Wednesday, and if I am let off, I'll get to Goshen long before you are up Thursday morning—at three minutes before five. I never was so concerned about the weather before. Please pray for sunshine—I know you have a better stand-in than I.

Yours always,
Ring

In accord with the customs of a more formal age, Lardner now had to ask Mr. Abbott's permission to marry Ellis. The following letter, written nearly six months after Ellis had first accepted his proposal, apologizes for his inability to make the request earlier in person:

Chicago, July fifth. [1910]

Dear Mr. Abbott,—

I'm sorry not to have been able to meet you this afternoon, for I know it would have been more satisfactory than writing. I intended leaving here last night, seeing you this morning and returning in time to attend the ball game here. The paper is very much opposed to allowing us to skip a regular game. There is some rule about not taking the signature off a baseball story during the championship season. Tonight we are going east again and, when we come back, about the first of August, I will manage to get over and see you for a few hours anyway.

Of course you have guessed by this time that I care a great deal for Ellis. I can't help it, although I realize that no one is really worthy of such a girl and do not flatter myself that I am. That she cares for me in return is my only excuse for this letter, which is a request for your consent to our marriage. I know the life she has been used to and know I am not "well off." But I do believe I can take care of her. She told me she would like to wait awhile, and, although I want her just as soon as possible, I know it will be better to wait until I have done some more saving.

My present work takes me from home too often to suit me and I intend to have another arrangement after this season ends. I can tell you more about it after this trip. I know how a father must feel about such things and all I can do is to give the assurance that I can take care of her now, and know that I will do better as time goes along.

I realize how much I am asking of you and Mrs. Abbott and Ellis' sisters and brothers. But I care so much for her I can't help asking and hoping that you will give her to me whenever she is ready.

We are going to stop for one day—tomorrow—at Cleveland, and from there will go to New York to stay from Thursday night until next Tuesday. I would like to hear from you and will be at the Somerset hotel.

              Sincerely,
              Ring W. Lardner

Among the Abbott family, Lardner had become especially close to Ruby, Ellis's older sister, whose interest in music he found especially congenial. When Ellis did not write as often as he wished, he wrote the following to Ruby:

Thursday
[Chicago, 4 August 1910]

Dear Ruby,—

You have a peculiar sister entitled Ellis Abbott. I write letters to her occasionally and I don't believe she reads them. At least, she pays no attention to anything in them. There's something I'd really like to know—namely, on what day in September is she coming to Chicago and about how long can she stay? You know I want to try to arrange my schedule accordingly. If you could find out from her and tell me, I'd do almost anything in your behalf.

Also, I ask you personally if you know a song by Robert Louis Stevenson and Mr. Homer called "Requiem"? Please don't let Ellis Abbott know I have communicated with you.

As a partial reward for your trouble, I send you a picture of myself called "Complete Bewilderment."

And please don't show that to her either.

I haven't much to do this afternoon, so I think I'll go to the ball game.

Please remember me to Dorothy, Florence and Jeannette.[1]

Your affectionate aunt,
Ringgold.
5042 Washington Park Place.

Tuesday night.
[Chicago, 9 August 1910]

Dear Girl,

Richard Lardner Tobin is the title of a new he brat out at our house. I haven't saw him yet and I'm not crazy to, for I never did see one that wasn't a fright. I think him and me will get along all right. I intend to show my authority right from the start. If he gets fresh, I'll slip him some carbolic acid. Please don't mention that to anyone. I'm going to teach him to talk Persian exclusively. Isn't it a shame he wasn't born a week ago yesterday so we could call him August the First?

You seem to think it strange that Paul[2] should be interested in me. I think it's very natural. I'm interested in him. Chiefly because he is your almost brother-in-law. I'll

---

[1] Ellis's younger sisters.

[2] Paull Torrence, Florence Abbott's fiance.

be in Pittsburgh just one more day this year—the eighth of October—and I'll look him up then.

The Lord is having lots of fun with me. At two o'clock this afternoon it was pouring down town, but not a drop fell at the ball park.—You were lucky not to be in Chicago. I ran into the parade twice and spent an hour and ten minutes getting across two streets. After I had sworn not to come to town in the daytime, too. But the arrival of R.L.T. upset my plans. He may be nice and you may like him, but I've got it on him, for I've kissed you and he hasn't.

I'm expecting a long letter from you tomorrow and I'm going to be disappointed if I don't get one. But I know I will, for you said you were going to write this morning. I haven't heard from Philadelphia yet, but I ought to tomorrow. Then I'll know whether I'm ever going to get the long lost letter or not. I want it because I hate to miss one from you.

I thought of you all day and had all kinds of trouble trying to pay attention to the game.

Good night, honey.
     Ring

Wednesday
[Chicago, 10 August 1910]

Honey,—

I was just introduced to R.L.T., who, for some reason, is known as B. around here. Tobe says he looks like me. I know he does not. He has the biggest nose I ever saw, just the right size for this part of town. He makes funny noises all the time, something like a recently caught fish.

I have more T.L's. for you, but you can't have them because you cheated me. And I trusted you, too.

Your letter was great and will be answered in detail. There is nothing new about the song. Some night this week is to be baseball night at the American Music Hall and Miss Mayhew is to sing it then.

The disappearing husband finally wrote to his wife and she told me where he was—down in Atlanta. So I wrote to him there. He hasn't answered and probably won't. The creditor is very nice about it and says I can have more time.

Your explanation about Monk[1] was satisfactory, especially the part about his being ugly. I'm glad of that.

I know I could get a day off if I asked for it, but I also know I ought not to ask for it. It's hard to be patient but I

---

[1] One of Ellis's escorts at Lake Wawasee.

guess it's best. I'm going to write to my colleague tonight and try to arrange the switching with him. But I'm a little afraid to ask him to change the first of September as that would necessitate his suffering an extra five days in St Louis, a town he hates heartily. But I'll do the best I can and let you know. Some day we can laugh at the weather and at the national pastime. I wish that day would hurry up and come.

B. has broken into a loud wail. One consolation— nothing like that ever disturbs my slumbers.

It's almost game time and no sign of rain today.

I love you.

Ring

Life in the Tobin household must have been hectic after the birth of Richard Lardner Tobin.

From the Tobin flat, Lardner wrote to Ellis about the new arrival and about White Sox night on Monday, August 15, at the American Music Hall. The song was "Little Puff of Smoke, Good-Night" (copyrighted on 13 August 1910), one of two songs that Lardner and White Sox pitcher Guy Harris "Doc" White had collaborated on and published (the other was "Gee! It's a Wonderful Game," copyrighted on 13 June 1911). Miss Stella Mayhew's performance of it was greeted with great applause, according to the account (obviously written by Lardner) the following day on the sports page of the *Tribune*. The fact that she was called back for five encores is not surprising, because the entire Sox team and the New York Highlanders were in attendance.

Lardner was even fonder of composing lyrics (and sometimes also music) than he was of writing his doggerel poetry, though only eight of his songs can now be identified as having been published.[1] Perhaps the best known were "Prohibition Blues" (sung by Nora Bayes in the 1919 musical *Ladies First*), and "June Moon" (the title song for his 1929 play in collaboration with George S. Kaufman). Lardner once estimated that if he were to measure his time devoted to composing lyrics against the money they earned, he would have a $10,000 deficit. But he loved to write them, and it was to a considerable extent his interest in music that sustained him in his last years.

---

[1] A few other songs probably were published, but no record survives. See Bruccoli and Layman, *Ring Lardner: A Descriptive Bibliography*, for a list of Lardner's copyrighted sheet music.

Because Ellis's father after six weeks had still not replied to Lardner's written request for permission to marry Ellis, Mrs. Abbott wrote to apologize and to invite Lardner to visit as soon as he could. Lardner framed the following response with obvious care.

[22 August 1910]

Dear Mrs. Abbott,
    I was awfully glad to get your letter, although I never was guilty of imagining that I had been unjustly treated. Ellis told me her father was sick and I was sorry to hear it. But I could not have blamed him for delaying his answer anyway, for I can guess how he must have felt about it—not knowing me at all. I know how a father or a mother must feel about giving up a daughter and especially one like Ellis, who is really so superior. I didn't dream she ever could care for me, and the knowledge that she could and would made me so happy as to cause me to forget for a time some things more important than my own happiness, such as hers, and her separation from her family. But I have thought of them since and can only hope that she will care enough for me to overlook a lot. I know she will not want for love, for she has all of mine.
    Of course I want her as soon as I can have her and I know I will be ready to take care of her by the first of the year, but I am *too* grateful over the prospect of having her at all to want to take her from you before you are ready to let her go.
    I challenge and defy her ever to discourage me and I don't believe I would care quite so much for her if she were more practical.
    I have been trying all summer to get down to Goshen, but I had to wait for rain, and it never came at the right time. However, I'm sure I'll have better luck next month and I will come the first day I can. Thank you for the invitation and also for writing.
                       Sincerely,
                         Ring W. Lardner
August Twenty-second.

Tuesday
[Boston, Mass.
30 August 1910]

Dearest Girl,—

It's cold in Boston, Mass., and the old shivers are present with me again. I don't think I ever could hold a job as an Arctic explorer. Anyway, I wouldn't care to try.

The Boosters club of Baltimore is stopping here and affording us almost as much enjoyment as the Boys from Amherst used to. Probably we amuse it, too.

I have an unpleasant task ahead of me. Frank Schulte's brother killed himself and I suppose I must write one of those awful letters. He is having a gay life with an insane mother and a brother who must have been as bad.

There was a letter from my mother this morning which was sort of song of praise for you. I suppose it was the result of Lena's home coming and her conversation about you. You sure are "in right" with the Lardner family. But don't you believe that the rest of them are as much in love with you as I am, no matter what they say.

I won't tell you now what your mother said about you. Perhaps I can use my knowledge in making bargains when I see you. She didn't knock you *very* much. If she had, I wouldn't have answered her letter.

I presume you have heard from Anne by this time. She says B. is becoming more reasonable every day, taking after his uncle Ringgold. Blood will tell.

Tomorrow night we will start west, stopping in Detroit for three days. Then we'll go home just for Labor Day and then to St Louis—Planters hotel—for five horribly long days. Then I will see you and that will be reward enough for recent hardships. You can't guess how I am longing for the arrival of the eleventh and for you. Don't dare to disappoint me.

Yours always,
Ring

Though Mrs. Abbott had invited Lardner to Goshen, the conference with Mr. Abbott could not take place until Lardner had the necessary free time, after the World Series. In the midst of this confusion, Ellis accepted a teaching position in the elementary school of the Culver (Indiana) Military Academy, which effectively postponed any possible wedding until the following June. Ellis explained that "we both need at least a year to try to learn to know each other a little better." She was also worried about her father's attitude toward Lardner, for Mr. Abbott in addition to being possessive about his daughters was concerned about Lardner's financial status and his professional association with "that damned sporting crowd."

The letter below, written to Ellis at Culver, refers to an "interview" between Ellis and her mother that was probably an attempt by Ellis to enlist her mother's assistance in urging Mr. Abbott to consent formally to the marriage, for he had still not responded to Lardner's letter of 5 July.

Sunday night
[Chicago, 11 September 1910]

My Honey,—

I don't know Mrs. Crandall[1] or whether or not she is to be trusted with anything so precious. Please don't let anything happen to you.

I mailed a letter to Goshen late Saturday night because I didn't know where else to send it. Perhaps it arrived too late. You can bet I'm anxiously awaiting news of the result of your interview with your mother. It means more to me than anything ever did, and to you, too, poor girl. I will give you two T.L.'s. in exchange for your two very nice ones, but I'm ashamed of John for wishing Ruby such hard luck. Mr. Eckersall said "You'd better hurry up and *grab* her before she wises up and quits you. She looks good to me." And Mr. Briggs: "Yes, because anyone is likely to try to steal her and you wouldn't have much chance in a real contest." When I pointed out the fact that I had won against a large field, they suggested the field was made up of Hoosiers, and that even I might look classy in such a race. While it isn't right for them to roast me—who really am or is a nice person—I forgive them because they speak well of you. I also have T.L's from my mother, but I'm not doing any credit business.

Perhaps we are going to have next Thursday off. If we do, I'll go home, I guess for I promised to do so some time this month. When that engagement is kept, I'll be free to see you some day next week, on my way to Cincinnati to join the Cubs.

When you write, tell me all about Culver. Also, that you love me.

Good-night, dear girl.
                      Always yours,
                          Ring.

---

[1] The wife of Captain Crandall, commandant at Culver, with whose family Ellis lived while teaching there.

On the 15th, Ellis was especially expressive of her love:

> My Sweetheart
> 
> I want you so! I want you so! I want you! I came home and did a few errands and went right out to the Fair. It was fun seeing the crowds and the races and all the people we knew. But *now* the excitement is over and I am just beginning to realize how hard it was to leave you. And isn't it dreadful? I might have stayed until the next train and been with you three hours longer. I'm so lonesome and blue. No one else helps at all. I need just you and next September *does* seem a long way off. I cant tell you about that definitely now but I will in a day or two.
> 
> I had such a nice time every minute I was in Chicago and I love you twice as much or a hundred times as much as I did before. If you think theres any chance of your ever not loving me *please* tell me now before it gets any worse. I'm thinking of you every minute and I need you.
> 
> Give my love to Anna and the baby and dont forget that I love you, love you, love you
> 
>                           Your own girl
> 
> I want to kiss you goodnight and I cant.

Lardner answered with an "ode":

> *Ode to Ellis*
> Before you came, I lived for something—
>     what, I never knew
> Until the day arrived when first I gave my
>     heart to you;
> Then living was a constant pain, a poignant
>     misery,
> Until the glorious day when first you gave
>     your heart to me.
> Now vainly fights the pain of knowing that
>     we're far apart.
> To overcome the joy of knowing that I
>     have your heart.

Ellis's "interview" with her mother was unsatisfactory. Ellis reported that Mrs. Abbott did not want Ellis to leave the home just yet but had agreed to talk to Ellis's father again about her marriage.

The following letter was written after Lardner had managed to see Ellis on two successive evenings. He had taken a train to Culver on a Thursday evening, stayed overnight at a hotel, and then, on Friday evening after Ellis had finished teaching, the two had gone to Niles and to Goshen to visit their parents.

Hotel Havlin
Cincinnati, Ohio
Monday morning.
[3 October 1910]

Honey,—
    Your small boy certainly has been making up for his days off. That Big Four train from Goshen got to Indianapolis an hour late. As we came into the station, the C. H. and D. was pulling out. I didn't have time to ask where it was going, but I hopped on and fortunately it was the right one. "Fortunately" is right, for I don't know what would have happened if I'd been late. I do know a lot of things did happen and have been happening ever since.
    In the game Saturday, Johnny Evers, one of the "stars," broke his leg and put himself out of the world's series. Yesterday's game made the Cubs champions of their own league and there sure was a celebration last night. Mr. Chance suspended the rules and said he would fine anyone caught drinking anything but wine and anyone caught paying for anything at all. So we signed his name to checks till they ran out of supplies and then we went to bed and were glad to get there.
    There's an important meeting of the commission today, and also a ball game, so business is still good.
    But I haven't forgotten you for a minute. You are still far more important than baseball in all its branches and I'm going to see you again the minute I can get away. I'm afraid that minute isn't coming very soon.
    Please don't forget me, dear. I think I'll have time to write the long letter when I get home Wednesday morning. Meanwhile, I love you.
                          Ring

Lardner did receive the following letter on the 5th. For the first time in the correspondence, Ellis begins to focus on domestic "stuff":

Dearest

I'm using my recess to the best advantage I know how—writing to you. I dont dare let the children see me or they'll say, "Miss Abbott is writing to her beau."

I am enclosing a picture which I know you'll enjoy. Do you think you can find me? George Ann Lacy took it last Sunday morning. Ruby and Helen Irwin (the middle one) and I stayed with her Saturday night and we did have a circus. It was such fun to be with girls again. There isnt a one here. George Ann is to be married in March or April and she wants me to play her wedding march. Did you ever hear anything so funny?

I got to thinking about housekeeping and expenses and things last night. Mrs. Crandall had been talking about her keeping house in a little flat when she was just married. Wont we want a little four roomed apartment and have you any idea at all about rent? I havent. You do want to go to housekeeping dont you? I guess you'll have to anyway because I *just wont board*. How much are you going to allow me a week for housekeeping? Is'nt it *funny* to be thinking about such things? Its such fun that now I'm started I cant think of anything else. It gives me such a funny little thrill to think of having a home of my very own and when I think that its going to be *our* very own it is a very big thrill. Do you think you'll get tired of it, dear? There'll be times when we're both tired and cross and everything will go wrong and I'll be spending too much money and you'll be discouraged with everything. But we can always remember that we have each other, cant we? And then things will look bright again.

Its a wonderful thing to think that someone will always be interested in you. We'll have some splendid talks when we are all by ourselves in our own little home wont we? And you'll tell me all you ever thought or did and all you want to do. I always love to know just how other people look at life, whether it means just the same thing to them as it does to me,

This has taken two recesses instead of one.

                    Dont forget my *long* letter.
                    Your own girl

Thursday
[Chicago,
6 October 1910]

Dearest Girl,—

I'm down at the office and I left your letters at home, but I can remember them I guess. First and foremost, I was awfully glad to get them because I heard from you for a long time.

I've been intending to order the paper for you, but the *country* circulation office manages to close before I get in from the ball game. I'll come down early tomorrow and do it.

I'm afraid, honey, I don't know any more about housekeeping expenses than you do. If this baseball season ever ends, I'll have time to talk things over with Richard and Anne, who ought to know something by this time. Encouraging to me are the thoughts that they got along all right—and he wasn't making any more than I am, although he always had more sense about his money.—and that I spent enough to take care of three people before you and the reform wave came. I know I can be as saving as Tobe because I won't want the things that cost when I have you. Don't worry, dear, you won't have to board. I'm looking forward too gladly to our own home to think of that. I think I'll be making enough by that time so that you can have some one to help you with cooking and other foolish things.

We must have five rooms in our flat. You are not to be shut off from your family and we want room for one or two or three of them whenever they want to come. I know *all* about rents, but that's *none of your business* and I don't think I ought to peddle my knowledge for nothing.

I want to be somewhere near Anne, so I can have an ally when you begin to think of leaving me.

You can't make me believe I ever will be discouraged or cross with you around. I'm afraid of one thing—you'll find out how little brains I possess in those talks of ours, and become disgusted [with] me. I guess my best play is to keep still.

I must quit.
                       Yours always,
                       Ring

After the World Series ended (the Cubs lost to Philadelphia, four games to one), Lardner went to Goshen for the long-anticipated interview with Mr. Abbott. Ring Lardner Jr. describes the situation thus:

Ellis complained to her mother that her father still hadn't answered Ring's letter, and Mrs. Abbott agreed to intercede for her, with the result that Ring was invited to pay a call on Mr. Abbott. Ellis was away at Culver, but some of her siblings and her mother were waiting outside the double doors when the two men emerged from their conference. Mrs. Abbott said she hoped Mr. Lardner could stay for supper, and Mr. Abbott said "Supper! He's staying all night," and everyone knew the meeting had been a great success.[1]

Ring Jr. also points out that since Ellis had announced her engagement and a June wedding at a luncheon three days earlier, Mr. Abbott must simply have wished to be able to say that he had met Lardner and to have adhered to the formal ritual of interviewing the man his daughter was to marry.

After some correspondence with Ellis's mother and with Ellis's sister, Ruby, in which Lardner worried that Ellis was working too hard at Culver, he reinforced this concern to Ellis:

Tuesday
[Chicago,
8 November 1910]

Dearest Girl,—

I didn't stuff your honorable family with untruths and you know it. I told some simple truths in the hope that said family would cooperate with me in making you mend your awful ways.

I didn't work yesterday. I staid home till after supper and then Tobe volunteered to mind the child while Anne and I went over to our new private theater on Fifty-first street. They had the world's series pictures and I made up my mind that you never would be allowed to see them. You would fall out of love with me pretty quick if you did.

If the dish towels are hemmed, I don't see why you can't get ready by February. I want you before June, and I hate to have you wearing yourself out down there. I can't forget that you said you didn't want to go back. Why should you want to? And the worst of it is that you don't

---

[1] Ring Lardner Jr., p. 56.

have to. We're going to have another quarrel when I see you.

I'm going downtown now to meet Doc White and be introduced to a music publisher—why, I know not. Also, I'm going to find out when I can get back to Indiana from Ithaca. Be sure to tell me where you are going to be. As soon as you do, I'll write you your orders.

Yours always,<br>Ring

Although Lardner was reluctant to leave the *Tribune*, where he felt at ease and had matured as a reporter, the new financial needs connected with his approaching marriage led him later that month to accept the managing editorship of the weekly *Sporting News* in St. Louis, when the job was offered by the owner, Charles Spink. The new position was prestigious (the *Sporting News* was even then regarded as "baseball's bible"), paid better, and did not require traveling.

However, the relationship with Spink was uneasy from the beginning. Hugh Fullerton later wrote:

> I tried to keep Lardner from going to the *Sporting News*, because I knew him so well and because I knew and loved Charley Spink so well. I was certain those two never would understand each other, and they didn't.[1]

Lardner would stay only three months.

Friday night.
[St. Louis, 2 December 1910]

My darling Girl,—

I'll tell you a little about St Louis, but not everything, for if I went that far, I'm afraid you would have to change your opinion of my cleverness. But first, please promise you will try to love me even if I can't hold this job. It's a lot heavier than I was led to believe and I started wrong today by heartily hating my employers at first sight. They're as much like the Tribune people as Mrs. Crandall is like Mrs. Frank P. Abbott. What was it I told you about my hours? The real ones are from 8 to 5:30 except on Sunday, when

---

[1] Fullerton's remark is quoted by Donald Elder in *Ring Lardner*, New York, 1956, p. 87. Elder's source is unknown.

there is only about an hour's work. So your father needn't worry on that score. New jobs always are awful, though, and I'm going to stick till I'm fired. It isn't half as bad as your work at Culver, and I guess I'm just so lonesome for you that I can't look at things cheerfully. March and June are farther away now than they were two days ago.

I looked up rooms this noon and called up one that seemed desirable. I came out to look it over tonight and got the wrong house—next door to the one I thought I was going to. But it didn't seem to make much difference. Both are regular boarding houses and both have pianos. So I decided to stick to this place. The landlady called me "dear" twice in the first five minutes of our acquaintance. Tomorrow my trunk is coming with its set of Balzac and from tomorrow night on, I'm going to divide my time— evenings—between him and you, with the piano once in awhile. I intend to retire at 9:30 every night, and arise at 6:45. Across from me there dwelleth a rather pretty young lady—and her husband. They seem so happy that I'm mad at them. They're the only ones I've seen of my new family except our common mother. I live at 5087 Fairmount avenue, but I guess you'd better send letters to the office for awhile.

Speaking of letters, honey, will you try your very hardest to write to me every day? Your letter today was a great big help and I don't know what would have happened to me without it. But you must get out of your head that ridiculous idea that I love you less than I did. I love you more, a million times more, and it's just plain hell to be without you. If you were here now, I'd kiss you and kiss you and make you promise never to leave me again. And I wouldn't let you cry ever again. But don't think I'm a beast when I say I'm glad you cried the other night. It hurt me to have you, but it made me feel surer of your love. Dear, you must tell me just how you feel all the time. I want to know everything about you, for really you are part of me, the bigger part, and I can't think of myself without thinking of you. This is a peculiar, mixed-up letter, but nothing makes any difference except that I love you and you love me. Sweetheart, don't get tired of me now.

I'm glad you didn't hear my speech at the "banquet" last night. They gave me a traveling bag and I had to thank them for it. It was awful. But I was all swelled up on myself because their efforts failed to knock me off the water wagon. Mr. Eckersall had tears in his eyes when he said farewell to me—they were extra dry tears. My boss said the Tribune job would be held open for me till the first of February. That was very nice of him.

> Tell me about your Niles trio. Also that you love me.
> Have you given Florence permission to write?
> > Goodnight, dear girl.
> > Ring

Ellis wrote back reassuringly:

> I'll still love you if you get fired a hundred times but Im dreadfully sorry you dont like the St. Louis people. I know how it is though I dont go quite so far as to "heartily hate" my many employers. Perhaps the hours wont be so long when you get things started. But, dear, dont you dare think of staying there on my account—(because of money or any thing else) if you dont want to. I wont think one bit less of you and neither will anyone else, if you give it up and come back to the Tribune. Of course they'll keep the job for you. Who wouldn't? I am keeping a place for you until June so you can see that I love you better—by four months—than they do. More than that I love you a hundred million times more than anyone else in the world.

In the social world of the Culver Academy, where Ellis was the only single young woman among a predominantly male faculty, a Captain Willhite was escorting Ellis to various academic functions. Ellis was flattered by his attention to her, and Lardner was jealous. On the 14th, Ellis teased him with some news that added to the frustrations he was experiencing in St. Louis:

> Captain Willhite came over yesterday afternoon and we went for a little walk—then he came over again in the evening at 7.45 P.M. and stayed until 11.15 P.M. Why he wanted to stay three hours and a half is more than I know unless he wanted a good listener. I was so sleepy I couldnt talk. More than that he offered to go to South Bend with me if I went Friday night and recheck my trunk for me but I am not going Friday night.

Lardner immediately communicated his concern that Ellis should have spent four hours alone with Captain Willhite: "I guessed him right, and if he keeps it up, I'm going to quit my job and make a quick trip to Indiana." A series of letters ensued on the merits and honor of the Captain. Though the flirtation was not serious on Ellis's part, she obviously enjoyed Lardner's jealousy.

Saturday night.
[St. Louis,
31 December 1910]

My dearest Girl,—
    I hope you aren't tired of records and statistics, for I'm going to give you some more of them.
    1. This is the last day of December. There were thirty-one days in this month, and during it I have written you thirty-one letters, *one every day.* I'm not boasting of their quality, but you'll have to admit and admire the quantity.
    2. During the thirty-one days of December, I have not gone outside the door of my boarding house once after supper. I went to Moore's for supper one night and was back here before nine that night. I claim this as a world's record for a single gent in good health, between the ages of twenty and thirty. Are you proud of me? There's really no reason you should be, for I wrote to you because I loved you and I staid in because I loved you and because the outside had no attraction for me. Sometimes I'm afraid you may grow tired of getting my letters. I'm still remembering the words of Mildred, who said you ceased to care for people when they cared too much for you. I don't know whether I love you too much or not, but I do know I love you more than anyone else ever loved anyone and that I'll die if March doesn't hurry.
    Tomorrow I will write you a beautiful New Year's poem if I remember it.
                       Yours always,
                         Ring

Ellis wrote:

> I am very proud of you but I dont see why you feel it necessary to stay in every evening. However if you stop writing to me every day I'll kill you. You needn't worry about caring too much. The more you love me the more I'll love you. You are the one grand exception.

    Unfortunately Lardner's records both in early evening retirement and staying on the water wagon fell on New Year's Eve, as his next letter reveals:

Tuesday night.
[3 January 1911]

My own Sweetheart,—
 Your threat to kill came today. Please don't carry it out, for I didn't know of it till after I'd missed two nights. And I would have written tonight anyway. I won't tell you why my beautiful record was spoiled for a minute or two, because of my New Year's resolution not to lie, and I don't want to tell you the truth. A piece of the truth is that I had been a little too good and something had to break. But everything's all right again now, and I'll try to keep it so.
 You must send me not only your own picture, but the family one as well. And I want them soon.
 Awfully sorry to hear your father wasn't well and I hope he's all right again. But I was glad you went to Niles. You weren't greeted by one hundred people, nor fifty—there were just eight outside the family and they were Bess and Florence and Nellie Burns and Effie Deam and Seely and Lottie and Marjorie Deam, and Lute Beeson. And here is some more dope from my mother's letter: "She (Mrs. Abbott) is a lovely woman; sweet-faced and motherly. I hope she likes me at first sight as well as I do her. She is bright and witty, too: and Ellis looks as she used to, I'm sure. Ellis is lovely to her (you see I use that word 'lovely' often, but advisedly) and now I can realize that the family is loving, *well-bred* and sympathetic: and I'm glad you have chosen a girl out of it.
 "We surely were delighted with her (Mrs. Abbott) and Ellis' affectionate care of her showed *the girl* in a still brighter light than ever. She is a 'peach' really. Perhaps you know that!"
 So you see, Miss Abbott, you mustn't jilt me now, for I never could face my family if I lost you. There are three things that could prevent the June 28th event—1. You might stop caring for me. 2. You might die. 3. I might die. I'll promise faithfully not to, if you'll promise not to let the other two happen. It's awfully hard sometimes to realize I'm going to have you and a thing like your going to Niles helps me to realize, so I like it. If you're absolutely sure your love will increase in direct proportion to mine, I'll tell you how much I love you—so much that there isn't a second when you aren't monopolizing my thoughts, nor when your face isn't between my eyes and my work, and you are my last thought at night and my first in the morning, and I like to go to the office better than I like to come "home" because, generally, there's a letter waiting for me down there; and it actually hurts me physically when there isn't and takes all my spirit away, and it also hurts me

to know always that I'm not fit for you and that it would be the most natural thing in the world for you to find it out. But if any of that makes you love me less, dear, please pretend I didn't say it.

Cold weather has come at last and it isn't fooling either. I hope you aren't cold at Culver and I hope also that your work won't be so awfully hard.

Please tell me the C.—W.— News. Do you know I suspect the reason you won't trust me with what you wrote to him is that you believe it would make me still more jealous?

If you had more than one kind of picture taken, you must send me all to choose from.

The three scarf pins incident was funny—that's why I told Anne I love my cameo and you, but I see plainly that my family is not to be trusted.

                Yours always,
                Ring.

Please forgive my sins.

If you love me, I want to know why.

Monday night.
[St. Louis, 9 January 1911]

Dearest Girl,—

For some reason this was the worst and most lonesome day of my St Louis existence. For one thing, there was no letter from you, but I didn't expect one because it was Monday. I had lots of work to do, but time dragged and I thought of you incessantly. June seemed a thousand miles away and things were just desperate. Will you answer me a truth question? Do you love me every bit as much as you said you did before I came down here? I don't know why it is, but I can't help thinking you've jumped down a little. If I had you here I'd make you tell me you loved me eight hundred times. You'd have to do it, too, or I'd punish you.

Mr. Spink is going on his vacation next week and I hope he stays away forever. It's getting so it irritates me just to look at him. But I won't inflict him on you anymore.

I dissipated tonight—Mr. and Mrs. Pretty and I going to a moving picture show. One of the stories was of a girl who forgot *him* when he went away and I didn't care for it a bit.

Ruby said she was having lots of *fun* embroidering napkins for *us*. I think it must be lots of fun and we'd better have some unembroidered ones in the house all the time for emergency amusement. I'll work on them while you read to me.

Tell me how school is going and how hard you are working and how you feel.

I love you, honey, and it's a continuous series of jumps up or jump ups.

Ring.

At this time, the newspapers were covering a number of demonstrations, particularly in New York City and Washington, D.C., supporting the Women's Suffrage Amendment (the 19th Amendment to the Constitution passed finally in 1920). In the following letter, Lardner takes a cavalier male view of the situation:

Tuesday night.
[St. Louis, 10 January 1911]

My dearest Girl,—

The agitation about Woman's Rights is a dismal joke. All the rights in the world are on the side of women and *girls*, which you are. For instance—you can tell me you're not going to write for three days and you won't tell me why. If I told you I wouldn't write for three days, you'd probably say, "Don't bother to write at all." But I can't say that, because if you didn't write at all I'd die. You can tell me you won't write for a month and I just have to bear it. But I have to write to you because I'm so desperately afraid of losing you and because I like to talk to you. All I can ask with about an even chance of getting a reply is: Are you ever going to tell me the wherefore of this neglect? and will you make up for it—partly—with a long, long letter? The next three days are going to be hard ones, honey. Please don't make me endure it longer than that.

Now that you can make hot rolls—which I know must be better than anyone else's—why should you bother any more about learning to cook? That's enough and I don't want you to work outside of school hours.

I burned my bridges today and after the craziest change of mind I ever suffered. I got a letter from the Tribune. It wanted to know if I wouldn't come back, but of course couldn't promise relief from travelling and night work. I sat down to write and say I would come if certain concessions were made, and, instead, I said there wasn't a chance for me to leave here and that it might as well go ahead and get a successor. Then I couldn't decide whether or not to mail the letter, but finally I did it. So, now, it's St Louis for awhile at least. I think I need a guardian. Do you want the job?

Goodnight, sweetheart.

Ring.

In his next letter, Lardner reminded Ellis of the significance of January 26—the first-year anniversary of the kiss on the Tobins' sofa:

Tuesday night.
[St. Louis, Missouri
24 January 1911]

Dearest,—
You aren't going to get a long letter tonight, because I've got to go to a "consultation," but if I didn't write at all, you'd probably think I'd fallen again, and I don't want you to think that.

You didn't go into details about the "lovely" things you got and you didn't tell me if you had a picture taken, which is one of the lovely things I want.

Today I sent you something; not much of a something and I won't vouch for its goodness. It is sent you provisionally: It is supposed to reach you on the 26th of January and you may keep it *provided* you know what great event occurred on that date. If you can't tell me, you must send it back (You'll probably want to, anyway). Here's a hint—January 26th 1911 is the first anniversary of the great event.

Being the younger brother of a Prince doesn't get me anything. You know the eldest is the heir to the throne.

It's only fair that a girl should have everything she wants when she's going to be married, for usually, she doesn't get anything she wants afterward.

Tobe's life insurance man came to see me today and landed me. He knew all about my "prospects." So I asked him if I couldn't make Mrs. R.W. my beneficiary and he said I couldn't because she didn't exist yet. So my "estate" had to be put down instead. You must pull for me to live till after June; you will be my estate then, but if I should die now, you wouldn't get a penny.

Write me a long letter, honey.
Ring

Ellis responded:

Indeed I do know what the twenty sixth is an anniversary of though I was'nt sure of the exact date. It was a very very happy day and a year from tomorrow will be even happier. Thank you in advance for whatever the something is and especially for remembering it . . . .

I hate the word insurance. Father has spent most of his life paying out large sums of money for insurance but it is my opinion that all men are alike when it comes to that so have it if you want it. What do you suppose I'll care about money if you aren't here. I am going to die too.

Thursday night.
*January 26*
St. Louis]

Sweetheart,—

A year ago tonight, you and I sat on the sofa at Anne's house and I read to you and Anne went out and while she was gone, something happened that made me happier than anyone who ever lived. I kissed you and, after awhile, you kissed me and told me you cared. And Anne came back, but we staid up after she had gone to bed. And we talked, and our conversation was the most interesting—to me—I ever took part in. A year ago yesterday noon you came to Chicago. A year ago last night we went to a play. A year ago this afternoon it was a matinee. You see I was trying to win you by showing you a good time—and a year ago tonight you rewarded me for the enormously good time I had shown you. In this year I've been happy most of the time (although the happiness was mostly prospective) scared often, sure sometimes that you didn't love me, and sure other times that you did.

Do you know what I'm doing tonight? You know I told you about a nurse's coming to take care of a little boy who was sick. He died today and I am sitting up. His mother, who hasn't slept for a week, keeps coming in all the time and looking at him. She just stares at me and I'm afraid she's going crazy. After awhile, when Mr. Perkins (alias Mr. Pretty) comes home, I think I'll make him take my place for a little while so I can take a walk over to the mail-box. I must go out for it's awfully hot in here and generally uncomfortable.

Here's a "New Year's" resolution. After this my letters are going to be different, for I don't believe you could like the kind I usually write. And after insisting that you keep on loving me, I'm never going to ask you another question, nor make any request of you whatever.

                Yours always,
                Ring.

Ellis answered by teasing him about the "anniversary":

Oh I meant to tell you! I know now what anniversary the 26th of January is. Its Captain Willhite's birthday—he told me so last night—he was thirty one.

As the following letter makes clear, Lardner had decided that working for Charles Spink was intolerable. Why Lardner considered him "dishonest" is unknown, but Lardner's implied comparison of Spink with Jesse James suggests that monetary ethics had something to do with their incompatibility. Lardner's ethics were higher than most, but Spink was a highly respected, if somewhat parsimonious, newspaper man.

Friday.
[St. Louis, 3 February 1911]

Dear,—
 I think I would rather be kicked downstairs than write this letter, but it's got to be written. But before I forget, I've been perfectly well and I'll tell you why I haven't written before when I see you, perhaps. Also, I don't understand why you, with the prettiest and most perfect teeth in the world, should have anything to do with a dentist unless you're going to act as an advertisement for him.
 Now for business—It didn't take me all this time to discover that Mr. Spink was dishonest. I knew it before I'd been here a month, but I decided to swallow it "for the good of the cause." He did something about a month ago without my knowledge that was against all newspaper rules, but I explained my innocence to the offended person and was believed. Day before yesterday he tried to put over something else, but he told me about it, and I kicked. I told him I'd quit if he did it, and he was afraid to have me quit because Ban Johnson, the president of the American League, which is responsible for his paper's success, recommended me. But we had some warm words and I told him I would just as soon work for Jesse James and that I was going to leave very shortly. Yesterday he tried to square things and I just listened to him and didn't say anything. If you care to listen to details, I'll tell them to you when I see you again. Anyway, I was invited to lunch yesterday by Billy Grayson of whom I have told you. He is owner of the American Association team in Louisville. He asked me how I'd like to be business manager of the Louisville Club. I told him not at all because it would necessitate my travelling. That closed the incident until today, when he took me to lunch again.

We talked for an hour and a half and he finally said he would fix things so I would have to take only one trip after we are married. The towns in that association are Louisville, Indianapolis, Toledo, Columbus, Milwaukee, Minneapolis, St. Paul and Kansas City. The trips never last more than fifteen days. I figured I could take you along on the only one after June—probably in August or September—and we wouldn't have to mingle with the athletes. The salary is the same I get here. He has promised me a bonus if he makes so much money. Here's how the matter stands now: I'll go with him if you can stand for Louisville. I don't know whether you know anything about the town or not. To boost it I'll say it is just as pretty and much cleaner than St Louis. Also, I'll say we don't have to stay there after the middle of October if we don't want to.

If I "accept the position," I'll probably quit here a week from next Tuesday. A week from Tuesday night, I'll start for Chicago, spend Wednesday and part of Thursday there, come to Culver Thursday night, take you to Niles Friday night, to Goshen Saturday morning and back to Culver Sunday afternoon. I do want to talk to you and convince you I'm not a grass-hopper because I jump around so much.

Here's what I want you to do: If you aren't awfully disappointed, if you think you can stand it, telegraph me, as soon as you get this, in care of the Sporting News. If you don't want to make the change, telegraph me to that effect. In either case, send the message collect and remember I love you.

Later—I've decided to mail this special delivery to Goshen, so you'll get it Sunday, so when you wire, address the message to 5087 Fairmont Avenue. And please don't say anything about this to anyone for awhile.

    Ring

The fact that Lardner was willing to risk Ellis's—and her father's—disapproval by changing positions three months before the wedding indicates how desperate he must have been to remove himself from a situation in which he felt he could not get along with his employer. From Goshen, Ellis immediately wrote back reassuringly, but with the alarming news that her father objected to the Louisville offer:

Dearest

  I just got your letter an hour or so ago and will do my best to answer it coherently. In the first place and before everything I want you to know that whatever you do will always be all right. I didnt know what to think when you got your letter—I am about as good at deciding things as a hedgehog—so I told father about it in spite of your telling me not to say anything about it. However I dont think he will spread the information. He quite agreed with you about staying with Mr. Spick and Span under the circumstances and so do I. I wonder you have'nt murdered him before this but I am very proud of you for having principles and sticking to them. I wish I had them. On the other hand dad thinks a "sporting man" is a "sporting man" and cant change his spots—and that his daughters are delicate and rare *things* and that they must not come in contact with that "damned sporting crowd." He is in fact quite strenuously opposed to the Louisville idea.

As far as I am concerned it does'nt make one bit of difference about the city we live in. Father wants to know whether it would be in any way possible for you to come up here before you decide definitely. But if it is'nt he says go ahead and do whatever you think best—that you know more about it than he does—which is very strange indeed. I want to do whatever you do—*honestly!*

I've got to hurry down town with this. I am dreadfully sorry you are having such a worrying time and wish I could help you more. I have'nt said much but the sum and substance of it all is—to do whatever you think best and it will be all right with me.
always
your own girl
There is one right thought in this business—that I may see you soon.

Lardner wrote the following letter to Mr. Abbott in an attempt to convince him that the Louisville position was a desirable one. This letter must have been difficult for Lardner, because many of his close friends were ballplayers or sportswriters and he did not share Mr. Abbott's low opinion of the sports world, even during a time in which most major league ballplayers were not particularly well educated or economically privileged. Many of the athletes in Lardner's fictional world are self-centered and insensitive, but most of them are depicted sympathetically.

St. Louis, February 5th
[1911]

Dear Mr. Abbott,—
    I just heard from Ellis, who told me of her conversation with you regarding my prospective change of cities and jobs. She told me you were opposed to the Louisville idea and I can quite understand your opposition. I myself am opposed to some features of it. However, it is a much different thing, in respect to my relation to the ball players, from my former job with the Tribune. Then it was up to me to mingle with them so that I might know what was going on. In the Louisville proposition, it will be to my interest and the interest of the owner, to keep away from everyone but the manager, who, in this case, is one of the most decent men I ever met. You can depend on it, Ellis won't ever have to see a ball player or a ball game. She can go to a game when she wants to, but I'm just as much opposed to her being "mixed up" in it as you are. It was impossible for me to delay my answer beyond tonight, so I told Mr. Grayson I would accept. He agreed to the conditions of my acceptance, which were that I would be allowed ten days off in June and that I wouldn't be obliged to make more than one trip after that. He also has a secretary who can do that travelling part of it a couple of times. My chief duty is to see that none of his employees, such as his ticket sellers and privilege men, are stealing from him, to oversee things in general, and have his books in such shape that he will know always how he stands. He's in a hurry to have me on the ground to prepare programs, advertising etc., for the coming season. He is in the lumber business here with his brothers and baseball is a sort of side issue with him. He wants to be able to leave Louisville any time his other business calls him.
    So I will leave St. Louis about a week from Tuesday. I want to spend a couple of days in Chicago, and I probably will be in Goshen a week from Saturday. Then I will explain things to you more fully. I don't intend to spend my life as "guardian" of the Louisville club. In fact, Mr. Grayson and I plan to start a paper of our own within a year. We were going to do it this spring, but we thought we had better wait until we had thought things out and been able to go into it with more certainty of making it pay. He, of course, is to furnish the capital, if we do make the plunge before I have enough capital of my own saved up to put in with his.
    As for The Sporting News part of it, it doesn't require knowledge of newspaper work to see that its publisher is not on the square. I will tell you this side of it when I see you, but I can assure you now that it's absolutely impossible for me to stay in his employ. It's a shame, too, because I liked

the work, when I was let alone in it, and I believe I could have improved the paper. The Tribune held my old place open until the first of February, but I couldn't go back there, because that would mean travelling about five months of the year, night work when I wasn't travelling, and it also would look as if I had failed to make good down here. I could have gone to work for one of the St Louis papers, but they don't pay as much and I would hate ever to work for less money than I had received before. So, as I had to have a job, I picked the Louisville one as the best, and I don't think I'll regret it. I waited for Ellis' consent, which came tonight, and then caught Mr. Grayson just before he started for Louisville.

You needn't be a bit afraid that she will be forced to meet an "athlete." I won't let her, but I guess she won't be so anxious that I'll have to "forbid" it.

       Sincerely,
5087 Fairmount Ave.  Ring Lardner

The specific events of the next two weeks are unclear, until Lardner writes in the following letter that he has taken a position as sports reporter on the Boston *American*. What seems probable is that, after ending his three-month ordeal under Charles Spink, he travelled to Goshen, where he found Mr. Abbott unalterably opposed to the Louisville job. In searching elsewhere for employment, Lardner probably consulted his old friend Hugh Fullerton, who had recommended Lardner for his first Chicago newspaper job on the *Inter-Ocean*. Fullerton recommended Lardner for the vacant post at the Boston *American*, one of the Hearst chain, and Lardner accepted, at the respectable salary of forty-five dollars a week—only five dollars less than he had been earning in St. Louis, and ten dollars more than he had received from the *Tribune*. In any case, we rediscover Lardner on 24 February writing to Ellis from Boston to describe his new job:

Copley Square Hotel
Boston, Mass.
Friday night
[24 February 1911]

My own Girl,—
 Writing to you from this room seems like old times and it would be natural to think I was going to see you in Northampton in a day or two.
 My experience this afternoon was almost as funny as you are. I called up the paper this afternoon (emphasis by

repetition) as soon as I got in and the managing editor asked me to come right down. When I got there I discovered I knew the sporting editor perfectly well, a welcome discovery. Before I had a chance to show humility befitting an employe, they began to exhibit gratitude at my condescending to take the job. They said they would be glad if I would go south with the National league team, but assured me they wouldn't make me do so against my will. I didn't want to give in too easily, so we left it open for discussion on Monday. I really don't care one way or the other and am happy in the assurance that I won't have to travel after the season opens.

I just got through supper, after spending most of the afternoon with my employers, one of whom is going to take me to the Follies tonight. There is a lot to tell you, but I'll save it until tomorrow when there'll be more time.

I went to sleep at Kendallville and staid asleep until Toledo. I thought of you at eight o'clock and all the rest of the time too. I retired shortly after eight and surely did sleep. During my waking hours, I tried to read The Egoist,[1] but your dear face was always between my eyes and the page so I didn't make a great deal of progress. Sweetheart, I am horribly lonesome, desperately lonesome, and I don't know how I'm going to stand it. I love you a thousand times more than I ever did before.

I'll write you a long letter tomorrow and tell you lots of things. I'll tell you now that I love you, love you, love you, and you must love me.

                Yours always,
                Ring.

I think it's safer to address this to Culver. Do you love me?

[February 24, 1911]

Sweetheart,—

This is the same night and I'll try to impart to you the rest of my new knowledge. Mr. Murdoch, new boss, took me to the show. He is to be married soon and gave me much information. He thinks it must be better to live in a suburb and says there are plenty of them, within fifteen minutes of town by train, which have desirable flats and apartments. However, I'm in no hurry and will do some looking around of my own; also some consulting with various people;

---

[1] Ellis's preferences in fiction were the nineteenth century English novelists Austen, Dickens, Meredith, and Thackeray. Meredith was her particular favorite.

before I make any move. If you want me to meet Miss Gibson[1] some time, perhaps she may be able to give me some dope. If they ship me south next week, I can call on her when I come back, which will be the second week in April. Here is something I think you wanted to know: During the baseball season, the first edition of the paper goes to press at eight in the morning. Some "gossip" is needed for this, gossip about the preceding day's game and the game to come. They think it's better to have that prepared the night before and I guess it is, for to get it ready in time in the morning, I'd have to be at the office at six. According to present plans, I won't have to be on the job until 10:30 or 11 A.M., then will work until between half six or seven at night, depending on the time the games are over, and games start earlier here than elsewhere. So, dear, I guess you'll have to learn to stay up later at night and get up later in the morning. In the off season, it will be different. That's about all I've learned since I came to Boston.

Except one thing—I love you better and better every minute and this evening has been about the longest I ever endured despite the theater.

Love me, my own dear girl.
Ring

Sunday
[Boston,
26 February 1911]

My Sweetheart,—
The longing for you gets worse every minute and I'll be glad to go to work tomorrow[2] so there'll be something sharing my mind with the thought that I want you and you are not here.

I walked down town after supper last night and ran into Bert Williams, who was on his way to the theater. I told him about an idea I had for a song and he approved it. He provided an idea for another one and told me to work on both of them and report to him later in the week. So I must try to do something this afternoon, although it's just about impossible to think of anything but you.

---

[1] Helen Gibson was Ellis's friend from Smith College. She and Arthur Jacks met at Lardner and Ellis's wedding and married each other the following year, with the Lardners as attendants.

[2] Lardner's first article for the *American* appeared in the 28 February issue.

Your picture is standing here in front of me and while it's nice to have it, looking at it makes me crazy for the original. Please remember, honey, that I want one of the big ones.

I'm rather hoping they'll send me south, as that will be a diversion and a help in killing time. I'm not like you at all. I wish it were June 15 right this minute and that I still had all my "plans" to make so that I'd have to hurry every minute. But my favorite occupation right now is planning and I have four or five different sets of arrangements already in my mind.

I'll send you my list of invitations and announcements in two or three weeks. I don't suppose there's such a rush for it, but such things make *the event* seem more real and nearer and that's the way I want it to seem.

I love you, dearest.

Ring

The allusion above to Bert Williams is significant, for Williams, a popular black singer, dancer, and comedian, had been one of Lardner's friends from Lardner's early days in Chicago. Ring Lardner Jr. speaks of his father's "contradictory" views of blacks.[1] Though he seems to have accepted the prevailing prejudice of his age that blacks were inferior, he greatly admired Williams and a number of other black performers.[2] In the Chicago days, Lardner and Williams frequently drank together at Stillson's tavern, a newspaper crowd favorite, and at numerous other saloons. Lardner wrote a number of lyrics for Williams, especially while Lardner was in Boston and Williams was a star of Ziegfeld's Follies. There was apparently correspondence between the two, but only the following letter from Williams to Lardner survives:

New York, March 14, 1911

Hello there Big Boy:
    Thanks so much for the laying out. But it was deserved. Have revamped the song so I am sure its a positive hit will write the music this week while I am

---

[1] Ring Lardner Jr., p. 27.

[2] See Lardner's letter of 7 March 1922 to Heywood Broun on Williams' abilities.

in Baltimore. Its not so cold here now but its not time yet to leave the overcoat home. Please during this spring practice get the *kinks* out of your arms—because I am going to beat you bowling and beat you *good.* I know you're having a *good* time "mongst the Pines" and when you see Bro' Dorey my regards—This week Baltimore, next Syracuse. If I hear from you there shall send you all the route into Frisco.
Good luck and health are the worst I can wish you.
Bert Williams

On the 25th Ellis wrote from Goshen of her plans for the wedding:

I'll tell you some of the plans for 'your' wedding. You are to be married in the back or north side of the library. You know you and the best man are just *there* and Ruby and father and I come downstairs and through the middle room. We are going to take the frames out of the windows that go out onto the front and side porch—and drape the porch with something, and hang lights out there. It will enlarge the space on that side of the house a lot. Then the wedding is to be in pink with pink sweetpeas and bride's roses for the flowers. I dont know whether you are interested in all that or not if you are I'll keep you posted as things develope . . . .

Sunday
[Greensboro, 2 April 1911]

Dearest Girl,—
The rats and I are spending a quiet Sunday in our room. Everybody attended the Elks' fair last night and I had three chances on a buggy. What would we have done with it if I'd won? The Southern Belles were very cordial as long as they were selling us chances, but froze up when they could get nothing more out of us. Such is hospitality in the South.
You know—or you ought to—that Saturday is my hardest day, because I have a Sunday paper, as well as the regular afternoon one, to look out for. You would have known that I was familiar with hell and high and low class swearing in all its branches if you could have heard me yesterday, for the operator was a bonehead, the Boston club used nineteen players and the score was 34 to 0. When

things like that happen after June, I'm going to give vent to my anger by beating you when I get home.

Anne informs me that Ethel Witkowsky Pick and Dora[1] want to know if you look well in the street. That's cruel and unaccustomed.

You made good on your poker prophecy. Here's one of mine which also will come true if it hasn't already: Captain Willhite will bring you one or more big red apples. He will say that he has been regretting all winter that he "declared himself" and thus deprived himself of the pleasure of evenings with you, but that his heart ran away from him; that if you will be so kind, he will resume his calls on a friendly basis and try to keep love out of his speech and his eyes, for his intercourse with you has been his only pleasure at Culver and he would give anything if he had never been so rash and wasteful of the precious hours. Then, after the friendly basis has been firmly reestablished, his heart will run wild once more and the former scenes will be repeated and then some. I'm not setting the hours and days on which these things will transpire, and I realize right this minute that jealousy is sharing my room with the rats and me; but, still, I'm willing to bet on my dope. You may name the amount of the wager and I'll trust you to decide whether or not I win. But please love me just the same.

My brain tells me that the twenty-fifth of June is twelve weeks from today, but my heart thinks that no time at all has been cut off my sentence since last Sunday although the week has been a year. I've quit waiting for the twenty-eighth and am thinking only of the twenty-fifth, for that date seems much nearer and much less impossible. You know I've seen you before and it's reasonable to expect I'll see you again; but I've never married you before and it's very hard to realize that I ever will.

Two weeks from today will be Easter. I'm going to Church at Brookline in the morning and, in the afternoon, I think I'll get my real estate and renting man to show me around. I'll tell you the result of my search provided you are very good in the meantime and not neglectful of your betrothed husband.

Before I forget it, please tell me the correct names of the Banta and Hawks furniture companies and of John Banta and Edward Hawks.[2] I think I have them right, but I want to be sure. Also, could you find out if I could tell one of them

---

[1] Dora McCarley Lardner was Rex Lardner's wife.

[2] John Banta of the Banta Furniture Company and Edwin W. Hawks of the Hawks Furniture Company.

about the other, without violating anything, so they could get together on the shipping proposition; although I don't suppose it will make much difference.

You see, if I find an apartment that fills the requirements, I'll want to grab it in May if necessary, to prevent anyone else's getting it. And, after I get it, I'll want something to put in it. I used to think moving into a place would be a horrible job, but I know I'm going to enjoy this. I will be moving into the home which is going to be to me the happiest home there ever was, and the process may make me realize that I'm really going to have you with me there.

I was doing some figuring awhile ago and I was convinced that we would be almost broke when our home life really started in spite of my economical Southern trip. But I'm not worrying about it because I'm too selfish to think much about your side of the case. If I were really and honestly unselfish, I wouldn't marry you at all. My only excuse, and it's a poor one, is that others have done it and got away with it.

This letter didn't mean to be such a long one. I wish you would forget yourself some time and write me one as long.

If you want me to meet Miss Gibson, I'll tell you my telephone number as soon as I know it.

I would like to hear Anne's instructions about the ring. My hand probably will lose its sense of aim entirely and I'll miss your finger when I shoot at it. It wouldn't be so hard if you had life-sized fingers. And that reminds me that I want the measurement of *the* finger. You can send me a piece of string or that little ring, the one that's absolutely guaranteed. Don't you dare to forget it.

We'll be in Roanoke only a short time tomorrow and I don't know whether I'll be able to write or not, but I'll try.

Tell me the latest "plans," all about Goshen, and that you love me, my dear, pretty girl.
Ring

Ellis responded:

You must'nt put anything in our house but the furniture we bought and perhaps your books. And don't you *dare* to buy anything else until I get there. I am very sure that I will change everything you arrange. Is'nt that encouraging? What difference does it make if we dont have anything in the bank when we start? I am going to keep just a few dollars—about twenty five—and if you have that much we'll start even. It is a very delicate subject—but I wish that sometime when you feel very confidential and practical you'd tell me *about*—you need'nt be exact if you don't want to—how much '*our*' monthly income is going to be. You see when I am learning to cook and sew etc. I'd like to know what sort of things we can afford to cook etc. And then of course I'm just naturally curious.

Less than three months before the wedding, Lardner still had not revealed to Ellis the precise amount of his income. The fact that Ellis was apprehensive and tactful in raising the question says much about their relationship and the conventions of the time. Lardner clearly saw Ellis as someone to be protected, and he saw himself as the breadwinner, who should assume all financial responsibilities. He replied with the details:

Saturday
[Lynchburg, Va.,
8 April 1911]

Sweetheart,—
 I almost missed today, for it rained and we decided all of a sudden to take a five o'clock train for Baltimore. But the train is over an hour late and I have borrowed a hotel across from the station in which to write. If the train goes without me it's your fault.
 Dear, I never feel practical and never confidential while I'm on the water wagon. We'll not wait for one of those moods, because you really have a right to know things. So I'll discuss the "delicate subject" briefly. I can't talk by months, for newspapers don't pay that way. The Tribune was giving me $35 a week and I went to St Louis for $50 and came down again to $45 at Boston. It's $45 now and still it isn't, and that's the delicate part. My family used to be "well off," but got over it. My father is kept busy paying for insurance and taxes, and he and my mother and Lena have to have something to live on. Lena makes something and there's no use arguing with her about it. My brother Billy helps when he can. Harry has a crowd for a family of his own, so you see it's up to Rex and me. Each of us ships home $10. Balance for me—$35. If you had been anyone but you, I would have felt obliged to say something before. But I know you. Lena would rather die than ask us (Rex and me) for anything and I guess she thinks I'm going to "stop" when I'm married. But I'm not. R.W. Lardner and Company, which is you, now possess about $800. About

$200 of this will go for the Goshen furniture and probably $150 or $200 for the furniture we are still to get. Another $200 for my typewriter (which I must have) and for my trousseau etc., and we'll be lucky to have $200 left when June comes, because I won't be able to save from now on. And I used to swear I'd never get married before I had $1,000 *laid away*. I hadn't known you when I swore that.

There'll be a pay-day on "Little Puff of Smoke" in July and perhaps something from other things some time. These can be used in helping to pay for a piano. I guess you know as much as I do now, and it's awful to leave you with all this. But you brought it on yourself. Perhaps I won't mail this letter, but I guess I will, for you'll have to know about things some time.

I don't want to meet Miss Gibson till you come. If you'll trust me with the flat choosing, there'll be no need of my bothering her. I thought you wanted her approval—of the flat and me.

I am interested in your dresses and you must tell me all about them.

In order that this may not be a business letter exclusively, I'll ask you to tell me you love me. You can pretend it isn't your business to.

I'm in a hurry to get back to Boston, but I suppose the days will drag just the same up there.

I love you and love you and love you and you owe me a long, long letter, with nothing in it but that you love me.

Ring

The Culver Military Academy school year ended early because of a measles and scarlet fever epidemic, so Ellis returned to Goshen earlier than Lardner had expected. But she was obsessed with the wedding plans and scolded him for expecting her to write every day:

> Your idea that I should take an hour off, everyday, to write to you is perfectly ridiculous. I love you dearly and think of you every minute of the day—but I simply have not an hour to spare.

In the meantime, Lardner was using his free time to search for an appropriate apartment. The following letter probably describes the apartment he leased, at 16 Park Drive in Brookline, Massachusetts.

Sunday Evening
[Boulevard, Mass.,
14 May 1911]

Sweetheart,—

I enclose another map and some measurements. I like the place more the more I see it and it's ours if you approve. The "built-in thing" isn't in the dining-room, but in a sort of vestibule that leads into the kitchen. The woodwork in the living-room, alcove and front bedroom is white and in the rest of the house oak, but a little darker than usual. The alcove is rather big—about seven feet by twelve and the people who live there now use it for a bed-room. It has a small, high window. The living-room windows are two in a row and the ones on the end of the dining-room are three—the middle one wider than the others. There are two clothes-closets opposite the bath-room, in the hall, and one in the front bed-room. The floors are to be done over and the living-room (including alcove) dining room and front bed-room repapered.

I wrote to John Banta and Mr. Hawks today, giving them directions, and I still have letters to write to my mother, Lena and Arthur Jacks.

Do you know what I did this morning? No, you don't. I read every letter I've had from you since I saw you. There's something particularly funny in one of them. I'll show it to you some time.

I didn't get a letter from you yesterday, so I guess you don't love me. But guess you'd better learn to, for it will pretty hard for you to live with me if you don't. It'll be pretty hard anyway, I guess.

Do you know what I'm going to do forty-two days from tonight? I'm going to kiss you. But it's going to be desperately hard to wait forty-two days. I love you, honey.

       Ring

I forgot to tell you—this apartment is on the first floor.

Monday night.
[Boston, Mass.,
15 May 1911]

Dearest Girl,—

I'm sorry, but I don't think we'll have time to go to the lake on Monday. I'll have things to do in Goshen in the morning—a marriage license must be procured for one thing—and we're going to Niles on the interurban because I'll have an errand or two in South Bend. But you've got to start when I do because I won't be separated from you any more than is absolutely necessary.

I know you're not interested in baseball, but I am, in one particular phase of it. They are using a new ball this year. It's livelier and that means more hitting, and more hitting means longer games, and that's the devil. It appears to be impossible to finish a game in less than two hours. It's bad enough now, but it's going to drive me crazy when it keeps me away from my own *home*.

Today's interminable game and other things have spoiled my usual sweet good nature and sunny disposition, and tonight my highest ambition is to kick somebody or something. Also, I'm lonesome and the time is passing slower than ever. I know that everything would be all right if you'd just come and kiss me. Never, as long as I live, will I forgive you for making it the twenty-eighth of June, when it could have been day after tomorrow just as well.

But I love you, and I can't write any more tonight.
                                                    Ring.

Tuesday night.
Boulevard, Mass.,
30 May 1911]

Sweetheart,—

I now have absolute, conclusive proof that you don't read my letters, but having gone thus far, I may as well continue to write them.

Listen, dear, if you want a husband who isn't a nervous wreck and a large, ill-tempered grouch, please don't skip any more days. It makes more difference to me because I do read what you write and the days which don't bring letters are awful. This waiting is bad enough without depriving me of the only thing that makes it endurable.

I don't believe Mr. Van Nuys[1] is going to marry us. I wrote to him over a week ago and he hasn't answered. Who is Goshen's most reasonable justice of the peace?

I am hoping that this coming Sunday will be busy. I'm going to spend the morning in our house, "arranging" furniture, and the afternoon and evening with the White Sox. I see by the Trib that the bum baseball song is published. Doc hasn't told me anything about it, but he'll be here day after tomorrow. You and I will always be living in hope of a windfall from one of our masterpieces.

I'm going to pay the first month's rent tomorrow and I'll pay for July before I come West so we won't have that to worry about. All I'm worrying over just now is you and

---

[1] The Reverend Van Nuys was minister of the Goshen Presbyterian Church.

whether you really want me or not. Do you know I'm going to be with you in just twenty-five days? And do you care? Arthur Jacks is going to meet us in Niles Sunday. Is he invited to the party? I guess he is, for I told him about it. Mrs. Tobin and her child will also be in Niles to greet us.

I'm tired to death of being alone, dear, and the queer thing about it is that I'd rather not be with anyone at all if I can't be with you. Hurry, and come to me.

Ring

The "bum baseball song" was "Gee, It's a Wonderful Game," which, as the following letter indicates, the Remick company publicized by having a quartet sing it at the White Sox ballpark before a game.

Wednesday night.
[Boulevard, Mass.,
31 May 1911]

My own Girl,—
I was hoping against hope that my mother would carry out my instructions regarding invitations, but she hasn't. She has sent some names to me and will send others to you—probably the same ones to both of us. I know it's too late to send the whole batch back to me for revision, so I guess you'll just have to take my list and her list and compare them and see that there are no duplicates. I hate to bother you about it, dear, but there's no help for it now.

Furthermore, there's no escape for you now, for Mr. Van Nuys has consented to do his worst. From what he has heard, Mr. Lardner will prove a worthy husband for Miss Ellis. That's a hot one on you and shows that folks have been talking about you to the minister.

Doc White comes tonight and I'll see him and your friend, Mr. Tannehill, tomorrow. Doc owed me a letter and was evidently afraid to meet me before he had answered it. Anyway, a letter came from him today, along with my contract from the publishers. I'm acquiring a great little collection of contracts. The Remick company, a decent concern, is it this time. It started advertising by having a quartet sing the song at the ball park in Chicago the other day. If Doc has any professional copies along, I'll send you one, absolutely free.

There was no letter from you today and I guess you'd pass me up if you had a chance. But it's too late. I'm going

to marry you three weeks from a week from tonight and then I won't care if the postman never comes.
*I I— y—.
Ring
*A prize for you if you can guess the missing letters.

Tuesday night.
[Boston, Mass.
13 June 1911]

My own Girl,—
It was kind enough to rain today and I did some shopping. First I made the required deposit with the gas company and then I went after a box springs and a mattress. I got, or ordered, the best they had of each. The springs cost five dollars less than the mattress, which is a hair affair. I was just wondering what I would do for funds when the man asked me if I wanted credit. I told him I certainly did. The dramatic critic on the paper has some sort of an interest in the place and that's why I was trusted. Now we can get the other things we need as soon as we want them, and the "Little Puff of Smoke" money, which comes on the fifteenth of July, ought to be enough to pay for the whole works. The mattress and springs are being made to order and will be delivered next Monday, which is going to be my busy day. It's a big store and seems to have everything.

I'm going to meet Jeannette, without the Bacons, Friday, and convey her from one station to the other. That's the day she leaves for Northampton. She says she has heard nothing from home since she left. You Abbotts are a fine bunch of correspondents and I'm glad I'm almost through with you.

Miss Gibson must surely visit us in August and for more than a few minutes. You will be very weary of just me by that time and, besides, perhaps she can cook.

I'll be with you in *eleven days* and two weeks from tomorrow night, you'll be all mine.

Write to me, dear.
Ring

Tuesday night.
[Boston, Mass.
20 June 1911]

This is my penultimate letter to you, sweetheart. And these days and nights are, without doubt or exception, the longest in history. Tomorrow is supposed to be the longest day in the year, but it can't possibly be any worse than this one.

I packed my trunk last night, and tonight I went down to our house and unpacked it again. I filled all the drawers in the chiff., but there's a little room left for you in the dresser. The place looks much better at night than in the day-time. I ran across many loving couples in the surrounding parks. Some night we'll pretend we're not married and we'll meet at one of the benches. Then we'll flirt. Oh yes, we will.

We'll have to make some very careful plans for our getaway. We ought to be able to manage somehow with the aid of Frank and Rex. The latter is perfectly trustworthy. He'll do a little lying for us if necessary.

Richard Tobin Sr. is not going to honor us with his presence. That's the one time in the month he has to work nights. I suppose he could make it if he had been on the job longer, but as it is, he's afraid to take a chance.

I think we'll put the Hawks table under the bed or between the dresser and chiff., so it will be among friends.

Please love me for four more days and then some. And remember you have an engagement for Saturday night.

     Signed—Ringgold Lardner,
       Horace Nordyke
       Irvin Coppes
       Stewart Gibson
       Loring Hoover
       Dean Taylor
       Ray Lindsay
       Fred Hurtz
       Harold Fonda
       Hugh Newell
       Jerry
        and
       old Cap Willhite

**Lardner was listing, besides himself, all of the men whom he knew to have courted Ellis in the past.**

Wednesday night.
[Boston, Mass.
21 June 1911]

I'm very tired of writing to Ellis Abbott, and I guess this is the last letter she'll ever get from me. Our correspondence has been a very pleasant diversion—really a necessity—but I don't think I can carry it on any longer, for paper and stamps cost money. I'll drop in and see her at Goshen Saturday night, on my way to South Bend and Niles, and see what she thinks about it.

I'm sure I've done my part toward keeping up our pleasant acquaintance. My letters have been as regular as the devil, and very interesting. Hers, I'm sorry to say, have been irregular as the devil, and sometimes they read as if they had been addressed to a stranger instead of a true and loving friend. But I suppose she was doing her best, and that is the most anybody can do. I always respect a man or woman who does his or her best. Nobody can do more, and one is prone to overlook faults in a person who is really trying.

I shall leave Boston—South Station—at 4:50 P.M. Friday afternoon. Pittsfield, 9:24 P.M., Utica, 1:13 A.M., Saturday morning, Erie, 8:28 A.M. Toledo, 2:05 P.M., Saturday afternoon. Train due at Goshen, 5:37 P.M., Saturday evening, but will be two or three hours late on account of heavy snows west of Toledo.

I went to our house tonight and put the springs and mattress to bed. The bed is now the prettiest thing in the house. It looks like Mount Tom.

I hope your boxes do arrive tomorrow, for I'll feel lots safer about them if they're here before I leave. But I may have time to look them up Friday.

Good-bye till Saturday, my own sweetheart. I want to kiss you and tell you I love you more than anything else in the world.

Ring

Ring Lardner and Ellis Abbott were married in Goshen on 28 June 1911, with subsequent coverage in both the Niles and Goshen papers and in the *Tribune*. The following account is from the Niles *Daily Star*:

> At eight o'clock last evening at the home of the bride's parents, Mr. and Mrs. Frank P. Abbott of Goshen, Ind., occurred the wedding of Miss Ellis Abbott and Mr. Ringgold Lardner, youngest son of Mr. and Mrs. Henry Lardner of this city. The ceremony was performed by Rev. Mr. Van Nuys, pastor of the Presbyterian church.
>
> The bride was given away by her father and was attended by her sister, Miss Ruby Abbott. Mr. Arthur H. Jacks of Chicago was best man. The ribbon bearers were Miss Wilma Johnson of this city, Miss Helen Gibson of Boston, Miss Julia Dole of Evanston, Miss Margaret Meyer of South Bend, Miss Ruth McGee of Toledo, and Miss Florence Abbott, another sister of the bride.

The wedding march was played by Noble Kryder, a young musical prodigy of Goshen, which was of his own composition.

The bride was gowned in Japanese hand-embroidered silk, trimmed with real lace, with tulle veil caught with orange blossoms. She carried a bouquet of bride's roses and lilies of the valley, and wore a cameo in antique setting, the gift of the groom.

The bridesmaid wore pink marquisette over pink satin and carried pink roses.

The ceremony which was witnessed by 175 guests, was performed in front of a beautiful screen of elderberry blossoms. Roses and hydrangeas were also used effectively.

The color scheme in the dining room was pink and green, where a three-course collation was served by caterers from Toledo.

Beautiful gowns were worn by the guests and the affair was one of the most elaborate ever given in Goshen.

The gifts were numberless and very beautiful, among them being a solid silver vegetable dish from "Doc" White, the noted Sox pitcher, who is a particular friend of the groom; from the Cubs, a 200-piece Haviland set of dishes; from Ban Johnson, Pres. of the American League, a cut glass dish; Chicago Tribune, of which the groom was formerly sporting editor, electric lamp; from Jimmie Callahan, another celebrated base ball man, set of glass-cut tumblers and pitcher.

Mr. and Mrs. Lardner left last night for Boston, where they will go to housekeeping at once, the groom having the home all ready. Mr. Lardner is now sporting editor of a Boston paper. The young man's many friends in Niles, where he was born and reared, extend best wishes, and offer hearty congratulations to the bride, who has also many friends here, having visited in Niles a number of times.

# Years of Fruition
## 1911–1925

Because there is no record of a honeymoon, one may assume that Lardner acquiesced to Ellis's earlier request that they move immediately into the Boston apartment. One week after the wedding, Lardner wrote from Boston to Ellis's mother, telling her how pleasant married life was:

[Boston, Mass.]
The Fourth of July.

Dear Mother II.,—

My wife and I are having a quarrel. She says I must show her this letter and I say I mustn't. I suppose she will win the argument.

People who said she didn't know much about keeping house and cooking were trying to deceive me. Last night's supper and this morning's breakfast—our first meals at home—were absolutely the best I ever tasted.

I wish I could make some sort of return to you for giving her to me, but I know I can't, so I'll just have to be grateful to you all the rest of my life.

You must come to us the first minute you can get away. I want you to, for my own sake as well as Ellis'. And you must stay a long time when you do come.

I'm having the best time of my life now. The next best times were spent at your house and I'm thankful to you for them, too.

It's desperately hot here now, but it can't last long. I hope it won't anyway, for I don't want Ellis to be utterly discouraged right at the start.

Give my love to yourself and the girls and tell Mr. Abbott I'm grateful to him, too, for my everlasting happiness.

                Ring

Lardner probably wrote the next letter later the same summer. He had been promoted to sports editor at the *American* at the time of the wedding and was busy in this promising position, while Ellis may have become bored with her conventional housewifely duties. However, because she became pregnant a month after the wedding, her life quickly became more complicated.

Sunday night.
[Summer 1911]

Dear Mother II,—
Your small daughter fell asleep while I was reading to her, so I am stealing a little time to write to you. I'm not allowed to do anything but read and try to play the piano while she is awake and I am at home.
I suppose you've heard that Mr. and Mrs. Lardner are to chaperone a house-party at Helen Gibson's the latter part of this week. It will be a novel experience but if it's half as nice as all the other novel experiences I've been having, I won't object a bit.
A new arrangement at "my" office requires me to work late every Saturday night. To make up for it, I don't have anything to do until Tuesday morning, and you may be sure I enjoy the Sunday–Monday vacation at home.
I think Ellis has been a little homesick once or twice, although she wouldn't admit it. It's a cinch she'll be glad to see Ruby and Frank and John—and any other members of the family who can be enticed away from home—when they come. It would be wonderfully nice if you, yourself, could come to see us.
We went to Andover a couple of Sundays ago to call on "Cousin Mary" and she proved to be quite the nicest person of her age I ever met. I'd like to go back there once a week, but my wife has a fiendishly jealous disposition, as was evidenced this instant. She awoke and asked me what I was doing and when I informed her I was writing to a girl, she went right back to sleep again.
All but two people have quit writing to me. The two are Mrs. Henry Lardner and Mrs. Abbott, and I hope they won't give up the practice.
Love to everybody, including yourself.
                    Ring

Early in September, Ellis told her mother of her pregnancy:

My Dearest Mother,
    This is going to be a very private letter so you'd better take it into the bath room to read. You have'nt written to me for a long time and I am afraid father

is'nt so well or you are sick yourself. Do write and tell me everyone is well.

Mother, dear, I have the most wonderful news for you. What would you think about being a grandmother? Well I think there is a very great probability that it wont be very, very, long before that happens. We are so happy about it mother, dear. Ring is just perfect. I wish you could know how nice he is. Just think of having a little baby all my own. I wont ever be lonesome any more—and it is lonesome all by myself in the day time. We had a doctor about a week ago and he said it was sure. I was sick last the tenth of July which makes it just eight weeks yesterday.

I am not a bit afraid, mother though I dont care much for this horrid feeling I have every morning. Its hard to sit down and plan dinner and order food when the very thought of it makes you ill.

Ruby must stay with me until Christmas and then you will come after Christmas wont you—if father does'nt need you. Anyway you will come for the last month won't you?

Please dont tell any one but Ruby and Florence and father and *dont* let anyone else find out for two or three months. I wish you would write me all the things I should and should'nt do because your little girl is all alone and does'nt know any thing. And ask Ruby if she knovs the name of that book Diana & Nell have by Dr. someone—Holt I think. I want to get it.

love to you all
your happy happy daughter

Ellis's pregnancy meant new financial responsibilities for Lardner; nevertheless, he abruptly resigned his post with the *American* that October out of a sense of family loyalty and personal honor. As sports editor, Lardner had earlier that summer added both his Chicago colleague Frank Smith and his brother Rex to the sports staff, but when he went to New York to cover the 1911 World's Series between the Philadelphia Athletics and the New York Giants, the Hearst newspaper in his absence fired both men as an economy move. A letter from Ellis in Brookline to Lardner in New York at this time reveals her anxiety about the situation:

I am wondering what you are going to do about this business at the office. I'd like to go out and murder Mr. Shore—or whatever his name is. I never *knew* anything so horrid as to wait until you got out of town and then make all this trouble. I dont think Rex cares very much as long as he has this job in Cleveland and I only hope Mr. Smith can get out of it as well. But it is the very devil for you and I'd like to kill people for making all this trouble for you—when you are working so hard any way.

What Lardner had done was to resign immediately, though he had little money on hand. Three weeks later, he wrote reassuringly to Ellis's mother:

Thursday, November ninth.
[9 November 1911]

Dear Mother II,—
    You are hereby ordered not to worry about us, although I'm free to admit that it is natural you should. We are through with the Boston American, but are finding out that we get along nicely without its help. I am doing some work for magazines that are not particular what they print, and waiting for a call to Chicago, New York, or some other city of size and importance. We have three meals daily, and some of your grand pickles and preserves are on every bill-of-fare.
    Ruby and Ellis have gone to their bridge club. It's a very interesting organization now that Helen is out of town, for none of the surviving members knows the others personally. Inasmuch as they can't get back before seven o'clock, I am going to get supper, and it will be good.
    Ruby is the only one in our family who gets any mail. But she is good enough to read most of it to us. If you don't mind, we'll keep her here always.
    My mother and father celebrated their golden wedding anniversary last Monday, the celebration consisting of staying at home and entertaining their grandson, Richard L. Tobin, and his mother.
    I must go to market.
                  With love,
                    Ring

Shortly afterward, Lardner and Ellis returned to Chicago, where Lardner worked briefly at the only job he could find—as a copy reader with the Chicago *American*. It must have been a difficult time both professionally and economically, until, in February 1912, he went to work again with the *Examiner* as a sports reporter, covering the White Sox.

Tuesday
[May 1912]

Dear Mother II,—
    I have returned to a state of activity and am going to the ball game this afternoon after a ten days' lay-off. I haven't yet learned what my ailment was, although the doctor gave me a big variety of things from which to choose, including typhoid fever, spinal maginnis, cerebro-spinal fever and grip. The last named seemed more simple than the others, so I picked it and got well much sooner than I would have from one of the others.
    Did you know Ruby was going to live with us hereafter? She has become indispensable to the welfare of our small family and will not be allowed to go to Goshen except for short visits.
    Ellis is awaiting the event with external patience. She seems well and I'm sure she'll be all right. She's the bravest young lady I ever met.
    Tell Mr. Abbott we all may surprise him by paying him a call some time before Summer.
    Love to you and the rest of the family.
                      Ring

The Lardners' first child, John Abbott Lardner, was born on 4 May 1912 in their Chicago apartment near the Tobins. (John would become an outstanding sportswriter, a noted World War II correspondent, and a columnist and essayist for *Newsweek*, *The New Yorker*, and other magazines before dying of tuberculosis and heart trouble in 1960.)
    The following letter to Ellis was written not long afterward, sometime during the 1912 baseball season, while Lardner was on the road with one of the Chicago teams. It describes humorously some dinner dialogue during an evening spent at a friend's home. The letter must be read carefully to distinguish when Lardner is speaking as himself and when he is reproducing conversation in much the same manner as in some of his later stories.

Friday.
[Summer 1912]

Sweetheart,—
 As predicted, I attended supper at the Leaming's last night. Roast beef, mashed potatoes, gravy, *beets*, peas in little round cups cooked with cracker crumb frosting, nut salad with something like maple syrup on it, biscuits, because Mr. Dehman, Mary's father, can't eat plain bread, coffee and strawberry shortcake, which needed sugar, but when it first came on Mary said she hoped, she certainly hoped, she had made it sweet enough this time because Harry was such a sweet tooth, and so, although I wanted sugar, I couldn't use any, and after dinner mints and cigars for me, you know Harry doesn't smoke at all and Mr. D. doesn't either, although he's a fiend for chewing tobacco, and has taken the cure twice and been cured of the habit, but has gone back to it again; he started chewing when he was sixteen and he is pretty old now, and the tobacco must have had the effect of making him nervous, for he talks in his sleep and sometimes even walks; you know he went with the band to Niagara Falls last year and it was the first time he had been on a sleeping car for eight years, and he and the cornet player shared a lower berth, and the rumbling of the car wheels made him dream that the machinery on the floor above the coffee room of the wholesale grocery in which he works was going to fall through the ceiling, and he dreamed that he was trying to escape by jumping out the window, and so he hauled off and smashed his fist through the car window, cutting his hand badly, and was going to throw himself out, when the cornet player awoke and grabbed him. It's hard to sleep on Pullmans when you're not used to it, but of course you're used to it. Don't you get tired of travelling? Mary often sits up in bed and talks and one night last week she dreamed Harry had hit Jack Johnson, the nigger, and that Jack had sworn vengeance, and so Mary thought Jack would kill Harry and she cried in her sleep. Does Ellis ever bother you at night? Gee, I love those Abbott girls. Gee, I love Florence. Gee, I love Ruby. You tell Ellis that I'll break her head for not coming here with you. Is Ruby engaged? When is she going to be married? What kind of fellow is Paull? Will he be good to Florence? Why, says Mary, I thought you knew him. Well, I just met him. Don't you think Wood Spitler is good looking? He's going to marry a little country girl, but she's a peach. He rides his bicycle out to see her. He says he'll trade his bike for my pony if the pony can get over the ground better. Mary sent him a pipe for Christmas and he said he thought at first that it wouldn't be any good because it was too fancy, but after

smoking it, he decided that Mary must have pretty good taste in pipes. Mildred certainly likes her beer and she likes to tell how much she can drink. Did you ever meet Aunt—? Well, then you missed the best of the lot. She isn't what you could call pretty, but she's all heart. She gave us this silver and the dining room set. Elizabeth's going to marry a pretty rich fellow, so I suppose Aunt— will spend a lot of money on something small but nice, instead of giving them any furniture. They want a sort of family reunion at Elizabeth's wedding, but it costs too much money to go. Marion and Margaret can travel as much as they please, for Marion gets passes. How can the paper afford to send you all around with the team? says Mary. Why, Lord, don't you know that nine out of every ten people read the sporting page first? Lillian is crazy about baseball, says Mr. D., and I wanted to ask you if it would be all right for a girl to go to the games alone in New York. When do you go to New York? Well, that's very good of you. I got a letter from her yesterday. I'll give it to you, for it has her telephone number and address. Don't you want the letter? says I. Well, yes, I'll tear off the part with the address on it.

I'll bet when you went home last spring you told Ellis all about the tough chicken we gave you. My, but Mary was ashamed of that. We have spoken of it a hundred times since.

Are there any crabs among the ball players? Does Ellis like to take care of the baby, or is it drudgery for her? I've got a picture of Ellis that looks just like a nigger. Why, Harry, it does not. Well, she looks dark.

Lillian finishes her study with Damrosch in June and then she's coming home. Mrs. D. says she thinks she'll make her do all her playing hereafter in the servants' quarters because she's so tired of listening to it.

Perhaps I'll get a letter from you in St. Joe.
R—

On 13 July, when Lardner was again on the road with the Sox, Ellis wrote to tell him that her sister Florence was to marry Paull Torrence in seven weeks, and she reminisced about their own courtship:

> It does'nt seem over a year since we were counting the days does it? Do you remember you wrote me once from Boston that in so many weeks we would be together never to be separated again? I think that was a pretty poor guess. Do you think that time will ever come? I love you so much, dear, and I need you every minute. Life is too short to waste so

many days apart. I wonder so many times if you are really as happy as you expected to be. Life means so much more to me than I ever thought it could—with my own husband and my baby—I am a very very happy girl—but I would be infinately happier if you could put your arms around me now —Ellis.

In March 1913, Ellis left John with her parents in Goshen and accompanied Lardner to the White Sox training camp in Oakland, California, so as to enjoy a lengthy vacation in a warmer climate. Also with the Sox that spring was Bill Veeck Sr. and his wife. At the time, Veeck, who would become president of the Chicago Cubs in 1917, was writing the Bill Bailey sports byline for the Chicago *American*. This California vacation marked the beginning of the Lardner-Veeck family friendship, a friendship that thrived until the Lardners moved to New York in 1919.[1]

When Ellis's father died early in September 1912, she inherited some money with which she and Lardner bought property in west suburban Riverside and began to build a house.

Friday
[Chicago, 18 April 1913]

[To Ruby Abbott]
Dearest Lillian,—
    You see Ellis already has written to your Ma and told her everything except a few inside facts. My Missus and boy spent Wednesday night at the home of my sister on South Park Avenue. I stopped there for them yesterday morning and we had breakfast consisting of boiled eggs, toast and coffee.
    John was very glad to see me. He nearly says Daddy and Dickie. I think he likes Dickie better than anyone, except, of course, his parents and his dear aunts.
    One of my annual practices is to see the Follies so that I can study the songs and acting of Bert Williams, my colored friend. So I deserted home and kindred last night and went. In the seats next to me were a man, middle aged or more, and his daughter. They talked of Helen Irwin several times and I sort of recognized them, but realized that they wouldn't know me from a dog (what an expression!).

---

[1] See Bill Veeck Jr.'s autobiography, *Veeck—As In Wreck* (New York: Bantam, 1963), pp. 10-16.

Finally a little Japanese girl came on the stage and the lady on my left said, "That must be the girl Helen saw on the train—the one who could say in English only 'Shut up' and 'I should worry,'" or something like that—and right then and there I recalled Miss Irwin's account of her California trip, and as sure as my name is Gus I knew those two must be from Goshen. What a small World this is after all.

One week from Sunday night I'm going to Detroit and perhaps, who knows?

If you want to carry on a regular correspondence with me, well and good. But I don't think it's fair to either of us to hold communication in this desultory way. I wrote you a long letter in February. You wrote me a short note late in April, and you wrote on account of no interest in me, but merely because you wanted to know where your sister had slept. For your further information let me say that she is sleeping right now—on a couch—in her own home—where she belongs.

You want us to build in Goshen. Why? Because you don't expect to be there long. Is that friendship? Is that sisterly?

In June 1913, Lardner replaced Hugh Fullerton (at Fullerton's suggestion) as author of the daily "In the Wake of the News" column in the sports section of the *Tribune*. The popular Hugh Keogh, who had written the column for years, had died some months earlier. The *Tribune* managing editor, James Keeley, hired Lardner on a three-months trial basis, and Lardner wrote his first column on 3 June 1913. Though Lardner had some uneasy moments while on trial, he was almost from the beginning a huge success, and his salary was soon raised to $60 a week. He wrote the column for the next six years, earning $200 a week on a three-year contract from 1916 to 1919.

Tuesday
[Winter 1913]

Dear Mother II,—

As you have undoubtedly discovered, Ellis forgot to enclose the Moffett Studio card. She wants me to tell you to write your letter to Mr. Anderson, c/o Moffet's Studio, 57 East Congress street.

Ruby is in Evanston, but we expect her back some time today. Her purchases are so pretty that even I know it.

When John saw the white snow on the ground this morning, he said, "Muck," which is his word for milk. We told him that it was snow and he pointed to his nose.

Everybody sends love to everybody.

Ring

Thursday
[January 1914]

Dear Mother II,—

A stiff neck has prevented my writing before to thank you for your kindness to me at Christmas time. I didn't deserve so much, and I appreciate it more than I can tell you.

I don't suppose I'll sleep, eat or otherwise enjoy myself in the old house again, but I assure you that I had some of my best times there and wouldn't have missed knowing it and its inhabitants for the world. The farm is bound to be a mighty pleasant place to visit, as would any house in which you and the rest of your nice family elected to live.

We have received all the property we left behind us in Goshen and ask your forgiveness for having caused you so much extra work. John is still wild about his hobby-horse and spends much time gazing at it and saying "Hoss" and "Duke."

The child has a new habit of sleeping soundly at night and continuing in slumber until eight in the morning, which makes life more enjoyable for Ellis.

Frank called on us Monday morning, but had to rush away on fraternity business.

Ellis made a mince pie the other day that was very good. She is repeating the performance today.

Love from all of us to you and Bill and "Hawn" and "Abe."

Ring

Early in 1914, in an effort to bring in some extra money, Lardner began to write his epistolary "busher" stories, consisting of fictional White Sox pitcher Jack Keefe's self-centered letters to his friend Al. Drawing on his association with an illiterate Sox pitcher for whom Lardner had compassionately read dinner menus aloud during the 1908 season, on his camaraderie with Frank Schulte, and on his general experience in the baseball world, Lardner drew his protagonist with a tolerant pen that rendered Keefe vividly real and oddly sympathetic. Later that year, Lardner achieved a breakthrough when George Horace Lorimer, editor of the *Saturday Evening Post*, accepted Lardner's stories for publication in that magazine, probably on the recommendation of Charles Van Loan, a *Post* writer whom Lardner knew through Hugh Fullerton. A number of stories have circulated about the circumstances of the acceptance of Lardner's stories, but Lardner's own version, in his letter of 7 October 1926 to Burton Rascoe, must be considered authoritative. Lardner received $250 for the first piece and subsequent increases of $250 per story between 1910 and 1921, until he was receiving $1250 a story, the *Post*'s ceiling at that time.

The following letter to Franklin P. Adams (popularly referred to as F.P.A.), a colleague who had already transferred to the New York newspaper world, foreshadows the move Lardner himself would make five years later.

Chicago, March 12 [1914]

Dear Mr. Adams:

I'm glad you liked the Post stuff and also glad that you took the trouble to write to me. It may not sound reasonable, but sometimes I almost prefer appreciation (from real guys) to dough. However, it's dough and the prospect of it that would tempt me to tackle the New York game. I think a gent in this business would be foolish not to go to New York if he had a good chance. From all I can learn, that's where the real money is. I'm not grabbing such a salary from the Trib. that I have any trouble carrying it home. But I do make a little on the side owing to my acquaintance with people hereabouts who want special stunts done—such as vaudeville acts, ads and alleged lyrics for stage songs. (Of course one might expect to get some of that work in New York after a reasonable length of time.) Moreover, I've just finished building a little house in Riverside, the suburb Briggs[1] lived in until he heard I was coming. I suppose I could sell it or rent it, and I mention it merely as a thing I have to consider. I could be torn away from here—and Riverside—for $8,000, and that's probably more than I'm worth. But you see how things are. It's not that I'm swelled on myself as much as some of our well-known diamond heroes, but that I'd have to get something like that to make the change pay. However, I suppose the sooner a person lands in New York, the sooner he feels as if he had a

---

[1] Clare Briggs was Lardner's friend and a cartoonist for the *Tribune* sports pages, before he moved on to New York.

permanent residence. This letter, I'm afraid, is unintelligible in spots. I hope you may be able to make some sense of it. It might have been clearer if Ted Sullivan[1] hadn't come in to see me twice during its composition.

                Sincerely,
                Ring W. Lardner

Happiest respects, as Jimmy Sheckard[2] says, to Briggs and Rice.[3]

The following letter, written in dialect as if by Ellis to her family, refers to the birth of the Lardners' second child, James Phillips Lardner, on 18 May 1914. (In September 1938, James was killed in the Spanish Civil War while fighting with the Abraham Lincoln Brigade—a group of American volunteers—on the side of the elected Republican government against General Franco's Fascist forces.)

Tuesday.

Dear Family:—

    This here baby I've got now is probably the best looking baby that every happened. He weighed 7 3/4. While he is good looking, he also is mad looking. His expression is one of permanent anger. I don't know why. He cries very little, but thinks a whole lot. All the nurses say he is the prettiest baby they ever saw. The alarm sounded about five o'clock Monday morning. I immediately told Ring to call up Dr. Courtright. Ring did so (He always does his duty) and also got me a taxi at some expense. The doctor was mad, as usual. He hurried with his shaving and cut himself twice. Then he had a quarrel with the hospital about the condition of the room, etc. Ring was mad because the taxi didn't come soon enough and the nurses were mad because the doctor bawled them all out. James Phillips was therefore born in an atmosphere of rage and he shows it. I expect to be in the hospital (Washington Park) two more weeks. Then I will move to Riverside, where James Philllips and I will be glad to see each and every one of you.

                Ellis

---

[1] Ted Sullivan was one of Lardner's colleagues on the *Tribune*.

[2] Jimmy Sheckard was the Chicago Cub centerfielder from 1906 through 1912.

[3] Grantland Rice was at this time a sportswriter on the New York *Herald*. After 1924 he was Lardner's closest friend.

The Chicago Tribune
Chicago, Ill.
[May 1914]

Dears Florence and Ruby:—
 This letter is written on an Underwood Typewriter No. 4.
 We will be glad to see you, Florence, especially if you don't forget to bring John.
 (We would also be glad to see you, Ruby)
 Ellis is very grateful, Ruby, for the candy. You, Florence, didn't send her any. But we'll be glad to see you just the same. The baby looks like John. He is supposed to be called Phil and not Barbara, as Ruby thought. He cries very seldom, sleeps very much and doesn't ask to be fed between ten o'clock at night and six in the morning. Ellis wasn't very well for the first two days afterwards. But Dora came to see her the third day and, on her departure, promised to give Ellis absent treatment. Sure as you live, it worked. Ellis now feels perfectly well and says she is much stronger than this long (or short) after John's arrival.
 The house will be done tomorrow, so I'm told. Not for a minute do I believe it. Write again soon.
R.W.L.
 P. S. I presume Paull meant that I should send him more details in telegraphic form, but, girls, I can't afford it.
 P. S. No. 2— Weight, 7 3/4.

The Chicago Tribune
Chicago, Ill.
Wednesday.
[End of May 1914]

Dear Mother II:—
 Will you please forgive the typewriter? I left my perfectly good fountain pen at the Grant Hotel, where I am now stopping.
 Ellis wants me to ask you if you will be kind enough to start shipment of the furniture and other stuff as soon as possible. It should be addressed to Riverside, but the bills of lading may be sent to me at the Tribune. The house is nearly done, but everybody is doing his part as slowly as possible. I suppose we'll have to wait a long time for electricity and gas.
 The new baby, James Phillips, has ears that stick close to his head. He hardly ever cries and doesn't eat between ten at night and six in the morning. Ellis is much better than she was yesterday, when she had bad after-pains and cramps.
 Love to everybody.

The house was not finished until the summer of 1914. Lardner drew on the economic frustrations of having a home built for a story, "Own your Own Home," originally published in *Redbook* in 1915, about the antics and anxieties of fictional Chicago detective Fred Gross during Gross's housebuilding venture. But Lardner appears to have been especially happy for a period of time immediately following completion of the house, with a secure position not requiring much traveling and the companionship of a wife and children.

The following letter was written to Ellis's sister Ruby, now married to Robin Hendry and the mother of a son named James Abbott Hendry.

[ca 1914]

Copy Cat! Copy Cat! I thought you certainly would be original and have a girl. And when I heard it was a boy, I thought, "Well, she'll at least display her natural ingenuity in naming him." But my Heavens! you've swiped his front name from my youngest son and his middle name from my eldest. My Heavens! And as he didn't come in the spring, poor thing, we can't even call him Robin. What can we call him? Nothing. We'll never be able to speak to him if he isn't looking at us, unless we yell, "Say, there! Listen!" My Heavens! While in Boston, I called on Helen, removing my shoes and stockings before entering her apartment. And I backed in and out to make her feel more at ease.

"Hello, kid," I said.

"Hello there, Ringlets," said she. "How's Ruby?"

I told her you were married and living in Detroit. She is going there to do her Christmas shopping—hosiery and the like—and will call on you. You owe me a debt of gratitude. I reached Detroit on the homeward journey at eight o'clock Sunday night. I then did an hour's work. I then had two hours and a half to wait for my train. But it was past Abbott bedtime when I got through work and I refrained from paying you a call.

We hope to see you and yours at the lake next summer. *James* Phillips and John *Abbott* Lardner send their happiest respects.

Your friend Reese McCarley.

The third of Lardner's four sons, Ringgold Wilmer Lardner Jr., nicknamed "Bill," was born on 19 August 1915. (Now the only surviving son, Ring Jr. has had a distinguished if controversial career as a Hollywood screenplay writer and an author. He won his first Academy Award at the age of 26 for the screenplay *Woman of the Year*. In 1947 he was subpoenaed as one of the "Hollywood Ten" before the House Un-American Activities Committee, where he chose on principle not to reveal whether he had ever been a Communist. Imprisoned for nine months and blacklisted by Hollywood for fifteen years, he reestablished himself in 1970 by winning a second Oscar for the script of the movie *M*A*S*H*.)

As early as 1916, Lardner seems to have considered writing for the movies. The following letter to R. L. Giffen, an authors' agent associated primarily with theater and movies, refers to twelve short comic baseball scripts that Lardner had agreed to write (though no evidence survives aside from this letter to indicate that he ever actually wrote them):

Riverside, Illinois
April 10. [1916]

Dear Mr. Giffen: —

In reply to your letter of the first, which I should have answered before, I will write the scenarios you desire (twelve in all, delivered one per month) at $250 apiece and an advance of $250.
Ring W. Lardner

The first five busher stories, all of which had appeared in the *Saturday Evening Post* in 1914, were collected and published by the George H. Doran Company in 1916, under the title *You Know Me Al*. In book form, this epistolary novel gradually achieved lasting popularity, primarily because its semi-literate, egoistic protagonist achieved larger-than-life comic stature, but also because, as H.L. Mencken was the first to proclaim, Lardner had captured the written language of the lowbrow American in a uniquely accurate way.

After the appearance of *You Know Me Al*, a larger midwestern publishing house, Bobbs-Merrill, arranged with Lardner to publish his stories in book form. In all Bobbs-Merrill published eight volumes of Lardner's work, before Scribner's purchased the rights in 1924.

The following letter, written two days after the University of Minnesota had defeated Coach Amos Alonzo Stagg's University of Chicago Maroons 49—0,[1] responds to an invitation by a Harold W. Gillen to speak at the University of

---

[1] In "In the Wake of the News," Lardner had predicted a Minnesota win, 34–7.

Minnesota M Club banquet. That year the Minnesota Golden Gophers had one of the better football teams in the country, though they were upset the following week by Illinois, 14—9, in what was termed the "greatest upset of all time." The letter is remarkable mainly because it is written in the semi-literate dialect for which Lardner was to become famous.

November 27 [1916]

Mr. Harold W. Gillen
Chairman of the General Arrangements
Minneapolis, Minnesota

Gents:—
Your flavor of the 16 with interest at hand and you says the m club was going to give a banquet on the 29 in honor of some football team and I suppose you mean the Minnesota college nine and if you do I am glad you are going to give them a banquet because I seen them down here last Saturday and they looked 1/2 starved.

You says also would I respond to a toast and I will be frank with you and tell you right out No, I won't because in the 1 place I can not come and in another place I been informed that I am pretty popular in Minneapolis and that is because they have not anybody up there ever heard me respond to a toast and another thing the last time I was to Minneapolis a man name John Ritchie took me around and I was sick afterwards for 3 wks. and could not eat or do anything only drink water.

You also says in your letter that it was needless to say that my presence would insure the success of your banquet and what I can not figure out is that if it was needless to say that what did you have to go and say it for.

You also says that if I could not come would I write a response to be read at the banquet and in any case you will of course stand all expenses so here is the response to be read at the banquet and the expenses connected with it is 13 cents allowing 1 cent for the stationery and 10 cents for the special delivery and 2 cents for the red stamp and that was the cheapest I could get at any of the post offices. I hope to hear from you by return of the mail.

I don't hardly know what to write about as I got no idear what was the name of the toast that I was to respond to it. I suppose you want something in regards to the football nine on account of me having seen them play last Saturday and probably you want my opinion on what is the matter with them. For 1 thing I think there is frictions on the team maybe on account of the different fraternitys and the men seems to be jealous of each other and don't help each other. If I was Dr. Williamson[1] I would try and root out the different clicks and get a little team work before your next game. Another thing I noticed was that the men did not act like they knowed what positions they was playing but kept moving around trying to get located and some of them was way out of place even when the ball was past. Dr. Williamson should ought to give them a lesson in the rules and tell them where the different players is supposed to stand. For instance you got a man named Baston[2] or something that the paper says he is supposed to play left end but he has not got no more idear where left end is than a rabbit or something and part of the time he was playing center and part of the time middle half back and part of the time right field. I thought the officials might of steered him right but I suppose they thought Stagg would think they were showing partiality. And another thing I noticed was that the defensive half backs did not hardly make a tackle the whole game. And another thing was the way your men catched the ball on the kick outs after touchdowns. Instead of standing up and catching the ball they dived on their stomachs like they was ball players that did not know how to slide. And another thing I noticed was that your line men loafed on offense and sometimes the half back that was carrying the ball run into an opponent and got tackled before he had hardly gained 18 yards. The line men's business is to make holes for the backs to come through and the holes your line men made was not hardly big enough to squeeze a delivery truck through let alone a fair sized half back. And if I was Dr. Williamson I would learn my men the multiple kick so as they would have a little variety to their attack.

But you got good materials to work with and if you can get the men to working together and try and fix up a versatile offense and let the half backs get a little tackling practice and find 4 or 5 good back field men to help out the line and learn the men the different positions so as they will know where to stand I would not be surprised if you would throw a scare into some of the teams you still got left to play yet and maybe even hold Ohio State to a low score.

---

[1] Dr. Henry Lane ("Doc") Williams had played football at Yale, had graduated from the University of Pennsylvania medical school in 1895, and was the head football coach at the University of Minnesota from 1900 to 1921. His record of 143 wins, 14 losses, and 12 ties is the tenth best coaching record in college football history.

[2] Albert Preston Baston was the captain and All-American left end of the 1916 Gophers.

That is about all I got to say except I seen Boles Rosenthal and Dr. Constance or something in Chicago Saturday night and I was surprised to see Rosenthal as I thought of course he would be scouting at some game, but I and he talked it over and he thinks the same as I do about your team, that you would be a whole lot better if you had a little harmony and adhesion.

And speaking of harmony that reminds me that I was in the Lambs Cafe late Saturday night and some of the Minnesota fans come in and sung their songs and without hurting nobody's feelings I would suggest that you better make some changes in your vocal faculty up there. But I never seen no better college spirits than they had and I guess they must of got it over to the college inn.

Well one of them come over to my table and asked a lady to dance and the lady happened to be my first wife so I answered for her and kind of discouraged him but after a while he come over again and there was a Minnesota man setting with us then and he told this here gent to get away and not bother us because I was Mr. Lardner. And the gent says: "Who the hell is Mr. Lardner?" So if the gent is there at your banquet here is some information for him. Mr. Lardner is the guy that is writing this letter which I will close.
                     Respectfully,
                     Ring W. Lardner

The following telegram, obviously a response to a request for copies of Lardner's stories, indicates again that Lardner did not bother to keep copies of his own work, once it was accepted for publication.

To Bobbs–Merrill Publishing Company
Collect
RIVERSIDE ILL 6P NOV 29 [1916]

BOBBS–MERRILL PUBLISHING CO
INDIANAPOLIS IND
    I HAVE NO COPIES OF STORIES ASK POST FOR THEM
                    RING W LARDNER

Most of Lardner's correspondence with Bobbs–Merrill was through its general editor, Hewitt H. Howland, who became a friend and, even in these early days of their relationship, a drinking companion. The story referred to below, "Three Without, Doubled," was the last of five *Saturday Evening Post* stories collected to form *Gullible's Travels.*

December 4, [1916]

Dear Mr. Howland:—
   I have no copy of "Three Without, Doubled," but I sent the proof back to the Post about ten days ago, so if you don't want to wait for it to come out, I think you will have no trouble getting it from them.
   Have seen Artie[1] but once since you were. He was in good voice, but I, being on the wagon, was not.
                              Sincerely,
                                 Ring W. Lardner

   The narrator of *Gullible's Travels* is, as Carl Van Doren observed, "a case-hardened low-brow . . . seeing the world with his slightly snobbish wife." The title story deals with the wife's unsuccessful attempt to elevate their social standing by spending a vacation at Palm Springs: "We'd be stayin' under the same roof with the Vanderbilts and Goulds, and eatin' at the same table, and probably, before we was there a week, callin' 'em Steve and Gus." They succeed only in getting acquainted with the hired help, and the devastating blow comes when Mrs. Gullible is mistaken for a maid. Another story relates the ludicrous efforts of the Gullibles and the Hatches to attain social status by attending an opera. "Three Without, Doubled" illustrates that the Gullibles do not fit into a higher social stratum even after they are tentatively accepted. They are invited to join the "San Susie" bridge club for one meeting, but Gullible plays miserable bridge and insults most of those present, so they are discreetly dropped from membership. Two other stories deal with Mrs. Gullible's attempts to help her sister catch a husband—a theme to be repeated with greater skill in *The Big Town*.

Chicago Tribune
March 2, 1917.

Dear Mr. Howland:—
   I apologize for not having answered your letter before. Inasmuch as I had resolved that February was going to be my last liquid month for some time, I was busy preparing for the dry spell. The book is, I think, very attractive and ought to be a go on its appearance alone. Our book department last Sunday said it had been one of the six best

---

[1] Artie Hofman (see page 51).

sellers in Chicago last week, but perhaps our book critic was using her imagination and merely wanted to help me out. I haven't sent a copy to F.P.A., but will do so; also will hand one to B.L.T., our own column conductor, who is widely read in these and other parts. Or No. I'm afraid I haven't another one to spare and will ask you to send him one. Just B.L.T., care of the Chicago Tribune, will reach him I enclose a brief letter to dealers, as you requested. Others to whom you might, to our mutual profit, send copies, are Grantland Rice of the New York Tribune, and the sporting editors of some of the larger metropolitan papers.
Sincerely,[1]

Chicago, Ill.
June 4, [1917]

Dear Mr. Howland: —

I just found in my desk your letter enclosing the cut which you wished to use in connection with advertising "Gullible's Travels." For some reason I overlooked the letter and never saw its contents till just now. I presume it is too late for me to write the stuff you wanted, but if not, please let me know and I'll try not to delay so again.
Sincerely,<br>Ring W. Lardner

On April 6, 1917, the United States entered World War I "to help make the world safe for democracy." Lardner entertained no such illusions. He scarcely mentioned the conflict in his letters or columns until, in the summer of 1917, he went to France as a war correspondent. He and Ellis sold their Riverside house, which they had outgrown anyway, and she and the boys stayed that summer at a lake resort in St. Joseph, Michigan.

Lardner was gone for eleven weeks, during which he saw the front lines only briefly, through field glasses. He did not cover military action but spent most of his time in military camps, staff headquarters, Paris, or London. The articles he wrote reflect his boredom with military bureaucracy and strain to find humor in his struggles with the French language.

When he returned in the fall, the family rented a house in Evanston. The fact that he rented rather than bought may indicate that Lardner was already considering a move to New York.

---

[1] Unsigned.

Chicago, Ill.
January 9, [1918]

Dear Mr. Howland:—
 I have just found your note unopened in a remote corner of my desk where a too-careful copy boy stored it.
 The manuscript business is very punk. I am just beginning a drive on the Post, but don't know whether they'll give way or not.
 Do you think my experiences in France, which are about to be wound up in Collier's, are worth printing in book form? Or have you read them? Lots of people haven't, I find.
                Sincerely,
                Ring W. Lardner[1]

Lardner's "experiences in France" had appeared as a series of articles in *Colliers* under the title "A Reporter's Diary." They were published in eight installments from 29 September 1917 to 19 January 1918. The articles are noteworthy only because they reflect Lardner's view that the backwash of war is boring. Nevertheless, Lardner's popularity in the midwest was such that Howland set about immediately, as the following letter shows, to obtain copies of the installments for publication as a book:

Chicago, Ill.
January 21, [1918]

Dear Mr. Howland:—
 You are shy two installments of the stuff—one of them about my visit to the American camp and the other, my stay in the vicinity of the British front. They were Nos. 4 and 5 in the series. I tried to save copies at home, but they have been torn up or hidden by offspring. They would come between the one about the first attempt to get to the American camp and the one about trying to get the major's car out of Paris. Because I didn't hear from you for quite a spell, I replied to a letter from one Paul Reynolds in New York, who said he could make a deal with the Century Company for the book. I told him I would listen to reason and this morning, with your two letters, I received one from him, saying Century would give me a fifteen per cent

---

[1] A note penciled on this letter reads: "Mr. Howland—Please get the Lardner matter in shape as we need it if it is good—and I may go east anytime—WBC"

royalty with an advance of $500.00, could get the book out within two months, and use Wallace Morgan's[1] illustrations, which I think are very good. I will not answer him until I hear from you. I, too, am dissatisfied with the title. My own title was "A Neophyte's Diary," but Collier's changed it. Also, Collier's cut out some verses that were in the sixth and eighth installments, and if I do say it as shouldn't, the verses did not deserve to be cut out. Perhaps I can remember or rewrite them.

My Evanston address[2] is 740 Hinman Avenue, but as a rule, I get things sooner at the Tribune.

Sincerely,
Ring W. Lardner

The Chicago Tribune
Chicago, Ill. March 12, [1918]

Dear Mr. Howland:—

I mailed the galley proofs—with one insert and some rather important corrections—this morning.

I have been unable to think of a suitably brief title that conveys the Innocents Abroad idea. How would "OVER THERE AND BACK" or "OVER THERE AND RIGHT BACK" do?

Sincerely,
Ring W. Lardner[3]

A good title for the book was the subject of several letters.

Chicago, Ill
March 19, [1918]

Dear Mr. Howland:—

I don't believe the "world's series" title fits very well. There is no baseball in the book, nor any war as far as that is concerned, and people thinking I was going to treat the war

---

[1] Wallace Morgan was an illustrator for such well-known novelists as Richard Harding Davis and Julian Street. Morgan was noted for his realistic drawings. When he died in 1948, he was described in the New York *Times* as "the dean of American illustrators."

[2] The house that the family rented after Lardner returned from France was at this address in Evanston.

[3] A pencilled note is below Lardner's signature: "Mr Chambers What do you think of these suggestions? HHH 3/13"

in a baseball way might be disappointed. Can I have a day or two more to think it over?
Sincerely,
Ring W. Lardner

Chicago Tribune
March 25, [1918]

Dear Mr. Howland:—

I was out of town for a couple of days and didn't get your letter till this morning.

I have been trying hard to think of a title, but can't seem to get one that would hit anybody "right in the eye." Would "My Four Weeks in France"—a sort of parody on Mr. Gerard's[1] "My Four Years in Germany"—be any good? The "Allies vs. Huns" one doesn't seem to get me. If I have an inspiration I will wire you. However, you are the best judge and if you think any of the ones we have discussed will do, I have no objection to your going ahead with it.
Sincerely,
Ring W. Lardner

Lardner's suggestion was accepted, and the book became *My Four Weeks in France*.

In the summer of 1918, Howland collected another series of Jack Keefe letters Lardner had written for the *Saturday Evening Post* as a wartime sequal to *You Know Me Al*. These letter dealt with Jack's army training camp experiences. Jack remains as imperceptive and inconsistent as he was on the baseball field. For example, as he is about to be shipped overseas after failing in several attempts to avoid military service, he asserts a strident patriotism:

> Well Al this may be the last time you will ever hear from me or at least for a long time and maybe never. I'm going over there old pal and something tells me I won't never come back. Well Al it's a big honor to be 1 of the men picked and it means they have got a lot of confidence in me and you can bet they are not sending no riff and raff over there but just picked men and I will show them they didn't make no mistake in choosing me.

---

[1] James Watson Gerard was a former ambassador to the German imperial court. His book was published in 1917 by Hodder and Stoughton.

The Chicago Tribune
Chicago March 28th.

Dear Mr. Howland: —
    I am mailing you an alleged picture of me, taken by "a staff photographer" yesterday. If you can wait a little while, I can send you one, taken by a flattering artist, which looks more human. But if you are in a hurry, this is the best I can do. I haven't an old one of any kind to my name.
                    Sincerely,
                        Ring W. Lardner

AUG 20 AM 12 21
CHICAGO ILLS
H H HOWLAND
    BOBBS–MERRILL PUB CO INDIANAPOLIS IND I AM GLAD STORIES DONT HAVE TO BE CUT NO OBJECTION TO USE OF "TREAT EM ROUGH" IN CONNECTION WITH TITLE IF IT IS MADE PLAIN THAT I AM NOT CLAIMING CREDIT FOR AUTHORSHIP OF THE PHRASE
                        RING W LARDNER.

Chicago, Ill.
August 30, [1918]

Dear Mr. Howland: —
    I enclosed a copy of the book contract, which I have duly signed in the presence of a beautiful young lady.
    I don't understand exactly what you want in the nature of a verse. Is it to be an ad for the book or something?
                    Sincerely,
                        Ring W. Lardner

    The references below are to more accounts of the overseas antics of Jack Keefe, which were collected in book form in 1919 as *The Real Dope*.

Chicago Tribune
November 5, [1918]

Dear Mr. Howland: —
    I haven't saved the Posts of dates previous to the first of October. As I remember, there have been four in the "overseas" series, the titles being "And Many a Stormy Wind Shall Blow—," "Private Valentine," "Strategy and Tragedy," and "Decorated." The Post now has one more,

called "Sammy Boy," and about two others will wind it up.[1] But if you are contemplating publication of another book, I would like to pass on the title and the illustrations. I don't think it was brought out clearly enough in the last one that I didn't claim authorship of the slogan "Treat 'Em Rough," and I did think it was understood that Mrs. Preston's[2] illustrations were to be used.

I had a letter from Bobbs–Merrill about two months ago, saying there was $280 or some such amount coming to me in October from "My Four Weeks in France" and "Gullible's Travels" and so far no check has arrived. Will you please ask somebody about it?

Sincerely,
Ring W. Lardner

Lardner wrote the following letter at the close of the war to his old friend and fellow baseball reporter John Neville Wheeler, while Wheeler was still with the Army in France. The letter indicates that Lardner by this time was definitely contemplating a move to New York. After leaving the *Tribune* some years earlier, Wheeler had established the Bell Syndicate to sell the work of well-known journalists, and obviously he had invited Lardner to write for him.

The Chicago Tribune
Chicago Nov. 8th.

Dear Jack:—

I haven't forgotten the "good old Bell Syndicate," but what can I do for it? However, I'm through here the first of next July and I presume you'll be through with the army by that time, and maybe we can put something over then. I don't want any regular job (if I can live without one), but what I would like to do is occasional stunts like national conventions, etc. I'll probably move east next summer and hang around N.Y. city till I can find a better place.

---

[1] Six stories were published as *The Real Dope*: "And Many a Stormy Wind Shall Blow," "Private Valentine," "Strategy and Tragedy," "Decorated," "Sammy Boy," and "Simple Simon" (previously published in the *Saturday Evening Post* issues of 6 July 1918, 3 August, 31 August, 26 October, 21 December, and 25 January 1919, respectively). "The Busher Reenlists," to which Lardner is probably also referring, was not included in the book.

[2] May Wilson Preston had illustrated *Gullible's Travels*. She did the illustrations for *The Real Dope*, in conjunction with M.L. Blumenthal, and later for *The Big Town*.

Mr. Howard, president of the United Press, cabled his company from Paris yesterday morning that the armistice had been signed and almost everybody got drunk. Mr. Crusinberry[1] and I, who have a bet up, decided to wait for Associated Press confirmation, and when the story was officially denied we were still bone dry. However, we've stood it six months and can wait a few, très few, days longer.

Of course you must come to Chicago as soon as you get back and Mr. Griffin will be invited to give us a party.
R.W.L.

Chicago, Ill
December 9, [1918]

Dear Mr. Howland:

I am trying to find a title for the new one and will fire it along as soon as the inspiration comes; not that I think "Let's Go" is at all bad, but there may be one that will fit better. The Post now has the closing two installments and I presume will print the first ones in two weeks or so. I know Mr. Lorimer wants to get through with his war stuff as soon as possible.

Is there any law in the Bobbs–Merrill company against sending a poor bird a check before it is due. If not—Well, it promises to be an unmerry Christmas on Buena Avenue.[2]

I had the pleasure of seeing Chicago with your townsman, Meridith Nicholson, Saturday night. We were fellow attendants at the farewell dinner to Ray Long, who, as you doubtless have heard, goes to Cosmopolitan as editor.

Remember me to Mrs. Howland and tell her Laurette sends love.
Sincerely,
Ring W. Lardner

Chicago, Ill.
December 23, [1918]

Dear H. H. H.—

"The Real Dope" seems to me a better title than "Let's Go." I am returning the galley proofs with some rather important corrections and the postscript you requested. I do

---

[1] James Crusinberry, a Chicago sportswriter, was an old friend. In the summer of 1909, he and Lardner had been members of a singing quartet that also included Artie Hofman and Jimmy Sheckard.

[2] After another summer in St. Joseph, the Lardners had rented an apartment on Buena Avenue in Chicago.

wish that instead of just the three stories, the whole six could be combined, winding up the series right and all at once. The Post has only one more installment, the final one, which no doubt they would send you ahead of their publication. The six installments together make a complete story of Jack's adventures from the time he sailed until he was invalided home, and I think purchasers of the book would be less likely to consider themselves "stung" if they got it all at once, no matter what the price. Besides, if the last three installments were published separately, it would be pretty late for war stuff, and I do want to be sure that the whole series is published if part of it is. The check was very welcome; also Mrs. Howland's message of cheer.
                        Sincerely,
                        R.W.L.

On 20 December 1918, Howland wrote offering Lardner "a flat royalty of ten cents a copy" on *The Real Dope*, on the grounds that Bobbs-Merrill could thereby offer the book at one dollar, rather than at a dollar and a half a copy. Greater sales, Howland explained, would make up the difference in the amount of royalty Lardner would receive.

Chicago, Ill.
December 27, [1918]

Dear Mr. Howland: —
    The "thin dime" royalty is all right with me. The main idea, I think, is to have the clients satisfied, which I'm afraid they wouldn't be if only the three stories were published. I'm glad you will try to get some of Mrs. Preston's pictures.
    Will you ask the editors or whatever they are to cut out the postscript which I wrote to tack onto the end of the three installment I received in galley proof. With the latest three stories added, there's no use of it.
    We had a dry Christmas, too, as I climbed back onto the cart the 18th., with a ticket good until the first of May.
                        Sincerely,
                        R.W.L.

David Ellis, the Lardners' fourth child (and fourth son) was born on 11 March 1919. (In 1944, while serving as a *New Yorker* correspondent during World War II, David was fatally injured in a land mine explosion in Germany as he was returning from the American First Army front.)
    Feeling the need for more income and remembering that his old contract with the *Tribune* was to expire in June,

Lardner went to New York early in 1919 to negotiate an agreement with John Wheeler to write a weekly column for Wheeler's Bell Syndicate. Of course, this agreement meant moving to New York. Lardner anticipated that his salary, which would be dependent on the number of newspapers that ran the column, would be substantially larger than the $10,400 a year he was receiving from the *Tribune*. In fact, his Bell Syndicate income would average close to $30,000 a year.

Because the agreement between Lardner and Wheeler was an oral one, Wheeler apparently became worried some weeks later and offered to provide Lardner with a written contract. Lardner wired him:

> If you knew anything about contracts you would realize we made one in the Waldorf bar before five witnesses, three of whom were sober.[1]

Needing additional money to finance the impending move, Lardner wrote to Howland:

Chicago, Ill.
May 5, [1919]

Dear Mr. Howland:—
I was in St. Louis two weeks ago and spent last week recovering; else I would have answered your letter before. I wrote a series of short stories about building a home three or four years ago. The series was printed in the Red Book and I don't know whether or not it could be obtained now; nor whether it would be worth printing.
I saw by the paper that you and Mrs. Howland were here last week, but my telephone told me nothing to that effect. Next time [you] come, you are supposed to call up.
                Sincerely,
                R.W.L.

On June 30, Howland telegraphed Lardner for permission to obtain the four stories from *Redbook* and publish them as a book titled *Own Your Own Home*.

---

[1] Quoted by John Wheeler, "The Unforgettable Ring Lardner," *Readers Digest*, 89 (October 1966), 115.

TOLEDO
3 05 P JUL 3 1919
H H HOWLAND
BODDS[1] MERRILL CO INDIANAPOLIS IND
ITS ALL RIGHT WITH ME
          RING LARDNER.

CHICAGO IL
1919 JUL 10 PM 3 16
H H HOWLAND
CARE BOBBS–MERRILL PUBLISHING CO
INDIANAPOLIS IND
WILL YOU PLEASE ASK TREASURER TO SEND ME
ROYALTIES DUE IN JUNE I NEED THE MONEY
          RING W LARDNER.

    By the fall of 1919, the Lardners were settled in a rented house in Greenwich, Connecticut. Lardner's first "Weekly Letter" for the Bell Syndicate, titled "Moving to the East," appeared on 2 November 1919.

33 Otter Rock Drive
Greenwich, Connecticut
[26 October 1919]

Dear Mr. Howland: —
    I enclose a copy of the "Own Your Own Home" contract, signed but not witnessed. The books came and are now on their way east by freight.
    Will you please tell your treasurer that I have a couple of royalty checks coming and the cost of living down this way is terrific?[2]
                  Sincerely,
                  Ring W. Lardner

    Round-robin letters among the Abbotts were a practical family convention. The eight Abbott siblings—Ruby, Ellis, Florence, Frank, John, Jeannette, Dorothy, and William—and their mother kept in touch by writing round-robins to which each recipient would add news and forward the whole to the next.

---

[1] Telegrapher's error.

[2] Royalties due Lardner in October, for sales of *Gullible's Travels, My Four Weeks in France, Treat 'Em Rough,* and *The Real Dope* during the first six months of 1919, amounted to $1017.36.

Ruby, the oldest child, married Robin Hendry. Florence married Paull Torrence (their courtship was renowned among the family for the fact that Florence fainted in a boat on Lake Wawasee upon receiving Paull's proposal). Jeannette married Francis R. Kitchell, and Dorothy, the youngest sister, married Howell W. Kitchell, Francis's brother.

Late in 1919, just after the U. S. Navy had commissioned a new destroyer the *James L. Lardner*, in honor of Lardner's great-uncle, who was a Rear Admiral, Lardner wrote the following:

Mrs. Abbott, Girls and Kitchell:—

    I note in the current "Round Robin" a suggestion from Mrs. Torrence that the husbands do the writing for once. Well, at least they wouldn't be illegible, though the only husband that has tried it to date is unintelligible which is worse. But I want to say that I would do the writing for this house only for two reasons:

    1. Why do they call it a Round Robin? When you think of the adverb round, what do you think of next? You think of Ring, not only that, but who was the first that married into the Abbotts? Torrence may have been the first to propose marriage and Hendry the first to consider, but who was the first that had the nerve to go through with it? Who set the pace by showing that his intentions were honorable? Furthermore who else does the adverb round fit? The only thing round about Paull outside of his physique is round Riverside, and who showed him round? The only thing round about Kitchell is his specs which he wears to keep people from taking a punch at him. (When Kitchell is mentioned in this letter, it means F. R. Kitchell. The other Kitchell is disregarded on account of his wife not taking part in the Round Robin. (What a name for it!) on account of being ashamed because she married the only man in the Navy that didn't get a medal except William Abbott. And speaking of the Navy, they recently christened a new destroyer "Lardner." The records don't show that there's even a cat boat named Torrence or Hendry or Kitchell.)

    2. If the husbands are supposed to write, what about John Abbott, who certainly can't claim shame-facedness on Dorothy's grounds, as he at least has a Victoria Cross, or at least she was down to the lake last summer when her so-called husband bid four and got set four and bawled her out for it, though she was dummy. Also what about the would-be husbands, Frank and William Chauncey? Why don't they write? Perhaps they will answer, "Because we have nothing to say." But did that ever prevent their talking?

In conclusion let me say that there is a show running in New York called "No More Blondes" and I consider it the truest word ever spoken as far as I am concerned, and when I say that I don't mean you, Victoria, nor you, Mrs. Abbott's favorite daughter, but the one I mean married the only man in the Navy that didn't get a medal except William Abbott, and won't write.
Guess who this is talking.

By the following February, Howland was also seeking Lardner's permission to publish *The Young Immigrants*, which had originally appeared as a lengthy story in the 31 January 1920 *Saturday Evening Post*.

GREENWICH CON
1920 FEB 9 PM 8 49
H H HOWLAND
　　CARE BOBBS–MERRILL CO INDIANAPOLIS IND
IF YOU THINK "YOUNG IMMIGRANTS"[1] IS LONG ENOUGH TO MAKE A BOOK I HAVE NO OBJECTION BUT I THINK CRAZY OLD FASHIONED PHOTOGRAPHS WOULD BE BETTER AS ILLUSTRATIONS
　　　　　　　　　RING W LARDNER.

Based on the family move from Goshen to Greenwich, *The Young Immigrants* is one of Lardner's funnier stories. Presented as if written by four-year-old Ring Lardner Jr., the account focuses on the obstacles encountered during the auto trip, and upon the numerous exchanges between husband and wife. One such exchange follows an encounter with newlyweds:

> A little latter who should come out on the porch and set themselfs ner us but the bride and glum.
> Oh I said to myself I hope they will talk so as I can hear them as I have always wandered what newlyweds talk about on their way to Niagara Falls and soon my wishs was realized.
> Some night said the young glum are you warm enough.
> I am perfectly comfortible replid the fare bride tho her looks belid her words what time do we arive in Buffalo.

---

[1] Probably a telegrapher's error.

9 oclock said the lordly glum are you warm enough.
I am perfectly comfertible replid the fare bride what time do we arive in Buffalo.
9 oclock said the lordly glum I am afrade it is too cold for you out here.
Well maybe it is replid the fare bride and without farther adieu they went in the spacius parlers.
I wander will he be arsking her 8 years from now is she warm enough said my mother with a faint grimace.
The weather may change before then replid my father.
Are you warm enough said my father after a slite pause.
No was my mothers catchy reply.

The book also contains this classic bit of family dialogue:

The lease said about my and my fathers trip from the Bureau of Manhattan to our new home the soonest mended. In some way ether I or he got balled up on the grand concorpse and next thing you know we was thretning to swoop down on Pittsfield.
Are you lost daddy I arsked tenderly.
Shut up he explained.

*The Young Immigrunts* is a parody of *The Young Visiters*, a book supposedly written by nine-year-old Daisy Ashford, for whom Sir James Barrie had written an introduction in which he hailed her as a child prodigy. Lardner and others suspected (probably incorrectly) that the whole affair was a joke perpetrated by Barrie (see letter of 22 February 1925 to William Orton Tewson).

NEWYORK NY
1920 MAR 10 AM 2 15
H H HOWLAND
BOBBS–MERRILL CO INDIANAPOLIS IND
DO NOT THINK THERE IS ANY REASON FOR CHANGE OF TITLE BUT IF YOU MUST CHANGE MAKE IT THE YOUNG MOORERS[1] INSTEAD OF YOUNG TRAVELERS
RING LARDNER.

---

[1] Telegrapher's error for "*Moovers.*"

The letter below responds to Howland's query as to whether a rumor he has heard from a friend in California is correct, that Lardner had run a series of fairy tales in the *Post* several years earlier.

Greenwich, Connecticut
April 2, [1920]

Dear H3:—
    I enclose the signed contract for "The Young Immigrunts."
    As for any fairy tales I ever wrote, the guy who said so is just a plain California cuckoo. Remember me to the family.
    And Oh, yes. Another cuckoo here wants two copies of "Gullible's Travels." Are there any left?
                    Sincerely,
                      R.W.L.

In the spring of 1920, the Lardners purchased a large house on East Shore Road in Great Neck, Long Island. His neighbors there included his brother Rex and many close friends, such as Arthur Jacks, Frank Adams, Herbert Swope, and, from October 1922 to early May 1924, Scott and Zelda Fitzgerald. Great Neck social life quickly became so hectic that Lardner often retreated to a New York hotel room to work.

Great Neck, New York
July 29, [1920]

Dear H. H.,—
    I hear that "The Young Immigrunts" has been out for some time, but so far I haven't seen nothing of it, as they say. I presume my copies were shipped to the various eastern coast points at which I have lived for the last 3/4 of a year, but they haven't caught up with me yet. I hope the above is our permanent address and if you have a few copies left, could you send them along?
    Please tell Mrs. Howland that I had a very pleasant two conventions with a guy named Irving R. Cobb[1] from

---

[1] Irvin S. Cobb was a journalist and humorous columnist who wrote several humorous books, the best known of which was *Old Judge Priest* (1915).

Parduchar in spite of the fact that his r's are all misplaced.
                    Sincerely,
                          Ring W. Lardner
Did you read about the reception that Laurette Taylor[1] got in London? I felt so sorry that I nearly broke down or up.

Great Neck, New York
September 16, [1920]

Dear Mr. Howland:—
    I have yet to see a copy of "The young Immigrunts" and I would like a few to distribute among my kin. I suppose I could go to New York and buy some, but I haven't been there for five weeks and hate to spoil the record. I don't accuse you of not having had my allotment sent, but Mr. Burleson[2] seems set on my not receiving same. Remember me to Mrs. Howland.
                    Sincerely,
                          Ring W. Lardner

    The following letter was written to William C. Abbott, Ellis's youngest sibling, then in his last year at the University of Michigan:

Great Neck, N. Y., Nov. 29 [1920]

Dear sir:
    Your sister, my wife by marriage, is too proud to write and asks me to tell you that yourself and friend (who we trust is of the male sex) will be welcome whenever you are ready to come. Let us know two or three days ahead so we can have the dishes washed.
    I'm sorry I was obliged to decline the kind invitation to make a speech at Ann Arbor, but if you'd ever heard me make one, you wouldn't have asked me. Trying to remain your brother-in-law,
                          R.W.L.

---

[1] Laurette Taylor was a famous actress and comedienne. She starred in such stage successes as *Peg O' My Heart* (1912), *Out There* (1917), *Happiness* (1918), and *One Night in Rome* (1919). In her last stage role she defined the character of the mother in *The Glass Menagerie* (1945).

[2] Postmaster General Albert S. Burleson was unpopular with the newspaper world because he favored higher bulk mail rates that would have affected newspaper prices.

Great Neck, New York
March 5, [1921]

[To Ellis's mother]
Dear Madam:—
 I enclose a check for the interest due you on March 6 and I trust my prompt attention to same will be appreciated in the proper spirit.
 My own Madam and I got back this morning from Washington where she made herself very conspicuous by trying to start conversations with all the prominent men. And on one occasion it was all I could do to restrain her from forcing a way into the White House. Hereafter she shall remain in woman's place—the home.
 Love to yourself and the Torrences and please overlook my expert use of the typewriter.
               R.W.L.
P.S. Ellis says that whatever you do with the cottage[1] is all right with her.

Great Neck, New York
March 5, [1921]

Dear Mr. Howland:—
 Will you please remind the bookkeeper of a $515 "Young Immigrunts" check that I was told was due in February?
 I have just finished for the Post the last of a series of five stories dealing with three newly rich Indiana people who moved to New York. Four of them—"Quick Returns," "Beautiful Katie," "The Battle of Long Island" and "Only One"—have been published. The fifth gets Katie marriedand is called "The Comic." How would this bunch do for a book under the title of "The Big Town."
               Sincerely,
 We declined an invitation to Herb Swope's[2] house the

---

[1] The Abbott summer home at Lake Wawasee.

[2] Herbert Bayard Swope, as a reporter on the New York *World*, won the first Pulitzer Prize for reporting (1917). When he was executive editor of the *World*, the paper was awarded a Pulitzer Prize (1922) for public service for its series on the Klu Klux Klan. In 1929, Swopte left the *World* to become a "policy consultant" to such major figures as Bernard Baruch and Dwight Eisenhower.

other night and found out afterward that Laurette and Hartley[1] were there. My God.

*The Big Town*, published later in 1921 by Bobbs-Merrill, is superior to any of the fiction Lardner previously had written, except *You Know Me Al*. The themes are again social-climbing and husband-finding, but Finch, his wife, and his sister-in-law are more broadly depicted than most of Lardner's previous characters. Finch is another version of Babbitt, thickskinned, prudish, never lacking in nerve, always sure of himself, and never indulging in self-analysis. As a member of the *nouveau riche*, he knows nothing of books and speaks only the jargon of business, card parties, and the sports world.

All five chapters of the book deal with the love affairs of Katie, the sister-in-law. The first is with a Wall Street broker who is more interested in Finch's wife, until Finch beats him up. The second is an elderly millionaire who has "seen baseball when the second bounce was out," but Katie foolishly falls for the chauffeur instead and swoons when she discovers the chauffeur has two children and a wife. The third suitor is an aviator who seems destined to marry Katie, until he is killed when his airplane develops engine trouble over Long Island. Callously, Finch's wife observes: "Sis is taking it pretty calm. She's sensible. She says if that could of happened why the invention couldn't of been no good after all. And the Williamses probably wouldn't of give him a plugged dime for it." The fourth suitor, an owner of racing horses, turns out to be as mercenary as Katie, and their "love" sours when Katie thinks he has given her a bad tip at the race track. Katie marries the fifth suitor and gets exactly what she deserves—a fortune hunter who works as a comic in the Follies.

Though nothing really is new in *The Big Town*, the social satire is more sharply depicted—the social-climbing *nouveau riche*, the snobbish upper class, the idiotically avid bridge

---

[1] J. Hartley Manners was the second husband of Laurette Taylor. Manners wrote many of the plays in which she performed, including *Peg o' My Heart*, *The Crossways*, *The Patriot*, *The House Next Door*, and *The Girl in Waiting*. They were married in 1912. After his death in 1928, she retired temporarily from the stage and isolated herself with a substantial supply of liquor. Reemerging some months later, she is reputed to have described the period as "the longest wake in history."

players, and the hypocrisy of prohibition. Moreover, the lowbrow narrator's language is perfect.

The letter below is yet another example of Lardner's nonchalance about keeping copies of his work.

Great Neck, New York
March 14, [1921]

Dear Mr. Howland:—

I suppose I ought to keep copies of my stuff, but I never have, so I guess the Post will have to be called on to provide you with the five that would go into "The Big Town." The titles are "Quick Returns," "Beautiful Katie," "The Battle of Long Island," "Only One" and "The Comic," the last named not yet published. May Preston did the pictures for all of them and don't you think it would be a good idea to have her illustrations in the book?

Sincerely,
Ring W. Lardner

Great Neck
April 11, [1921]

Dear Mr. Howland:—

I haven't heard when the Post is going to publish "The Comic," the last story in The Big Town series, but presume it will be in two or three weeks. I enclose the contracts, which I haven't signed on account of Clause No. 2, providing that I offer the next two books to Bobbs–Merrill. If this clause is in every contract I sign, it means that I sign with Bobbs–Merrill not only for life, but also for the two books afterwards, and while I have no fault to find with Bobbs–Merrill's treatment of me and see no immediate prospect of switching to another company, where would I be at if Doran or Appleton or some one else should go crazy and offer me a million for book rights to some future set of stories?

Can you have this clause removed?

Sincerely,
Ring W. Lardner

In a letter dated 14 April 1921, Howland agreed to remove the clause to which Lardner objected.

Lardner's magazine articles were by this time much sought after, as demonstrated by the following comunications with George Horace Lorimer, editor of the *Saturday Evening Post*. From the time the *Post* accepted the busher stories, Lardner had favored that magazine.

Great Neck, New York, April 11. [1921]

Dear Mr. Lorimer:—
   Some time ago, at Hughie Fullerton's solicitation, I wrote one of those things for The American Magazine on "How it Feels to be Thirty-five." Mr. Siddall has asked me several times since to write him two or three more of the same kind. I've told him that my time was limited and I didn't have much to spare for any but my Post and syndicate stuff. When he called up the other day, however, I said I'd see if I could arrange to do two or three short stunts for him. I don't want to do them unless it's all right with the Post, so I'm writing to see how you feel about it. It really doesn't make any difference to me one way or the other.
                Sincerely,
                Ring W. Lardner

Lorimer answered: "If you have time to write two or three pieces for the American, why not do them for the Saturday Evening Post?"

Great Neck, New York, April 15.

Dear Mr. Lorimer:—
   That's very complimentary, and to return the compliment—I thought perhaps the pieces I intended writing for the American might not be good enough for the Post. However, if I do write them (I have no ideas for them yet), I will send them to you.
                Sincerely,
                Ring W. Lardner

Lorimer replied: "My dear Lardner: The answer is to make them better. We must not degrade our art."

Great Neck, New York
May 11th.

Dear Sister—and Brothers—and Night School-in-Law: —
   I don't suppose anybody will be surprised to hear that we have another baby. I had it myself this time and it's a girl and we have named her Frederika Beauvais. I started for the hospital Saturday night and found it Sunday morning and was back home in time for Sunday night supper. The doctor said he had never enjoyed a more obstetrical weekend. The baby weighed 9 1/2 pounds stripped. The boys are wild about her and she has already taken a fancy to David, whom she calls "Curly."

Mr. and Mrs. Fred Nymeyer and mother-in-law, Mrs. Crewell, were here the night after the baby came and I played bridge with them till nurse made me stop. Ellis is in town today, having lunch with Grace and Helen Hawks. Speaking about bridge, Ralph Crews, our Riverside neighbor, and considered a very good player out there, told me a while ago that he was totally lost in a New York bridge game and warned me to keep out of same, but I got roped into one at a party next door the other night, and before we started, the lady who was to be my partner, asked me what conventions I played. So I kind of stalled and said I always liked to play my partner's conventions, so she rattled off seven of them. Then it was announced that we were playing for 2 1/2 cents. I won $20 and I don't have to tell you that I held good hands, and whatever her bid was, I raised it. After the first lead, the declarer generally slapped the cards down on the table and said it was a grand slam or a small slam and that ended it. Ellis and I have since bought two books on bridge by New York experts and in three or four years I will expect her to know that when I lead the four of spades, it means I haven't the trey of diamonds.

Dear Vic:— If you are as empty as you say and John is bankrupt, I'm very much afraid we'll have to call you the vacuum cleaner, and next time I telephone you I'll say, "Hollow."

Dear Howell:— There are two l's in your Indianapolis brother-in-law's first name. Let's try to keep our spelling pure and be as different as possible from the children's round robin.

Dear Paull:— If you do want to help that Link Belt friend of Kitch's, I'd strongly advise against your mentioning the fact that he went to Wisconsin with a couple of hoodlums.

Dear Robin:— My golf seems to have gained in accuracy and lost none of its brilliance. The other day I was playing over in New Jersey and George Ade[1] insisted on my

---

[1] George Ade was a well-known newspaperman (on the old Chicago *Morning News* in the 1890s), a writer of humorous stories in dialect (e.g., *Fables in Slang, More Fables, Forty Modern Fables*), and, later, a musical comedy writer (e.g., *The Sultan of Sulu*). Lardner's interests paralleled Ade's, and they seem to have been good friends, though Ade was nineteen years older. The high esteem in which Lardner held Ade is evident from Lardner's comment during a 1917 New York *Times* magazine section interview:

> Well, I wouldn't consider Mark Twain our greatest humorist. I guess that George Ade is. Certainly he appeals to us more than Mark Twain does because he belongs to our own time. He writes of the life we are living, and Mark Twain's books deal

trying his spoon. I did, and the ball hit George in the colon bacillus. Vic can tell you where that is. Also, Bill Fields of the Follies said he met a brother-in-law of mine on a party in Detroit. Don't let Ruby open this one.

Dear Kitch:— I pray God you'll have nerve enough to dictate to a stenographer next time. It will save everybody time and may make you less obscene.

I didn't feel like writing this today, but the other letters had been in the house since Monday and were just beginning to spell.

R.W.L., five times a Father.

The following letter to Churchill Williams, an associate editor at the *Post*, responds to an expressed fear by the *Post* editors that publication of Lardner's story "The Battle of the Century" might result in a libel suit. Sarcastically so titled, the story was a thinly disguised narrative of the Dempsey versus Carpentier heavyweight title mismatch of 2 July 1921.

Great Neck, New York
August 4.

Dear Mr. Williams:—

Before I forget it, will you please tell whom it may concern that my address is *Great Neck New York, not Greenwich, Conn.* The last three or four communications from the Post have been sent to Greenwich and forwarded to me from there. I have gone over the proof of the fight story carefully and this is my dope on it:

There is nothing Tex Rickard[1] possibly could object to, as all the references to him, as "Charley Riggs," are boosts for him. He is the man Kearns[2] (Larry Moon) wants as

> with the life which we know only by hearsay. I suppose my forebears would say that Mark Twain was a much greater humorist than George Ade.
>
> But I never saw one of Mark Twain's characters, while I feel that I know every one about whom George Ade writes. You see, I didn't travel along the Mississippi in Mark Twain's youth, so I don't know his people. Harry Leon Wilson is a great humorist, and Fiunley Peter Dunne is another. But I'll bet Finley Peter Dunne is sick of writing in Irish dialect.

[1] Tex Rickard was the boxing promoter largely responsible for developing boxing into a million-dollar sport. The Dempsey–Carpentier fight that he promoted had the first million-dollar gate in boxing history.

2 Jack Kearns was Jack Dempsey's manager from 1917 to 1925.

promoter because he is the only man big enough for the job. And later there is a boost for the way he handled the fight. As I see it, the fall guys in the story are Crawley and Guthrie, who are supposed to have been fooled by the Cuban waiters.[1] "Crawley" and "Guthrie" are supposed to be Cochrane,[2] the English theatrical man, and William A. Brady.[3] I don't believe there is anything even remotely libellous about them, but it is possible they might not relish being represented as gullible. If you think best, I will fix the story so that their identities will be more obscure. As for Jack Kearns (Larry Moon), I don't like to brag, but he is a friend of mine and wouldn't be offended at anything I wrote, even if he happened to read it. Moreover, I think he is proud of his part—a mighty big one—in "building up" the fight. Besides all that, he is too busy defending suits to start any. But to play it perfectly safe, I'll show him the proof of the story, not saying anything, of course, about the possibility of libel, but merely telling him I don't want to have it printed if there's anything in it that he objects to, and will let you know what he says. He is at the Belmont in New York and I think I can see him in a day or two. I'll do it as soon as possible and then return the proof to you.

Please let me know if you think it necessary to "cover up" the Crawley and Guthrie characters. I enclose Runyon's Wednesday stuff[4] which corroborates the opinion

---

[1] According to Nat Fleischer's 1972 biography *Jack Dempsey*, the deception practiced through the Cuban waiters was connected with the Dempsey-Willard fight of 4 July 1919. Rickard was unwilling to match Jess Willard with the unproven Dempsey. Kearns introduced the Cubans, who could not speak English, to Rickard as representatives of a syndicate that would promote the fight if Rickard would not. The ploy worked, and Rickard began serious negotiations for the championship bout, which Dempsey won by a TKO after three rounds. Lardner simply appropriated this incident for his attack on the promotion of the later fight.

[2] Charles B. Cochran was a British theatrical producer and sports promoter.

[3] William A. Brady was a New York theatrical impresario who had managed both James J. Jeffries and James J. Corbett.

[4] The famous columnist Damon Runyon obviously shared Lardner's view of the fight.

of everybody that knows the fight qame—i.e. that the Dempsey–Carpentier match wasn't a match at all.
Sincerely,
Ring W. Lardner

If you think it advisable, I can also show the story to Rickard, who is friendly, too.

Great Neck, New York
August 10th.

Dear Mr. Williams:—

I enclose the proof of the fight story. You will notice that I have indicated a couple of changes on Page 3 which would cover up the identity of Cochrane and Brady. I don't believe the changes are necessary, for safety's sake, but if you want to make them, all right.

I saw Jack Kearns, Dempsey's manager, yesterday. As I thought, he saw nothing in the story to object to; in fact, seemed to take it as a boost for him. He wanted to know how I had found out about the Cuban waiters, which he said was true. By chance two friends of mine were with me and heard all he had to say, the important part of which was, as truly as I can report it: "You don't have to show me nothing that you write. Anything you write about the champ and I is O.K. with us. I don't know how you found out all them things or remembered them. But they's nothing in there that ain't right."

He also told me (this not for publication) that he is going to Europe soon to try to arrange another bout between Dempsey and Carpentier in Paris. I asked him how he expected to get away with a thing like that and he said he thought the French would be as eager to see it as if the Jersey City fight had never taken place. "They don't believe nothing that happens over here," he said.
Sincerely,
Ring W. Lardner

When Williams continued to express fear that Tex Rickard "has good grounds for a suit if he chooses to bring one on the ground that he had promoted a phoney fight," Lardner sent the proofs to Rickard's secretary:

Great Neck, New York
Friday.

Dear Ike:—

Here is the dope and if you will ask Tex to take time to read it (it isn't long) and say whether it's all right with him, I'll be much obliged.

Will you please send it back to me as soon as possible in the enclosed envelope?

R.W.L.[1]

Lardner then enclosed that letter with another to George Horace Lorimer:

Great Neck, New York
September sixth.

Dear Mr. Lorimer:—

Here is the fight story again, with the note I wrote to Ike Dorgan (Rickard's secretary and press agent) and his and Rickard's expressions of approval. The cipher message in blue pencil means "OK, G.L.R. (George L. Rickard)."

If the libel experts have others in mind who they think might be sensitive, I wish they'd send the whole list at once, as the story is in danger of losing something of its timeliness.

Sincerely,
Ring W. Lardner

"The Battle of the Century"[2] appeared in the 29 October 1921 *Post*.

When Hewitt Howland passed on to Lardner an invitation from the Advertising Club of St. Louis to come with expenses paid and speak for twenty minutes on anything in which he might be interested, Lardner made clear his aversion to making public speeches:

---

[1] Inscribed on the page in large letters are "OK / GLR" and "Ring—/ Listens good / Ike."

[2] Reprinted in *Some Champions*.

GREATNECK NY   1921 SEP 23 AM 11 44
H H HOLLAND[1]
BOBBS–MERRILL CO INDIANAPOLIS IND
NOT A CHANCE TELL THEM AM BUSY WITH
BASEBALL STUFF
                              RING W LARDNER.

Howland also wrote to ask Lardner if he would write an article of five or six hundred words on "anything you have to say about books, the reading public, styles in literature, revival of interest in books, what in a book creates conversation among those who have read it; does the American public give English authors preference, etc., etc." The article was to be part of a series syndicated by the "All-the-Year Round Bookselling Committee" for the purpose of "stimulating the buying of books."

Great Neck, New York
September 28, [1921]

Dear Mr. Howland:—
　Please let me beg off on that assignment. Whenever I attempt anything in the line of serious discussion it sounds like a seventh grade essay on The Ethics of Veterinarianism.
　　　　　　　　Sincerely,
　　　　　　　　R.W.L.

When D. Laurence Chambers, president of Bobbs–Merrill, wrote, during Howland's visit to New York at World Series time to propose newspaper syndication of *Own Your Own Home* if the rights were available, Lardner responded just after the Series:

Great Neck, New York
October 14, [1921]

Dear Mr. Chambers:—
　I would have replied more promptly to your letter, but the world's series has had me jumping. My newspaper syndication rights are all in the hands of the Bell Syndicate, with which I am tied up. Moreover, I'm afraid the "Own Your Own Home" stuff is out of date. In it are many references to prices of material etc. which were considered

---

[1] Telegrapher's error for "Howland."

out of all reason when I wrote the stories, but which would be mighty cheap nowadays.
I saw Mr. Howland at one world's series game and expect to have a chance to visit with him before he goes.
Sincerely,
Ring W. Lardner

Below is the first of several letters to H.L. Mencken, one of the first literary critics to identify Lardner as a major American fictionist and to praise especially Lardner's ear for capturing dialogue accurately. In the first edition of *The American Language* (1919), Mencken had written:

> In his grotesque tales of base-ball players, so immediately and so deservedly successful and now so widely imitated, Lardner reports the common speech not only with humor, but also with the utmost accuracy.... The result is a mine of authentic American. In a single story by Lardner, in truth, it is usually possible to discover examples of almost every logical and grammatical peculiarity of the emerging language, and he always resists very stoutly the temptation to overdo the thing.[1]

In 1920, while they were both covering the Republican Convention, Lardner and Mencken became good friends. They shared a number of views, notably distrust of the American politician and skepticism of an electoral process dependent on the good judgment of the American "boob." For the second edition of *The American Language* (1921), Lardner wrote two "amusing specimens of the common speech" (see fourth edition, p. 425n).

Great Neck, New York
October 24th. [1921]

Dear H. — L. —
"The Girls"[2] is in the house, but I haven't had my turn at it yet. I just got through with "If Winter Comes" and

---

[1] H. L. Mencken, *The American Language,* first ed. (New York: Alfred Knopf, 1919), pp. 190-91.

[2] *The Girls* was a novel by Edna Ferber about three spinsters, each symbolizing an era. Published by Doubleday, 1921.

thought it was over-touted,[1] possibly because I was fed up with English stories.

I'm glad you liked the Post story.[2] I didn't hate it myself, but I have a hunch that the editor wasn't so keen for it.

Are you going to the disarmament conference? I am, for some reason another.
R.W.L.
The above is where I live.

The next letter was probably written in 1921 just after Lardner had returned from covering the Disarmament Conference in Washington.

Great Neck, New York
November 23.

Dear sir:
Thanks for the Declaration, which I read and enjoyed. I intended to tell you this face to face at Washington, but didn't run across you, probably because I stuck to the dry spots.

I think it only fair to warn you that a certain back biter whom we will call Harry Hyde[3] and whom I have nicknamed Dr. Jekyll and Harry Hyde is spreading a report about you the substance of which is that no matter what you seem, you have a kind heart.
R.W.L.

Lardner's addressing Howland below as "Hewitt" is probably a result of the social meeting predicted in the letter to D. L. Chambers of 14 October above. Subsequent letters to Howland exhibit a more relaxed tone.

---

[1] *If Winter Comes* was a novel of sentiment by Arthur Stewart-Menteth Hutchinson, published by Little, Brown and Company, 1921.

[2] "Some Like Them Cold," which had just appeared in the 21 October *Saturday Evening Post*.

[3] Henry M. Hyde, a reporter on the Chicago *Tribune* from 1915 to 1920. He went from that newspaper to the Baltimore *Sun* (Mencken's home base for years), for which he was Washington reporter.

1. Niles, Michigan, in 1906

2. The Lardner family home in Niles

3. The Lardner family circa 1900.
Left to right: Lena Lardner (the older sister of Ring Lardner),
Reginald (Rex), Lena (Ring Lardner's mother), Anne, and Ring,
with Mrs. Parret (a neighbor), in front of the Lardner home
before its portico was removed

4. Left to right: unidentified, Anne, Ring, Rex Lardner

5. Lardner shortly before he met Ellis Abbott

6. Wilma Johnson, the friend who introduced Lardner to Ellis

7. Left to right: Ellis Abbott with companions Helen Irwin and Ruby 2 October 1910, Goshen, Indiana, some thirty miles south of Niles

8. Lardner at the Chicago *Tribune*, 1913, shortly before writing *You Know Me Al*

9. Ellis and Ring Lardner on vacation in the early 1920's

10. Bud Fisher—the creator of "Mutt and Jeff"— Jack Dempsey, and Ring Lardner

11. John Golden and Ring Lardner in a publicity fight in Miami Beach, 1921

12. At the White House, 1921
Left to right: President Warren Harding, Grantland Rice,
Lardner, Henry Fletcher

13. The Lardners at the Great Neck house in 1923
Left to right: Jim, Ellis, David, Ring Jr., Ring, and John

14. With Gene Buck in Great Neck

15. Lardner in the early 1920's

16. Lardner in 1925

17. Maxwell Perkins, the famous editor at Scribners, who, in addition to working with Lardner, was the editor for Fitzgerald, Hemingway, Wolfe, and Edmund Wilson

18. Lardner's most important literary contact, F. Scott Fitzgerald

Photograph by Nikolas Muray

16, 17. The Fitzgeralds in their apartment in Rue de Tilsitt in Paris, 1924 (F. Scott Fitzgerald with his wife, Zelda, and daughter, Scottie)

19

His sharp features and sly smile made Lardner a favorite with caricaturists.
See frontispiece for Covarrubias; above a drawing by an unknown hand (19)
and by Ralph Barton (20)

21

22

21, 22. Margaret Freeman's caricatures of the author of *The Story of a Wonder Man* (1927)

23. Dorothy Parker
Photograph by George Platt Lynes

24. Theodore Dreiser, with whom Lardner corresponded briefly at the end of his life

25. H. L. Mencken, who warmly endorsed *How to Write Short Stories* and predicted the longevity of Lardner's writing

26. Lardner with his sons on Long Island

27. Ellis Lardner in 1931

28. The house in East Hampton, New York, to which the Lardners moved in 1928

29. Lardner in 1931

30. One of the last pictures of Lardner, taken by Ring Jr. in 1932

Great Neck, New York
November 20, [1921]

Dear Hewitt:—
    I'd like two or three copies of "The Young Immigrunts" if it isn't too much trouble.
                         R.W.L.

The following letter to Heywood Broun[1] (as quoted by Broun in his New York *Morning World* column of 9 March 1922) responds to Broun's column of 7 March on Bert Williams,[2] who had died on 4 March:

    When I read your line, "It did not seem to us that Williams was a great comedian and certainly not a great clown," I thought to myself—
    But then I thought, "This guy ain't stupid so the answer must be that he never saw a Williams and Walker show, and is judging Bert by Bert in the Follies, well, sir, you might just as well judge Babe Ruth's pitching on his 1920-1921 showing with the Yankees."
    And besides being the greatest comedian and one of the greatest clowns I ever saw, Bert was a great natural musician and a masterly singer of "coon songs," and when I say singer, I mean singer.
    The people who wrote the Williams and Walker shows knew how to write for Bert. The Follies people didn't, and he lacked the energy to write for himself. Besides, he was under the impression, the delusion, that Follies audiences were drawn by scenery and legs and didn't want to laugh. He used to say, "I'm just out there to give the gals time to change."
    In my early Chicago days, Williams and Walker played long runs, mostly at the Alhambra and Great Northern theaters. My allowance for spending money was about $5 a month. I used to spend $3 of it on their show, going once a week at 75 cents a trip. It was Williams who drew me and he meant to me a sacrifice of sixty beers a month. He had a

---

[1] Broun began his career as a rewrite man on the New York *Tribune*. He became a sportswriter, drama critic, and columnist, moving to the New York *World* in 1921, where he began writing "It Seems to Me." In 1930 he was a losing candidate for the House of Representatives on the socialist ticket. He was one of the founders of the American Newspaper Guild and its first president.

[2] See Williams' letter to Lardner of 17 March 1911, with preceding commentary.

song—"My Castle on the Nile"—in the chorus of which there wasn't a funny line; yet they (we) made him come out and sing, or dance, that refrain twenty-one times in one show.

Speaking about his dancing, if you'd seen him just dance in the old days, you'd have pronounced him comedian and clown as well as the champion eccentric "hoofer" of all time.

In my record book he leads the league as comedian and can be given no worse than a tie for first place as clown, pantomimist, story-teller, eccentric dancer and a singer of a certain type of songs. Otherwise, he was a flop.

At income-tax time, Lardner wrote to the *Post* :

Great Neck, New York
February twentieth.

Dear Mr. Lorimer:—
Will you please ask the cashier to send me, for income tax purposes, a statement of what the Post paid me in 1921?
Also, I was in Cuba the early part of this month and thought of writing a piece about it. But two or three people have told me they thought the subject was covered not very long ago by Mrs. Putnam[1] or somebody. Will you let me know whether it was or not?
Sincerely,
Ring W. Lardner

The statement Lardner received from the *Post* shows a total payment of $6,000 ($1500 for each of four pieces—"The Comic," "A Frame-Up," "The Battle of the Century," and "Some Like Them Cold"). Lorimer also encouraged Lardner to write about Cuba "if the subject is handled in your well known josh style."

Lardner also asked Bobbs-Merrill for a statement:

---

[1] Nina Wilcox Putnam was a well-known contributor of stories and articles at that time to periodicals such as *Ainslee's Magazine* and *The Saturday Evening Post*. Like Lardner, she wrote for the motion pictures and also later wrote a syndicated news column.

Great Neck, New York
March 1, [1922]

Dear Hewitt:—
 Will you be good enough to ask the bookkeepers to let me know how much Bobbs–Merrill paid me in 1921?[1]
 Also, thanks for that letter you wrote to the guy on the Brooklyn Eagle.
Sincerely,<br>R.W.L.

Howland's response included the query as to what Lardner might think of making a booklet out of "A Caddy's Diary," which had appeared in the 11 March 1922 *Saturday Evening Post.*

Great Neck, New York
April 1, [1922]

Dear Hewitt:—
 I think we'd better lay off'n the caddy's diary. In the first place, it's too short and in the second, I may follow it up, though probably not.
Sincerely,<br>R.W.L.

Great Neck, New York
June 12, [1922]

Dear Hewitt:—
 I received notice in February that a royalty on the "35" story, amounting to $293.66, would reach me in May. It hasn't arrived, so will you please nudge the bookkeeper?
 Nina Wilcox Putnam and I have written one of those double stunts,[2] like the one Irvin Cobb and Mrs. Rinehart wrote on men and women;[3] ours will appear in the

---

[1] Notations, probably by someone at Bobbs–Merrill, on this letter indicate that Lardner received a total of $522.09 from Bobbs–Merrill in 1921.

[2] The "double stunt" was a combination of Lardner's *Say It With Oil; A Few Remarks About Wives* with Putnam's *Say It With Bricks; A Few Remarks About Husbands.* The two books were bound together back to back, inverted, with separate title pages and pagination.

[3] *Oh, Well, You Know How Women Are!* by Irvin S. Cobb, with *Isn't That Just Like a Man* by Mary Roberts Rinehart; inverted, with separate title pages. Published by George H. Doran Company, 1920.

November American and Doran wants to make a book of it. Mrs. Putnam, as you doubtless know, is signed up with Doran, so I told them it was all right with me, though I was going to tell you about it first. Between you and me, I don't think the book will set the world afire, but it may help toward the mortgage.
      Sincerely,
      Ring W. Lardner

 Astonishingly, in March Lorimer had rejected Lardner's "The Golden Honeymoon" on the grounds that "the humor in it is so quiet that . . . the average reader would miss it." In April Lorimer had rejected another piece (probably "My Week in Cuba"), saying that "this story and the one before it are rather a slip-back for you considering what you have done for the Post." When Lardner subsequently began sending his work to *Cosmopolitan*, T.B. Costain, one of the *Post*'s associate editors, wrote suggesting that they "talk matters over."

Great Neck, New York
July seventh.

Dear Mr. Costain:—
 I am going to have young visitors from the middle west all week, so I'm afraid I can't make a lunch or dinner date. But I'll try to get to town some time Wednesday or Thursday and look you up.
      Sincerely,
      Ring W. Lardner

 Lardner did meet with Costain, at which time they discussed a possible series of football stories. Although Lorimer and the *Post* continued to solicit Lardner's work, he did not publish again with the *Post* until 1931.

Great Neck, New York
August 7, [1922]

Dear Hewitt:—
 Will you please ask the boys to send along the $574.44 which was supposed to be due on "The Big Town" last month?
      Sincerely,
      R.W.L.

By this time, the Lardners and the Fitzgeralds had become close friends. Though Lardner was eleven years older than Fitzgerald, they shared common interests in writing, in literature, in people, and in socializing with friends. Lardner maintained a public facade of provincialism, but he was actually widely read and could participate in most intellectual discussions. Many of their marathon evenings spent drinking and talking are now legendary. Lardner enjoyed Fitzgerald's enthusiasm for new ideas, and Fitzgerald appreciated Lardner's cynicism and common sense. Lardner was also attracted to Zelda and once wrote: "Scott is a novelist and Zelda is a novelty." Ellis admired Zelda, though she never quite approved of the Fitzgeralds' unrestrained lifestyle.

Zelda Fitzgerald's scrapbook contains the following Christmas poem that Lardner sent to her in 1922:

A CHRISTMAS WISH—AND WHAT CAME OF IT.

Of all the girls for whom I care,
And there are quite a number,
None can compare with Zelda Sayre,
Now wedded to a plumber.

I knew her when she was a waif
In southern Alabama.
Her old granddaddy cracked a safe
And found therein her grandma.

A Glee Club man walked up New York
For forty city blocks,
Nor did he meet a girl as sweet
As Mrs. Farmer Fox.

I read the World, I read the Sun,
The Tribune and the Herald,
But of all the papers, there is none
Like Mrs. Scott Fitzgerald.

God rest thee, merry qentlemen!
God shrew thee, greasy maiden!
God love that pure American
Who married Mr. Braden.

If it is dark when home I go
And safety is imperilled,
There's no policeman that I know
Like Zelda Sayre Fitzgerald.

I met her at the football game;
'Twas in the Harvard stadium.
A megaphone announced her name:
"It's Mrs. James S. Braden!"

So here's my Christmas wish for you:
I worship Leon Errol,[1]
But the funniest girl I ever knew
Is Mrs. Scott Fitzgerald.

The following letter was to Kenneth Gilbert, a newspaperman who was in 1922 the editor of the Seattle Press Club's annual publication, *El Toro*. Gilbert had invited Lardner (along with Irvin S. Cobb, George Ade, and Hugh Wiley) to write anecdotal pieces for that year's *El Toro*, but neither Lardner nor the others were interested in writing for no pay.

Great Neck, New York
December 30, [1922]

Dear Mr. Gilbert:—
My desk is a mess and your letter, written in December, got lost in it. I'm sorry. And I hope you haven't thought I was in the habit of just not paying any attention to correspondence.
      Sincerely,
      Ring W. Lardner

Miami Beach, Florida
Sunday, February eleventh
[1923]

[To George Ade]
Dear Geo,—
This will introduce a old pal of mine Mr. J. C. Andrew.[2] He is a member of the Pardon Board of the Indiana State Penitentiary. So if you ever get in the state which he is in, beg his pardon. I was sentenced for a year, but he

---

[1] Leon Errol starred as a comic in the Ziegfeld Follies from 1911 through World War I. His most notable success was in *Sally*, with Marilyn Miller. Later, he went to Hollywood to make the film version and became a star in short film comedies.

[2] A member of the Indiana Prison Board, Jess C. Andrew went on to serve eight terms in the Indiana House of Representatives and to become president of the International Livestock Exposition.

commuted me 48 pints. He is a Indiana boy and played a half back on Purdue the year they scored. They call them the Boilermakers on acct. of him getting everybody boiled. Please treat him as a equal.
                    Respy,
                    A Michigan Boy.

Great Neck, New York
February 21st. [1923]

Dear Mencken:—
Your letter was waiting for me on my return from your old friend the South. "Champion" (a story of which I am a great admirer) was published first in Metropolitan and later syndicated. The gent who had the syndicate rights is trying to unearth a copy for me and if he does, I'll send it on. The German Authors' League is welcome to the receipts.
                    R.W.L.

Great Neck, New York
February 26. [1923]

Dear Mencken:—
Here's "Champion," copied by a $2.50 stenographer who paid no attention to jumps in the story which were indicated by spaces.
I have put in x's to show where they were. If it isn't too much trouble, will you return the copy when you are through with it?
I guess the Who's Who is all right. My four grandparents were all born in America, of Irish descent on the father's side and English on the mother's.
I'll pay you back the $7 in liquid form at the next Democratic convention.
If you go to Miami, get far enough ahead in your work so that you can spend the week following your visit in bed.
                    R.W.L.

Great Neck, New York
June fifteenth [1923].

[To Francis R. Kitchell, Jeannette Abbott's husband]
Dear Kitch:—
I'd send this to your office if they didn't insist on all communications being addressed to the A.C. Lawrence Leather Co. *not* to an individual.
If Mr. Ely is in his dotage he might like "Gullible's Travels," but I'm afraid there is no way of trying it on him. The author has no copy. The bookstores evidently never

heard of it. I wrote to the publishers two or three months ago, requesting that they send me six copies, but have had no reply. If I ever get hold of one, I'll send it.

I'm sorry we didn't see more of you and Bingham, but I had to get back to work, and when one is touring with the Abbott girls, one has to allow for retreats every two or three hundred miles to recover what they left at the last stop.

Tell Jane she might as well make up her mind to the western trip en famille; there is an overwhelming majority in favor of same.

I am one of the grafters sailing from Boston Tuesday on the Leviathan, but won't get there till Tuesday morning and the last tender is supposed to leave at ten o'clock.

Ruby, Ellis and I were at Fitzgerald's Sunday night, but left early on account of dullness. Half an hour after we had gone, Scott nearly killed Gene Buck's sister-in-law's husband. The last named had confided to me earlier in the evening that there weren't no real decent fellas nowheres but in the south. He himself is from Texas where men are oil men. Scott is nursing a broken hand as a result of hitting him in the head. This was the semi-final bout. The wind-up was won by Mrs. Buck, who hit Mr. Buck three times in the nose for not taking his brother-in-law's part. My sympathies are with Mr. Buck.[1] What is this world coming to if you have to take your brother-in-law's part?

Thanks for the Collier clippings. The Herald will lose some day.

R.W.L.

*The following was written to C. O. Kalman. The Kalmans were old friends of the Fitzgeralds from their St. Paul days. Beginning on the same paper is also a note from Fitzgerald. Both notes were apparently written during a drinking session:*

---

[1] Gene Buck was Lardner's Great Neck neighbor, and a songwriter and producer for Florenz Ziegfeld's Follies and Midnight Frolics. His songs included "Hello, Frisco," "Tulip Time," "Maybe," "No Foolin'," and "Garden of My Dreams." As a male talent scout for Ziegfeld, he "discovered" Ed Wynn and Eddie Cantor. Buck's range of acquaintances is indicated by diversity of the one hundred honorary pallbearers at his funeral in 1957. They included Bugs Baer, J. Edgar Hoover, William Randolph Hearst Jr., Fritz Kreisler, Deems Taylor, David Sarnoff, Oscar Hammerstein, and Eddie Rickenbacker.

Great Neck
Long Island
5.30 A.M.
(Not so much up already as up still)[1]
[ca. November 1923]

Dear Kaly:—
I hear that you have given two seats to this nonsensical game between the Yale blues vs. the Princeton Elis, to F. Scott Fitzgerald. For what reason, is what I want to know.
                                Ring W. Lardner

The note by Fitzgerald follows:

Dear Kaly:
This is a letter from your two favorite authors. Ring & I got stewed together the other night & sat up till the next night without what he would laughingly refer to as a wink of sleep. About 5.30 I told him he should write you a letter. The above is his maudlin extacy.

The tickets arrived and I am enclosing check for same. I'm sorry as the devil you didn't come. We could have had a wonderful time even tho the game was punk.

We took Mr. & Mrs. Gene Buck (the man who writes the Follies & Frolics.) This is a very drunken town full of intoxicated people and retired debauches & actresses so I know that you and she to who you laughingly refer to as the Missus would enjoy it.

I hope St Paul is cold & raw [I discover this telltale evidence on the paper][2] so that you'll be driven east before Xmas. Everything is in its usual muddle. Zelda says ect, asks, ect, sends ect.
                Your Happy but Lazy friend
                F Scott Fitzgerald.

The friendship between Fitzgerald and Lardner appears to have developed from a mutual recognition of the ways they

---

[1] This return address and comment are in Fitzgerald's handwriting

[2] Editor's brackets. Fitzgerald here inserts this comment and draws an arrow to a circular stain obviously made by the placement of a wet glass on the paper.

complemented each other. Fitzgerald admired Lardner's deflating humor, stoical cynicism, insistence on accuracy, and general knowledge of human nature, and he saw Lardner as potentially a great literary talent. Lardner was amused and challenged by Fitzgerald's exuberant ideas, respected Fitzgerald's judgments about literature and the jazz age, and appreciated the precision of Fitzgerald's prose style. Whereas Lardner often imposed restraints on Fitzgerald's enthusiasms, Fitzgerald apparently succeeded in convincing Lardner to take himself more seriously as a writer of fiction.

Early in 1923, Fitzgerald enthusiastically recommended to Maxwell Perkins that Scribners publish Lardner's uncollected stories. As Scribner's leading editor, Perkins enjoyed even then—before his great successes with Wolfe and Hemingway—considerable fame as a personable editor who recognized talent and uncannily obtained remarkable effort from his writers. Perkins agreed with Fitzgerald about the quality of Lardner's work and wrote to Lardner, eventually persuading him to join Scribner's coterie of authors.

Though Perkins did not achieve the same degree of success that he did with Fitzgerald, Wolfe, and Hemingway, he did establish a personal friendship with Lardner as well as a professional relationship, and he undoubtedly influenced the sometimes reluctant Lardner to write more quality fiction than Lardner might otherwise have produced.[1]

In a letter dated 2 July 1923, Perkins initiated his correspondence with Lardner:

> I read your story 'The Golden Wedding' [i.e., "The Golden Honeymoon"] with huge enjoyment. Scott Fitzgerald recommended it to me and he also suggested that you might have other material of the same sort, which, with this, could form a volume. I am therefore writing to tell you how very much interested we should be to consider this possibility, if you could put the material before us. I would hardly have ventured to do this if Scott had not spoken of the possibility, because your position in the literary world is such that you must be besieged by publishers, and to people in that situation their letters of

---

[1] See Clifford M. Caruthers (ed.), *Ring around Max: The Correspondence of Ring Lardner and Max Perkins* (DeKalb, Illinois: Northern Illinois University Press, 1973).

interest are rather a nuisance. I am certainly mighty glad to have the chance of expressing our interest though, if, as Scott thought, you would not feel that we were merely bothering you. Would you be willing to send on any material that might go with "The Golden Wedding" to form a volume, or to tell me where I might come at it in periodicals?

Lardner was agreeable, though he was surprised by the prospect of being transformed into a "literary" man. Known chiefly as a newspaper humorist, he was by this time easily one of the ten best known names in America, and he was earning over $30,000 a year. Such acclaim necessitated the tact with which Perkins approached Lardner, who had not even bothered to keep copies of his stories. Eventually, to assemble *How To Write Short Stories*, Perkins had to photostat back copies of magazines in the New York Public Library.

Great Neck, New York
December fifth.

Dear Mr. Perkins:—
    I enclose a (and, I guess, the only) copy of "Champion," which Scott tells me you have been looking for. I'm sorry to have kept you waiting.
                    Sincerely
                    Ring W. Lardner

Great Neck, New York
February second.

Dear Mr. Perkins:—
    The arrangement and terms are satisfactory to me. I'm sorry you have had so much trouble gathering the stuff.
    Why not visit Great Neck again? It's safer now, as Durand's pond is frozen over.
                    Sincerely,
                    Ring W. Lardner

The reference above to Durand's pond has to do with Fitzgerald's auto driving. A favorite eating and drinking place on Long Island was Rene Durand's restaurant at Manhasset, where on one occasion Perkins, Lardner, and Fitzgerald apparently discussed the composition of Lardner's projected volume of short stories. Fitzgerald imbibed too freely and, while attempting to leave, drove Perkins into a nearby pond. A year later, Perkins recalled the incident in a letter to Fitzgerald:

> I had yesterday a disillusioning afternoon at Great Neck, not in respect to Ring Lardner, who gains on you whenever you see him, but in respect to Durant's where he took me for lunch. I thought that night a year ago that we ran down a steep place into a lake. There was no steep place and no lake. We sat on a balcony in front. It was dripping hot and Durant took his police dog down to the margin of that huddle of a lily pond,—the dog waded almost across it;—and I'd been calling it a lake all these months. But they've put up a fence to keep others from doing as we did.

On 18 February 1924, Perkins described to Lardner the publication plans for *How to Write Short Stories*:

> I considered first more or less grouping the stories but gave up the idea and went in the other direction;—that is, I aimed at variety. I thought that the several baseball stories ought to be scattered through the volume, for instance. The question of the first story was a hard one, but it could not be "The Golden Honeymoon" because that had appeared in the "Short Stories of 1922" volume. I did not think it ought to be a baseball story anyhow, because we want to place the emphasis differently in this whole scheme. I finally hit upon "The Facts" because it will please everybody, male and female, of every sort. Then I followed with "Some Like 'em Cold" because it seemed to me to be a masterpiece in that sort of writing. At this point it seemed well to get in one of the baseball stories and "Alibi Ike" is a corker. I am sorry "Champion" comes so late in a way, but publishers probably exaggerate the importance of an early position. People don't begin at the beginning and read a book of stories straight through. The stories that follow I have arranged on the principle of variety.

At Perkins' suggestion, the collection was to parody then-popular manuals on the art of writing short stories through the title *How to Write Short Stories*, mock introductions to individual stories, and a burlesque preface on the "technic" of writing the short story. The suggestion at least for the title may have come originally from Fitzgerald (see Lardner's letter to Fitzgerald of 24 March 1925). The preface contained such advice as:

> How to begin—or, as we professionals would say, "how to commence"— is the next question. It must be admitted that the method of approach ("L'approchement") differs even among first class fictionists. For example, Blasco Ibanez usually starts his stories with a Spanish word, Jack Dempsey with an "I" and Charley Peterson with a couple of simple declarative sentences about his leading character, such as "Hazel Gooftree had just gone mah jong. She felt faint."

In light of the overall quality of this collection, such promotional gimmicks would seem unnecessary, but then Perkins had to consider that Lardner's audience at that time consisted largely of newspaper readers rather than literary scholars, and that such satiric introductions were likely to cause a stir, even if they were deplored by such critics as Edmund Wilson, who later accused Lardner of "a guilty conscience at attempting to disguise an excellent piece of literature as a Stephen Leacock buffoonery."

March 27.

Dear Mr. Perkins:—
    I will try to show up in your office on Monday with all the galleys and everything. I think that would be the simplest way of getting things finished up. I will call you Monday forenoon. And that's the last sentence I intend to start with an I till my next letter.
                Sincerely,
                Ring W. Lardner

In mid-April the Fitzgeralds abandoned the social life of Great Neck for France, in an effort to find a "new rhythm" for their lives. Though Fitzgerald was earning in excess of $30,000 a year, he had been spending more than that on booze and lavish parties. On their departure, Lardner sent Zelda another poem:

## To Z.S.F.

Zelda, fair queel of Alabam',
Across the waves I kiss you!
You think I am a stone, a clam;
You think that I don't care a damn,
But God! how I will miss you!

For months and months you've meant to me
What Mario meant to Tosca.
You've gone, and I am all at sea
Just like the Minnewaska.

I once respected him you call
Your spouse, and that is why, dear,
I held my tongue—And then, last Fall,
He bared a flippancy and gall
Of which I'd had no idear.

When I with pulmonary pain
Was seized, he had the gumption
To send me lives of Wilde and Crane,
Two brother craftsmen who in vain
Had battled with consumption.

We wreak our vengeance as we can,
And I have no objection
To getting even with this "man"
By stealing your affection.

So, dearie, when your tender heart
Of all his coarseness tires,
Just cable me and I will start
Immediately for Hyeres.

To hell with Scott Fitzgerald then!
To hell with Scott, his daughter!
It's you and I back home again,
To Great Neck, where the men are men
And booze is 3/4 water.

My heart goes with you as you sail.
God grant you won't be seasick!
The thought of you abaft the rail,
Diffusing meat and ginger ale,
Makes both my wife and me sick.
                    Ring W. Lardner

When Perkins asked Lardner for a publishable photograph, Lardner invited him and Mrs. Perkins to dinner:

Great Neck, New York
May 9, 1924.

Dear Mr. Perkins:—
Sorry you have a cold. We never have them in Great Neck.
I will be home all day every day next week excepting Monday. My wife says (and we speak as one), can you and Mrs. Perkins come to dinner Tuesday night (or Wednesday, Thursday, Friday or Saturday night)? The telephone is Great Neck 103. If you drive out and can't find the place, call up from the drug store and we'll come and pilot you. Dinner is at seven o'clock and I have outgrown my dinner clothes. If you accept this invitation I will give you my photograph.
Sincerely,
R.W.L.

This informal evening was a great success: thereafter both men continued the correspondence on a first-name basis.

Great Neck, New York
May 19, 1924.

Dear Mr. Perkins (or Max):—
I suppose you saw Burton Rascoe's little piece.
Here are some more names:
Percy Hammond, 17 West 10th. Street New York.
Alexander Woollcott, the City Club, New York.
Quinn Martin, Greak Neck, N.Y.
Harvey T. Woodruff, c/o Chicago Tribune, Chicago, Illinois.
W.O. McGeehan, New York Herald and Tribune.
Sincerely,
R.W.L.

P.S. Next time you come out here, which I hope will be soon, I will be different.
P.S.S. also—adding to names—Herbert B. Swope, New York World.

When Perkins did not reply immediately to the letter above, Lardner cautiously resumed a formal salutation. After Perkins' letter of the 24th, beginning "Dear Ring," reached him, he addressed Perkins as "Max."

Great Neck, New York
May 27th.

Dear Mr. Perkins:—
I enclose what I have nicknamed the perfect blurb.[1] Thanks for sanding me the Post's.
I also enjoyed Scott's "Absolution" though some of it was over my partly bald head.
Mencken writes that he is reviewing my book at length in the July Mercury.
Did I put James J.Montague on that list? I meant to. His address is c/o The Bell Syndicate, 154 Nassau Street, New York City. And another one is Hugh S. Fullerton, c/o Liberty, 25 Park Place, New York City. I hope I haven't overdrawn my account, but anyway I promise this is the finish.
                                    Sincerely,
                                    R.W.L.

In the preceding letter and the following one to Mencken (then editor of *American Mercury*), Lardner's pretense at not understanding "Absolution" is probably a reaction to sexual overtones in Fitzgerald's story, which deals with the psychological frustrations of a priest. For Lardner, the expression "over my head" was often the ultimate dismissal. His standards for good taste were as high as his standards for professional skill, and he was emphatically prudish about vulgarity and sexual innuendo. He lived by a prewar midwestern moral and social code in which both the world of the flesh and the world of the mind had fairly prescriptive limits.

Great Neck, New York
May 27th. [1924]

Dear Sir:—
Thanks for the tip on the Boilermakers' Journal and the Journeyman Barber. I'll try to find some copies of them. My wife says the American labor leader has already got into fiction, but she can't remember where. That's the woman of it.

---

[1] Lardner included a piece from the Boston *Transcript* advertising *How To Write Short Stories* straightforwardly thus: "Ten short stories by an American humorist, with a brief prefatory explanation of methods of writing them."

I liked Scott's "Absolution" in the current Mercury (my favorite magazine) though parts of it were over my head.

I'm going to Cleveland and if we do meet (I expect to stop at the Hotel Cleveland), I'll take steps to repay in part the debt I have owed you since the return trip from San Francisco.

Your attention is called to "Why I Didn't Die" by Harold Bell Wright[1] in the June American Magazine.

R.W.L.

The Mencken review of *How to Write Short Stories* appeared in the June 1924 *American Mercury*. After deploring academia's failure to recognize Lardner's talent, Mencken focused on that talent:

> His studies, to be sure, are never very profound; he makes no attempt to get at the primary springs of passion and motive; all his people share the same amiable stupidity, the same transparent vanity, the same shallow inconsequentiality; they are all human Fords, and absolutely alike at bottom. But if he thus confines himself to the surface, it yet remains a fact that his investigations on that surface are extraordinarily alert, ingenious and brilliant—that the character he finally sets before us, however roughly articulated as to bones, is so astoundingly realistic as to hide that the effect is indistinguishable from that of life itself. The old man in "The Golden Honeymoon" is not merely well done; he is perfect. And so is the girl in "Some Like Them Cold." And so, even, is the idiotic Frank X. Farrell in "Alibi Ike"—an extravagant grotesque and yet quite real from glabella to calcaneus.

When the Fitzgeralds departed, they left Lardner to rent their hastily abandoned house and to take care of assorted expenses. Lardner conscientiously restored order to Fitzgerald's chaotic financial arrangements and even covered

---

[1] Harold Bell Wright was a clergyman and novelist, best known for *The Shepherd of the Hills* (1907). The article, "Why I Did Not Die," describes a collision between Wright, while on horseback, and a car, and a subsequent lengthy but successful struggle in the Arizona desert with tuberculosis.

his Great Neck bank account later that year when Fitzgerald overdrew.

Lardner's subsequent letters to Fitzgerald are more affectionate, informational, and personal than any other letters he ever wrote to anyone outside his own family.

Thursday, June 5. [1924]

Dears Scott and Zelda:—

Why and the hell don't you state your address, or haven't you any? I'm going to send this registered to plain Hyéres, with a prayer. First the financial news, which I am afraid is bad, but I am enclosing plenty of documentary evidence to support it.

The day after you left, Miss Robinson called up to say that she had rented the house to Mr. and Mrs. Gordon Sarre, née Ruth Shepley, for $1600. "But listen, Miss Robinson," I remonstrated; "Mr. Fitzgerald told me that if you rented it right away, the rent was to be $2000." "But listen, Mr. Lardner," said Miss Robinson: "Mr. Fitzgerald called me up just before he left and said I was to rent it as soon as possible for $1600 as he had given up ideas of making a profit and just wanted it off his mind." Well, she seemed honest so I said all right and I hope it was. Now then, it seems that William and Sally had kind of let things get dirty in out of the way places and Miss Robinson said that both the house and yard needed a thorough renovating, which ought to be at the expense of the last tenants. Not knowing the ethics, I asked Ellis and she said this was according to custom. So I said go ahead and renovate, and all you were soaked for that was $50. Then there was the matter of the oven door, mentioned in one of the enclosures. I said I thought it was up to the owner to repair oven doors, but she said no. I don't think it will amount to more than a very few dollars and will be subtracted from the next rent check.

The Sarres paid $500 down. There was subtracted from that $50 for the cleaning and $80 for Craw's commission, leaving a balance of $370, which I deposited to your account in the Guaranty Trust Company.

Then along came a water bill for $22.08 which I paid because if I hadn't, the company would have shut off the water and Ruth and Gordon would have had to join the Kensington Association in order to use the pool. Sarre is a French name and they ought to get along without baths, but they are kind of Ritzy.

The balance of $1100 in rent is to be paid partly in July and partly in August. Anyway I'll see that it's paid and deposited to your account.

In regards to "How to Write Short Stories": The notices have been what I might call sublime; in fact, readers might think I was having an affair with some of the critics. I'll send the most important ones when I get them all — Mencken, Bunny Wilson[1] and Tom Boyd[2] are yet to be heard from. But listen, if I do send them, will you please send them back? Burton said I was better than Katherine Mansfield, which I really believe is kind of raw, but anyway it got him and Hazel an invitation to come out and spend Sunday with us. Hazel was on the wagon, but her husband was *not*. I enclose his Day Book for June 1 which mentions several of the best writers.

Max Perkins and wife came out to dinner one night. Max brought along twenty-five books for me to autograph (not to sell) and it just happened on this occasion that I could hardly write my name once, let alone twenty-five times. I have promised to be sober next time I see him and her.

John Golden[3] wants me to write a play based on "The Golden Honeymoon," but I don't see how it could be done without introducing a pair of young lovers or something.

Personally I am now reading "The Beautiful and Damned."

We have a parrot which talks, laughs and whistles.

We are going to Cleveland Sunday night for the Republican convention.

Victor Herbert dropped dead a week or so ago.[4] The papers said he spent the forenoon with his daughter, then had lunch with Silvio Hein and died soon after lunch, but Gene says he was with him virtually all day up to the time he died. How he missed being with him when he died or put him in the death business is a mystery to me. Anyway he

---

[1] In 1924, Edmund Wilson was managing editor of *Vanity Fair*. He was then in the process of becoming one of the ablest American critics and editors of the 20th century.

[2] Thomas A. Boyd was one of Scribners' authors at that time.

[3] John Golden produced more than a hundred plays on Broadway. His first hit was *Turn To the Right* (1916); his last, *The Male Animal* (1953).

[4] The death of operetta composer Victor Herbert was a shock to the New York theatrical world. According to the New York *Times* of 27 May 1924, he became ill after luncheon at the Lambs Club, went home after cancelling an appointment with Ziegfeld's producer, decided to visit his doctor, and collapsed while climbing the stairs to the doctor's office. Gene Buck was an honorary pall bearer.

was the leading pall bearer. I didn't find out whether or not your stunt was going into the Follies because all we could talk about was Victor's death which came like a bolt from the blue.

There's a great murder case in Chicago. Two Jew boys named Loeb and Leopold, aged nineteen apiece, both of whom had graduated from both Michigan and Chicago at the age of eighteen with the best records ever made, were trapped and confessed murdering another Jew boy aged thirteen. It has since been brought out that they had previously murdered two or three other guys and helped themselves to important glands.

Ellis says she will write as soon as she is through with the dentist. Personally I have written a thousand words. Love to one of you.

Mary Esselstyn.

The same day Lardner also wrote to the *Saturday Evening Post* on behalf of a young writer:

Great Neck, New York
June fifth.

Dear Mr. Costain:—

Nick Flatley,[1] a rising young Boston Irishman, has written a golf story in which he thinks the Post might be interested. He asked my advice as to whom to send it to, being one of the boys who think that a manuscript addressed merely to The Editors is thrown into the nearest open fireplace unread. Anyway, I've taken the liberty of telling him to address it you and you'll probably get it in a few days.

Sincerely,<br>Ring W. Lardner

The following letter is probably to Kate Rice, wife of Grantland Rice. Lardner and Rice were acquainted before the move to Great Neck, but as neighbors they became the closest of friends for many years, sharing particularly interests in sports, bridge, and gambling, although their attitudes about the sports world and life in general were very different. These two great sportswriters each wrote columns that transcend their own time, but Rice was an eloquent glorifier of sport, while Lardner was an incisive debunker.

---

[1] No story by Nick Flatley appeared in the *Post*.

Nothing demonstrates the scope of Lardner's talents as clearly as the fact that he was the close friend of two such different colleagues as Grantland Rice and Scott Fitzgerald. While Lardner shared with Rice the ability to memoralize great moments in sport, he also shared with Fitzgerald the capacity to expose the foibles of the 1920s sympathetically in fiction.

Ellis Lardner and Kate Rice also became close friends; as a result, the Lardners and the Rices annually took winter vacations together during the 1920s.

Ring Lardner
Great Neck, Hew York
June 12.

Dear Madam: —

I trust this will put a stop to the innuendoes regarding my alleged indebtedness to you. Three dollars of it is for what you say I owe you at golf, God knows how; five cents is for a telephone call which I was going to make to you, but decided not to, and twelve dollars is for flowers for the funeral of Mr. Morse Sr.[1], though I swear I had nothing to do with his death and would have preferred the demise of another member of the family.
                        Cordially,
                          Sister Stanislaus.

Though Lardner's political views were conservative, his irritation with the Democrats in the following letter to Perkins is the result of his frustration with the machinations of the 1924 Democratic National Convention, which he covered as a reporter. At the Convention he suffered through 103 ballots while William McAdoo, considered the spokesman for small town protestant America, and Al Smith, the leader of the eastern liberal establishment, struggled for political control. Eventually the party labor groups sought to promote Robert M. LaFollette, and the moderates supported John W. Davis. Davis was finally selected (though the "Progressives" later ran LaFollette as a third-party candidate), but he lost the election to Calvin Coolidge by seven million votes.

---

[1] Theodore Morse was a composer. He had just returned from accompanying Victor Herbert to Washington to testify in the hearing on the copyright law when he died, on 26 May 1924.

Perhaps more interesting is Lardner's reluctance in this letter to use profanity. He was quite prudish in this respect. In 1932, he angered many people in the popular music field by conducting from his hospital bed a crusade in his *New Yorker* "Over the Waves" column against popular lyrics he considered profane or sexually suggestive. Lardner did not include such language in his fiction. In a 1934 *Esquire* piece, Ernest Hemingway described himself as an "early imitator and always admirer" of Lardner and argued that the reluctance to use profanity was Lardner's only flaw as a master of realistic dialogue.

Great Neck, New York
July twenty-first.

Dear Max:—

    I do hope you will overlook or forgive or something my rudeness in not replying sooner to your letters or telephone calls—my alibi is the Democrats, God      them.

    Now then (1) 1 am trying to get up nerve enough to ask for release from the "comic" strip,[1] which is me bete noir as the Scotch have it; if I do that I will have a lot more time to spend on short stories. (2). I'll come to one of those literary luncheons if you think it advisable, but it is my secret ambition not to. (3). I enclose a letter from Mr. Darrow which I ought to have answered. Will you please tell him that I had a letter from Mr. Beach,[2] in which he not only repeated the request that I write something for his Book Notes, but also he wrote it himself as he thought I ought to write it and I wished you could see it; he put every

---

[1] From September 1922 to January 1925 Lardner wrote a comic strip for the Bell Syndicate called "You Know Me Al," which featured Jack Keefe as protagonist (the strip continued to appear under Lardner's name until September 1925). The cartoons were drawn first by Will Johnston and, after February 1923, by Dick Dorgan, brother of the well-known cartoonist Tad Dorgan, who was a friend of Lardner. The strip appeared in over a hundred newspapers and brought in about $20,000 a year, but Lardner found it boring and in January 1925 turned it over completely to Dick Dorgan, who apparently wrote those strips that appeared between September 1925 and May 1926, when the strip ceased.

[2] Probably Harrison L. Beach, a newspaperman.

gag into it except Alabama casts 24 votes for Underwood.[1] If Mr. Darrow thinks I'd better write something for them, I'll do it, but between you and me I have nicknamed the editor the Beach Nut. (4). I very much appreciate the way you are pushing the book. (5). I have virtually gone down on my knees to the Bobbs–Merrill people for a copy of Gullible's Travels, vainly. I haven't a copy myself. Gene Buck has, and if you just want to read it, I'll try to get it away from him for a few days. It isn't that he is so fond of it, but they have got great big bookcases.

I wish you would call up and get into a confidential conversation with me, the gist of which would be that we'd make an engagement for you and Mrs. Perkins to come to Great Neck and I'd promise to be cold sober and nice, but not amusing.
Sincerely,<br>Ring W. Lardner

*How to Write Short Stories* had sold moderately well in 1924—about 3,500 copies by the end of June, enough for Perkins not only to encourage Lardner to write more stories for another book next year but also to seek the rights to Lardner's earlier books so that Lardner could fully join Scribner's "stable of authors." Because Perkins had not been able to obtain a copy of *Gullible's Travels*, he had appealed to Lardner, who in the above letter referred him humorously to Gene Buck. While Lardner liked Buck, he was frequently amused by Buck's professional brainstorms and pretentious lifestyle.

Great Neck, New York
July 27. [1924]

Dear Francis:—

I enclose proof that the second payment of $500.00 (being Ruth Shepley's rent) has been deposited to your account. I also enclose the letter about the frozen water pipes in the garage and the plumber's bill for fixing same. I asked Charley Goddard who was responsible for frozen water pipes in a garage (he being an experienced landlord)

---

[1] During the struggle through 103 ballots at the 1924 Democratic National Convention, Alabama continually cast its 24 votes for its own Senator Oscar W. Underwood, in hopes either of promoting him as a compromise candidate or of waiting until that block of votes could function significantly in a swing to another candidate.

and he said the tenant was responsible; that the tenant ought to have seen that the water was turned off.

Meanwhile, I have told Mrs. Sarre (Ruth Shepley) that I had sent Hines's bill to you and that if Hines bothered her, to refer him to me. If you want to pay it, all right; if you don't, let me know, and I'll send the bill to Mrs. Miller.

Furthermore, Huntington Smith, of Craw's office, wrote me that you hadn't paid the rent for July, and he wanted me to pay it for July and August, as Mrs. Miller was squawking. I called him up and told him I knew it was an oversight on your part and if Mrs. Miller would be patient a few weeks, she would get her money. He seemed satisfied and said he would pacify her.

Now for the bad news:—

She whom I married and I are going to leave for France on the Paris, September tenth; will stay in Paris a week or so, and then go to the south of France, where I have a first cousin, aged about 60, in Montpelier, and we may possibly drop in at San Raphael, but if we do, we're going to stop at a hotel, because we have agreed we don't like the service in private homes. We'll try to find the Villa Marie, and if we do, don't let me forget to tell you the many peculiar things that have happened in Great Neck. Most of them have happened to nobody but me, but I always like to talk in the first person.

Give my fondest regrets to her whom you so generously married.

R.W.L.

If we do come, I'll wire you from Paris or Montpelier the approximate time of our arrival. Could you go to Biarritz or Spain with us? I want to see a bullfight.

Great Neck, New York
August 24th. [1924]

[To Scott and Zelda Fitzgerald]
Gents:—

I'll bring some of the clippings with me and then I'll be sure of getting them back.

Met Gordon and Ruth at a wild party the other night and they gave me a check for the final $600.00 and I will deposit it and either bring you the duplicate or send it to you, though the Guaranty Trust Company says it attends to that itself. I am still arguing about the $29.00 Plumbers bill, but will do my best to get it passed on to Mrs. Miller. Of course it isn't the Sarres' business and I don't see why it's yours, but plumbers will be plumbers.

We leave here September 10 and will stay a week in Paris before going south. I hope you and Thelma or whatever her name is can be ready to go with us to Biarritz for a day or two.

The book has now gone into the fifth edition of 3,000, which is better than I expected.

We'll wire you or write you from g-y P-ar-is

Don't forget to let me tell you the latest Great Neck news when we arrive.

Our address in Paris from Sept. 17 to 24 will be the Crillon, in case you can come up.

Sam.

The Lardners left New York on 10 September, disembarked at Le Havre, and, after spending a few days in Paris and Montpellier, joined the Fitzgeralds at St. Raphael. Fitzgerald drove the four of them to Monte Carlo, where they won modestly at the roulette wheel. The Lardners then returned to Paris, went on to London, and finally came home on the *Mauretania*.

As before, Lardner seems not to have been greatly impressed by Europe; his series for *Liberty* based on the trip is a pale burlesque of *The Innocents Abroad*, lacking the spontaneity of Twain's work. Curiously, Lardner also says little about the visit with the Fitzgeralds, which came during a trying period for Scott and Zelda. Zelda's involvement at St. Raphael with the French pilot Edouard Jozan had caused a crisis not fully resolved at the time of the Lardners' visit, and Fitzgerald in addition was revising *The Great Gatsby* for publication the following year. After this visit, Fitzgerald and Lardner would see each other again on only two brief occasions.

As early as March 1924, Perkins had been considering the possibility of obtaining from Bobbs-Merrill and Doran the rights to Lardner's previous books, so that Scribners could publish a uniform edition of Lardner's works. Lardner had written a letter in April to Hewitt Howland, indicating his approval of Perkins' plan, which evoked the following agonized reply:

The Bobbs-Merrill Company
Publishers—Indianapolis
April 19, 1924

Dear Ring:

Your letter sent me to the hospital for repairs; hence the delay in replying. I am still running a temperature, clear up over the transom, as Riley used to say, and am dictating this letter while the doctor and the nurse have their backs turned—not on each other.

As Brown says when Smith dies! Why, I can't believe it. I saw him only three days ago and he never looked better. If you were going to some—but are you really going? And why do you have to "stick with 'em" as you say, just because they happened to have an idea? This getting an author with the uniform edition bait is such an old wheeze. Listen—if I lose you I'll probably lose my job, and it's a long time since I worked. I'd starve and you'd have me on your conscience and be most uncomfortable.

You ask if we'd set a price on the plates of your books. As for me, I'd as soon sell my fee simple in my brother-in-law. But Lawrence Chambers will be in New York next week. Get hold of him, and there may be another story, as the girl said to the soldier.

The doctor and the nurse have come to and are saying that if there is any dictating to be done they'll do it. And if you could see the nurse!

By October 1924, an agreement was reached whereby Scribner's paid the George H. Doran company $500 for the plates, existing stock, and rights of *You Know Me Al* and $2,000 to Bobbs-Merrill for the stock, plates, and rights of *Treat 'Em Rough*, *Own Your Own Home*, *The Young Immigrunts*, *Gullible's Travels*, *My Four Weeks in France*, *The Big Town*, *The Real Dope*, and *Symptoms of Being 35*. *You Know Me Al*, *Gullible's Travels*, and *The Big Town* were reissued by Scribner's in 1925 as part of a five-volume set including *How to Write Short Stories* and *What of It?*

Great Neck, New York
November 11th.

Dear Max:—
I enclose a letter to Bobbs-Merrill as you requested.
I'm so desperately far behind in work that I don't believe I'll be able to get to town for a couple of weeks.

We had a pleasant session with the Fitzgeralds. Scott likes his new book,[1] which he was revising when we left.
Sincerely,

The above letter included a copy of the following letter to Bobbs–Merrill:

Great Neck, New York
November 11, 1924.

Bobbs–Merrill,
Indianapolis, Indiana.

Gentlemen:—
Charles Scribner's Sons have informed me of an agreement with you, depending on my approval, by which they are to take over those books by me which you have published with the idea of forming a uniform group of them and of others for publication. This is to tell you that the arrangement has my approval and that I am grateful for your cooperation in connection with it.
Sincerely,

On 29 November, Perkins wrote to Lardner:

I'm delighted with Scott's book. It's got his old vitality,—vitality enough to sweep away the faults you could, critically, find with it;—which relate, in my view, chiefly to Gatsby himself. Large parts of it are almost incredibly good and there is in it a sort of strange mystical element which he has not exhibited since "Paradise"—an element that comes partly, perhaps, from once having been a Catholic. Well—I am one of these 'jaded' readers, or ought to be and I read it straight through and thought it much shorter than it was.

Great Neck, New York
December second.

Dear Max:—
I am tickled to death with your report on Scott's book. It's his pet and I believe he would take poison if it flopped.

---

[1] *The Great Gatsby*, published the following year.

Ellis and I have both read "Three Flights Up"[1] and both liked the two middle stories best. My favorite is "Transatlantic." The last story is way over my head.

I think I am going to be able to sever connections with the daily cartoon early next month. This ought to leave me with plenty of time and it is my intention to write at least ten short stories a year. Whether I can do it or not, I don't know. I started one the other day and got through with about 700 words, which were so bad that I gave up. I seem to be out of the habit and it may take time to get back.

Don Stewart's "Mr. and Mrs. Haddock Abroad"[2] was a blow to me. That is the kind of "novel" I had intended to write, but if I did it now, the boys would yell stop thief.

Five "articles" on the European trip are coming out in Liberty, beginning in January[3]. I don't know whether or not they will be worth putting in a book.

I'm coming to town early next week to call on a dentist. As soon as I know when, I'll telephone you and try to make a date. Not that we don't want you in Great Neck, but I realize that it's no pleasure trip.

Sincerely,
R.W.L.

Great Neck, New York
Dec. 10.

Dear Max:—

I enclose the pieces I think more worthy. I am sending the others in a separate envelope.

I have put new titles on the ones here enclosed, titles of which I am not proud, but which I believe are at least better than the Syndicate's. As soon as I think of a general title, I'll call you up.

It seems to me that the year and month when they were written ought to be put at the bottom or top of each piece.

Sincerely,
R.W.L.

---

[1] *Three Flights Up* was a collection of short stories by Sidney Coe Howard, published by Scribners in 1924.

[2] Donald Ogden Stewart, a friend of the Lardner family, was a well-known humorist, playwright, and screenwriter and was briefly, at his friend Philip Barry's request, an actor.

[3] Published in the 14, 21, and 28 February and the 7 and 14 March issues of *Liberty*, all under the title "The Other Side."

No record survives of Lardner's preferences, but presumably the "pieces" to which he refers in the letter above were selections from a list Perkins had compiled of Lardner's syndicated articles that Perkins felt were worthy of republication. Titled *What of It?*, this volume of miscellany appeared in 1925 and sold a respectable 8,000 copies in its first year. It is remarkable chiefly for the inclusion of *The Young Immigrunts* and *Symptoms of Being 35*, and for three "nonsense" plays that anticipate such later absurdists as Pinter, Albee, or Beckett: "Clemo Uti—'The Water Lilies,'" "I. Gaspiri," and "Taxidea Americana." As the following dialogues illustrate, these plays dramatize a non-sequitur world in which people talk, but no one listens:

    First Stranger
Where was you born?
    Second Stranger
Out of wedlock.
    First Stranger
That's a mighty pretty country around there.
    Second Stranger
Are you married?
    First Stranger
I don't know. There's a woman living with me, but I can't place her.

And:

    Pat
I certainly feel sorry for people on the ocean tonight.
    Mike
What makes you think so?
    Pat
You can call me whatever you like as long as you don't call me down.

Several critics have suggested that this mad world reflects a deepening cynicism in Lardner's later years, and that it explains why Lardner felt unmotivated to attempt the novel Perkins continually urged him to write. Some lines in these plays seem also to satirize specific values; the following stage direction, for instance, appears to deplore the emphasis on stage naturalism: "The curtain is lowered for seven days to denote the lapse of a week."

In December 1924 Lardner sent the following printed Christmas postcard verse to a number of people, including Frank Crowninshield (the humorist and critic, perhaps best known for his work as editor and writer for *Vanity Fair*), whose card survives:

How utterly ridiculous
You'd feel, how damn unpleasant,
If you sent just a card to us
While we sent you a present!

In order that no such a thing
Can happen to you comma
This card is all you'll get from Ring,
His kiddies or their mamma.

The followng letter to the Fitzgeralds captures the tone of Great Neck life in early 1925.

[Great Neck, Long Island]
Friday January 9, 1925.

Dear Wops:—
You would get a lot more mail from me if you had a decent and permanent address. I hate to write letters and think all the time that they'll never get anywhere.
I have talked with Max Perkins several times since he received Scott's novel. He is very enthusiastic about it, saying it's much the best thing Scott has done since "Paradise," that parts of it are inspired, and etc. He wasn't crazy to have anybody use it serially on account of the delay it meant in getting out the book, but he told me today that "College Humor" had made a good offer which he thought you might accept. "College Humor" seems to be l——y with money and careless of how it spends it—not knocking Mr. Fitzgerald. My brother was strong for the book and wanted "Liberty" to run it, but some of the readers thought it was better as a book than it would be as a serial, meaning that it couldn't be arranged so that the reader would be left in suspense at the end of each installment.
I've been on the wagon since Armistice Day and Ellis and I have seen a lot of shows. Laurence Stallings' play[1] is a bear, even with a few of the words left out. I see no reason

---

[1] *What Price Glory*, by Maxwell Anderson and Laurence Stallings, then playing at the Plymouth Theater in New York City.

why it shouldn't beat a record or come near it. Dorothy Parker's[1] "Close Harmony" got great notices and was, we thought, a dandy play, but it flopped in three weeks. Dorothy, Beatrice Kaufman[2] and Peggy Leech[3] gave a party at the Algonquin six or seven weeks ago. I was enjoying an intellectual conversation with Mary Hay[4] when Peggy tore me away to talk to a lady who seemed kind of lonely. The lady was Mrs. Ernest Boyd[5] and I'd have been with her yet if June Walker[6] hadn't come in with a bun and rescued me.

We got back from the other side (Europe) in time to see the Yale-Princeton game. Art Samuels[7] was host to a huge party of us—Swopes, Brouns, etc.—at lunch at the Cottage club. The Princeton team, which had made a sucker of Harvard the Saturday before, acted on this occasion as if football was a complete surprise and novelty. We stood up all the way home and I swore it would be my last trip to old Nassau.

---

[1] Dorothy Parker wrote plays, poetry, and short fiction but was best known as a literary critic. Discharged from *Vanity Fair* in 1920 because her drama reviews were considered too harsh, she thereafter wrote drama and book reviews for the *New Yorker*. She was a "charter" member of the Algonquin Round Table, where she regularly exercised her caustic wit.

[2] The wife of George S. Kaufman, Beatrice Kaufman was an editor with *Harper's Bazaar* and several book-publishing firms. She herself wrote two plays, the first in collaboration with Peggy Leech (*Divided by Three*) and the second in collaboration with Charles Martin (*The White-Haired Boy*).

[3] Margaret (Peggy) Leech was the author of two novels and a number of non-fiction works. She won a Pulitzer Prize in history for *Reveille in Washington* (1941), and another for *In the Days of McKinley* (1960). She married Ralph Pulitzer in 1928.

[4] Mary Hay was a Ziegfeld girl and an actress. She married Dick Barthelmess, the actor, in 1920; they were divorced in 1926.

[5] Madeleine Boyd, wife of the critic, eventually wrote a novel based on her life with her husband, titled *Life Makes Advances* (1939).

[6] June Walker made her debut on Broadway in the chorus of *Kitchy Koo* (1916). She is especially remembered as the original Lorelei Lee in *Gentlemen Prefer Blondes* (1926) and for her starring role in *Green Grow the Lilacs* (1931).

[7] In 1923, Art Samuels had written a successful musical, *Poppy*, starring W.C. Fields. His career included stints as a managing editor with the *New Yorker*, *Home and Field*, *Harper's Bazaar*, and *House Beautiful*. He was a regular member of the Algonquin Round Table.

Instead of working on the ship coming home, as I intended, I did nothing but lap them up. But as soon as I was home and on the wagon, I wrote the five European articles in nine days.

I have quit the strip and Dick Dorgan is doing it, with help from Tad.[1]

The Society of Composers and Authors, of which Gene is president, gave him a clock for Christmas that must have cost $1000 at least.[2]

Gene and Helen were over the other night and in the midst of one of Gene's stories, Helen said, "Stop picking your nose, sweetheart." That's all the dirt I know.

Speaking of noses, Rube[3] and Irma gave a New Year's Eve party to which 150 people were invited and 300 came. Rube said he never saw so many strangers in his life. Billy Seeman[4] had a lot of the Follies people there to help entertain, but the affair was such a riot that little attention was paid to the entertainment. Ellis and I missed this party. Speaking of noses again, I was in the hospital having my antrum cut open. I'm nearly all right again now, I think, though if I get up suddenly or stoop over, a regular Niagara of blood pours forth from my shapely nostrils.

I took "Vanity Fair" (Thackeray's, not Crowninshield's) to the hospital with me and one day the nurse asked me what I was reading and I told her and she said, "I haven't read it yet. I've been busy making Christmas presents."[5]

Ellis is at present in Danville, Illinois, where her last brother is being married tomorrow to a gal named Bredehoft. I was kept at home by my nose. We are leaving next Tuesday, with the Grant Rices, for Miami and then Nassau, to be gone till nearly the first of March. Our address

---

[1] See p. 162.

[2] Gene Buck was one of the founders of the American Society of Composers, Authors and Publishers and its president from 1924 to 1941.

[3] Rube Goldberg, the famous cartoonist, was one of Lardner's neighbors in Great Neck.

[4] William Seeman was a young man-about-town, the son of a wealthy food processor. He would marry Rube Goldberg's sister-in-law, Phyllis Haver, in 1929.

[5] In "Zone of Quiet," a story published originally in the June 1925 *Cosmopolitan*, Lardner used this experience with a nurse's ignorance of Thackeray's *Vanity Fair*.

at Nassau will be New Colonial Hotel. I think I'll take up golf again, but won't stick to it if I don't like it.
And I think you've staid away long enough.
Mrs. Nell

The following letter was written during a vacation in Miami and Nassau with the Grantland Rices, from 13 January 1925 through mid-February.

The New Colonial
Nassau—Bahamas
January 31, 1925.

Dear Max:—
How about *What of It?* as a title. This is Grantland Rice's suggestion and it sounds pretty good to me.
I'll send you the prefaces in not too short a while.
R.W.L.

The following letter is to William Orton Tewson, editor of the New York *Evening Post* Literary Review section, who had invited Lardner to review *The Prince of Washington Square*, a novel supposedly by nineteen-year-old Harry F. Liscomb. Written in a mixture of semi-idiomatic formal and colloquial English, this story of a newsboy's life obviously reminded Lardner of *The Young Visitors*, the narrative supposedly written by nine-year-old Daisy Ashford, which Lardner had parodied in *The Young Immigrunts*.

Great Neck, New York
February 22, 1925.

Dear Mr. Tewson:—
I was away for six weeks and I guess some of my mail went astray; anyway, the enclosed note is the only one I received about "walnuts."
As for "The Prince of Washington Sguare," I think it had better be reviewed by some one less skeptical than I. I didn't, and don't believe Daisy Ashford in spite of Swinnerton's testimony and that of other "witnesses," and this new book is, to me, palpably conscious humor written by somebody much older than they say the author is.
Sincerely,<br>Ring W. Lardner
P.S. I don't mean to say the Stokes people are trying to put something over, but that they have been deceived. (Though some of the lines and paragraphs in the book are

so "raw" that it is hard to know how they could fool anybody)

Great Neck, New York
March 11, 1925

Dear Max:—
　The principal cause of delay has been lack of an idea. But I've also been fighting a cold; the kind that relieves you of all pep.
　　　　　　　R.W.L.
　Did you have the wrap changed on You Know Me Al?

　When Perkins read Lardner's short story "Haircut" in the 28 March issue of *Liberty*, he wrote to Lardner:

March 16, 1925

Dear Ring:
　I read "Hair Cut" on Friday and I can't shake it out of my mind;—in fact the impression it made has deepened with time. There's not a man alive who could have done better, that's certain.
　Everyone will tell you this, or something like it I guess, so there's little use in my doing it.—But it is a most biting and revealing story and I'd like to say so.

Lardner's reply was succinct and typically modest:

Great Neck, New York
March Seventeenth.

Dear Max:—
　Thanks.
　　　　　　　R.W.L.

　Perkins' judgment has been sustained: "Haircut" remains today Lardner's most anthologized short story. With artful irony, Lardner exposes the variance between the narrator-barber's insensitive interpretation of an "accidental" death and what actually occurred. The story reveals powerfully the need among human beings for sensitivity, kindness, and sympathy—a theme that runs through much of Lardner's fictional world.
　Curiously, Lardner had written no short stories between "The Golden Honeymoon" (*Cosmopolitan*, July 1922) and

"Haircut" (*Liberty*, March 28, 1925), though he had written a number of short fictional sketches (e. g., "What of It?" and "In Conference") for *Hearst's International* and *Cosmopolitan*. In the next year and a half, however, he wrote twelve stories, nine of which were published in *The Love Nest*, after appearing in *Cosmopolitan* or *Liberty*. A significant factor in Lardner's resumption of writing stories was probably the offer that Ray Long, editor of *Cosmopolitan*, had made to Lardner in London in the fall of 1924: "For your next six short stories, $3000 each, or, for your next twelve short stories, to be delivered at intervals of not more than 45 days, $3500 each."[1] During the remainder of 1925, Lardner alternated his stories between *Cosmopolitan* and *Liberty*, where his brother Rex was an editor. When Rex was dismissed near the end of the year in one of *Liberty*'s frequent reorganizations, Lardner sent all his short stories to *Cosmopolitan*, where Rex shortly was hired as an associate editor.

At this time, Perkins, frustrated by the last minute revisions Fitzgerald had continued to send, mailed Lardner a copy of *The Great Gatsby* proofs, an action that suggests both the closeness of Lardner's friendship with Fitzgerald and Perkins' trust in Lardner, who proofread the copy and, as he explained to Fitzgerald in the letter below, suggested a few minor changes in the interest of a more accurate representation of New York City.

March 24th. [1925]

Dears Mr. and Mrs. F.—

Max Perkins reports that Mrs. F. is or has been sick, which we hope isn't true, but would like to know for sure.

I read Mr. F's book (in page proofs) at one sitting and liked it enormously, particularly the description of Gatsby's home and his party, and the party in the apartment in New York. It sounds as if Mr. F. must have attended a party or two during his metropolitan career. The plot held my interest, too, and I found no tedious moments. Altogether I think it's the best thing you've done since Paradise.

On the other hand, I acted as volunteer proof reader and gave Max a brief list of what I thought were errata. On Pages 31 and 46 you spoke of the news-stand on the *lower level*, and the cold waiting room on the *lower level* of the

---

[1] Quoted by Elder, p. 219.

Pennsylvania Station. There ain't any lower level at that station and I suggested substitute terms for same. On Page 82, you had the guy driving his car under the elevated at Astoria, which isn't Astoria, but Long Island City. On Page 118 you had a tide in Lake Superior and on Page 209 you had the Chicago, Milwaukee & St. Paul running out of the La Salle Street Station. These things are trivial, but some of the critics pick on trivial errors for lack of anything else to pick on.

Michael Arlen, who is here to watch the staging of The Green Hat,[1] said he thought How To Write Short Stories was a great title for my book and when I told him it was your title, he said he had heard a great deal about you and was sorry to miss you. He also said he had heard that Mrs. Fitzgerald was very attractive, but I told him he must be thinking of somebody else. Mike is being entertained high and low. He was guest of honor at a luncheon given by Ray Long. Irv Cobb and George Doran sat on either side of him and told one dirty story after another. Last Sunday night he was at a party at Condé Nast's,[2] but who wasn't? I was looking forward to a miserable evening, but had the luck to draw Ina Claire[3] for a dinner and evening companion and was perfectly happy, though I regretted being on the wagon. The last previous time I saw her was at the Press Club in Chicago about eight years ago and she says I was much more companionable on that occasion. George Nathan[4] said he heard you were coming home soon. George, they say, is quitting the associate editorship of the Mercury, but will continue to write theaters for it.

---

[1] Michael Arlen dramatized his own novel, *The Geen Hat*, in 1925. The play starred Katherine Cornell and was the basis for two later films. He wrote thirteen other novels, none of which had the success of *The Green Hat*. His works were carefully calculated to appeal to popular taste.

[2] The publisher of *Vogue, Vanity Fair,* and *House and Garden*, Condé Nast was known as a bon vivant, entertaining frequently in his thirty-room Park Avenue apartment.

[3] Ina Claire made her first appearance on Broadway in the Ziegfeld Follies of 1915. She became a star in *The Gold Diggers* (1919) and played in vaudeville, musical comedy, and "drawing room" comedy, eventually starring in movies.

[4] George Jean Nathan began his career as a drama critic in 1906. He was associated with H.L. Mencken on both *The Smart Set* and *American Mercury*. His articles appeared in *Vanity Fair, America Spectator, Saturday Review, Esquire, Scriber's, Newsweek, Theatre Arts,* and *Liberty*.

So far as I know, Zelda, Mary Hay and Richard are still together; they were when I met them.

Beatrice Kaufman and Peggy Leach have gone abroad.

We had a dinner party at our little nest about two weeks ago; the guests were the Ray Longs, the Grantland Rices, June Walker and Frank Crowninshield. As place cards for Ray, Crownie and Grant, we had, respectively, covers of Cosmopolitan, Vanity Fair and The American Golfer, but this didn't seem to make any impression on June and right after the soup she began knocking Condé Nast in general and his alleged snobbishness in particular. Finally Crownie butted in to defend him and June said, "What do you know about him?" "I live with him," said Crownie. "What for?" said June. "Well," said Crownie, "I happen to be editor of one of his magazines, Vanity Fair." "Oh!" said June. "That's my favorite magazine! And I hate most magazines! For instance, I wouldn't be seen with a Cosmopolitan." After the loud laughter had subsided, I explained to her that Ray was editor of Cosmopolitan. "I'm always making breaks," she said, "and I guess this is one of my unlucky evenings. I suppose that if I said what I think of William R. Hearst, I'd find that even he has a friend here or something."

The annual Dutch Treat show comes off this week. I have a sketch in it which is a born flop.

I met Gene on the train the other day and he said, "Come over and play bridge with us tonight," and I said I couldn't because Arthur Jacks was coming to our house. When I got home, I called up Arthur to inform him of this and he said it was tough luck, but it just happened that he had been invited, several days before, to dine at Gene's that very night.

Write.

Bob Esselstyn.

Great Neck, New York
March 25.

Dear Scott:—

Thanks for the idea, which I think I can use. I wrote to you yesterday, but don't mind doing it again as I left out one piece of news which may be of interest, namely that George Jean and Lillian Gish are often seen together these days. And a handsome pair they make.

Looked up Capri in the encyclopedia and learned that the water supply for drinking was unsatisfactory. Hope to God this is not ruining your stay.

Mr. Lambert, when questioned, said he was taking the best of care of your stuff. He said he had sent the wrong graphophone south or something, but had got it back again.

Visited Mr. Perkins yesterday, had myself sketched by a lady named Anderson,[1] and saw the wrap of your book, which looks good. Then dined at the Princeton club with Art Samuels and attended a Dutch Treat rehearsal, after which I went backstage at the Follies and turned down three offers of drinks, one from a lady, or at least a female.

Must close and nibble on a carrot. Love to the little woman.

Buckie.

The following letter is to Walter Yust, associate editor of "The Literary Review" and "The Literary Lobby" in the New York *Evening Post*.

Great Neck, New York
April 4, 1925.

Dear Mr. Yust:—

If you don't mind, I'd like to consider my brief book reviewing career at an end.[2] There is more work ahead of me

---

[1] The original of this sketch, by Ellen Graham Anderson, is now in the University of Virginia Library.

[2] Lardner had written a review four years earlier of John V.A. Weaver's *In American: "What Is the 'American Language'?"* *Bookman*, 53 (March 1921), 81–82. In the following excerpt from that review, his precise scrutiny of the common American's careless speech is particularly evident:

> We can't hope to land the old K.O. on the writer's jaw, but we can fret him a little with a few pokes to the ear.
> For the most part this organ has served Mr. Weaver well. But I think that on occasion it consciously or unconsciously plays him false. It has told him, for example, that we say *everythin'* and *anythin'*. We don't. We say *somethin'* and *nothin'*, but we say *anything* and *everything*. There appears to be somethin' about the *y* near the middle of both these words that impels us to acknowledge the *g* on the end of them. Mr. Weaver's ear has also give or gave (not gi'n) him a bum hunch on *thing* itself. It has told him to make it *thin'*. But it's a real effort to drop the *g* off this little word and, as a rule, our language is not looking for trouble. His ear has gone wrong on the American for *fellow*, *kind of*, and *sort of*. Only on the stage or in "comic strips" do we use *feller*, *kinder*, and *sorter*. *Kinda* and *sorta* are what us common fellas say.

than I can possibly do, and besides, I can't be even half way entertaining unless I knock, and I don't like to knock.
Sincerely,
Ring Lardner

On 20 April, Perkins wrote to encourage Lardner to complete another volume of short stories:

> I just ran into John Wheeler at lunch and he told me of two stories written and one in early expectation. These with "Haircut" make four. In "How to Write Short Stories" we had ten, but we would not need quite that many for another book and what Wheeler said was encouraging.

Great Neck, New York
April 25th.

Dear Max:—
I do think there ought to be at least nine stories in a book and I am fairly well on the way to that number. Besides Haircut, Mr. and Mrs. Fix-it, and Women (a baseball story) for Liberty, Ray Long has two stories—Zone of Quiet (which, I think, will be in June Cosmopolitan) and The Love Nest (which I sent him this week). I intend to have one and possibly two more done for Liberty by the end of May. The quality of the five already written averages better than the stories in How To Write Short Stories and if we give 'em fair quantity too, they ought to be satisfied.
I'm glad to hear that Scott's book is going.
R.W.L.

Great Neck, New York
May 4, 1925.

[To H. L. Mencken]
Gents:—
Your stuff about Scott in the Sunday World was, it seemed to me, close to perfection in criticism.
And you have the right dope on the pains he took with Gatsby. He rewrote the whole book four or five times and had Scribner's crazy at the finish with revisions by cable.
R.W.L.

*The Great Gatsby* had been published on 10 April. It received some of the best critical reviews Fitzgerald ever got, but the sales were disappointing by Fitzgerald's standards—just over 20,000 copies during the first year. Perkins theorized that Fitzgerald's audience had reacted negatively to a book that was quite short in comparison with Fitzgerald's previous books.

Great Neck, New York
June 25, 1925

Mr. H.L. Mencken
1524 Hollins Street
Baltimore, Md.

Dear Sir:
    If you will be a little patient I will autograph all my books and all Dickens's and most of Cobb's.
    I have been kind of sick but I did like what you said about me.
Sincerely,<br>R.W.L.

On 27 July, Perkins advised Lardner that they should delay publication of the next volume of short stories. He cited as an example the disappointing sales of *The Great Gatsby*:

> The temptation is to get the book out . . . and it is certainly very hard for me to resist it, because I think the stories almost incredibly good. "The Love Nest" is a marvel. But I do honestly think from a farsighted view, that we should act more wisely if we waited—and after all, it would mean only four months—until you had several more stories, so that the book would not look slim and perhaps padded, in half titles, etc. and a widely spaced page and all, along side of "How to Write Short Stories." It is bound to be compared with that and the fact that it was not its equal in quantity,—at least it would not in the eyes of the trade:—they began by washing their hands of the whole matter when they saw how few pages there were in "The Great Gatsby" compared with his other books.

The following is again to Fitzgerald:

Great Neck, August 8, 1925.

Dear Sir:—

I enclose a fragment from one of your former letters. Zelda isn't here, but when I see her I certainly will give her your best love.

I might consider visiting Paris if you will guarantee me an introduction to Miss La Gallienne[1] who is my favorite actress and with whom I have been secretly in love ever since Liliom.

Thanks to the Great Neck Playhouse we hardly ever have to go to New York any more. Nearly all the shows play a night or two here before going to Broadway. Twenty-two try-outs are booked for this season and you can buy season tickets if you want to.

Gene didn't make any comment on "The Love Nest," but evidently had no suspicion.[2] Anyway, we are still pals. He told Dorothy Parker in my presence one night that the new house had been bought as a memorial to the kiddies.

Dorothy visited the Lardners for a week at my invitation. She had been having an unfortunate affair and for some reason or other, I thought a visit to us would cheer her up. I got into this sympathetic mood on the seventh of May and it lasted till the tenth of July; during the two months I was constantly cock-eyed, drinking all night and sleeping all day and never working. Fortunately I was eight weeks ahead in syndicates before the spree started.

One night during Dorothy's visit, Herman Mankiewicz[3] called up from Petrova's and said he would come and see us if we'd come after him. We did and I took them, Mank and Dorothy, to Durand's, Ellis (very sensibly) refusing to go. The place was full of Durand's big, husky Irish clients.

---

[1] Eva LeGallienne established herself on the New York stage with *Not So Long Ago* (1920). She also starred in *Liliom* (1921) and *The Swan* (1924). She founded the Civic Repertory Theatre in 1926.

[2] Though Lardner admitted that "The Love Nest" (a portrait of an outwardly happy marriage that is in reality blighted by the husband's possessiveness, the wife's sense of unfulfillment, and her subsequent dipsomania) was actually based on the Buck household, Buck never gave any sign of having read the story or of having been offended in any way. His wife was Helen Faulkner, a former Fred Stone showgirl.

[3] Herman Mankiewicz was a foreign correspondent for the *World* who subsequently became drama editor and critic for the New York *Times*. He went on to become a screenwriter for Paramount and to share an academy award for *Citizen Kane* (1941).

After a few drinks, Mank remembered that he had been in the Marines and ought to prove it by licking all the inmates of the joint. I (as usual) acted as pacifist and felt next day as if I'd been in a football game against Notre Dame. We finally got Mank home (our house) and put him to bed and he arose next day at ten and said he had to go right to town and do some work for the Sunday Times. Ellis gave him a few highballs to brace him up and he finally left at five in the afternoon.

George Nathan and Lillian are still very thick so far as I know.

Harry Frazee,[1] who is making millions out of "No, No, Nanette" (with four companies in America, three in England and two in Australia), promises to stage a small revue, written by Jerry Kern and me, late this fall. But you know how those things go.

Dick Barthelmess[2] is living in Great Neck and we see him occasionally. The papers announced that Mary was through with him, though she didn't intend to get a divorce.

Mrs. Lardner and I will be highly honored by the dedication of your book to us.[3] I hope "The Great Gatsby" is going better. It certainly deserves a big sale. I think it probable that the reason it got no notice from Frank Adams was that he was on a vacation and getting married about the time it came out. Max Perkins said he thought the size of the book was against it (in the eyes of the buyers). That is a great commentary on American life and letters. What is your new novel going to be about?

Gene called up the other day and said he had sold the play "we" wrote to Ziegfeld, but that it would have to be rewritten into musical comedy form. Ziegfeld had given him contracts for us to sign. There were clauses in them which I wouldn't sign even with a manager I could trust. I told Gene so and he cabled Ziegfeld, who is now in France, and said we objected to certain clauses. Ziegfeld cabled back that he wouldn't make any changes. Gene then wanted me to sign the contracts as they stood and I wouldn't. So that's that. I've got a story coming out in "Liberty" for October 3, of

---

[1] Harry Frazee produced *No, No, Nanette* (written by Vincent Youmans). He owned the Boston Red Sox from 1916 to 1923.

[2] Dick Barthelmess was a leading man in many movies from 1916 to 1941.

[3] Fitzgerald had dedicated *All the Sad Young Men* to the Lardners.

which Flo is the hero. When, and if, he reads it, he won't offer me any more contracts, even lousy ones.[1]

On the Fourth of July, Ed Wynn[2] gave a fireworks party at his new estate in the Grenwolde division. After the children had been sent home, everybody got pie-eyed and I never enjoyed a night so much. All the Great Neck professionals did their stuff, the former chorus girls danced, Blanche Ring[3] kissed me and sang, etc. The party lasted through the next day and wound up next evening at Tom Meighan's,[4] where the principal entertainment was provided by Lila Lee and another dame, who did some very funny imitations (really funny) in the moonlight on the tennis court. We would ask them to imitate Houdini, or Leon Errol, or Will Rogers, or Elsie Janis; the imitations were all the same, consisting of an aesthetic dance which ended with an unaesthetic fall onto the tennis court.

Charley Chaplin's new picture, "The Gold Rush," opens here next week and we are going to a party in his honor at Nast's.

I seem to have written a good many words, most of them about myself, and not many of them of much interest.

We do miss you and Zelda a great deal. Write again and tell her to write, too. And I might add that I have a little money to lend at the proverbial six percent, if worst comes to worst.

Bucky.

Signing this letter "Bucky" reminded me that Bucky bought himself a Chevrolet or something and nobody would ride with him but Isabelle, so he took her riding and drove her into a tree and raised hell with the bridge work.[5]

---

[1] The story, which depicts an insensitive, mercenary producer, was "A Day with Conrad Green."

[2] Ed Wynn performed in the Ziegfeld Follies in 1914 and for several years thereafter. In 1921, his title role in *The Perfect Fool* established his comic style.

[3] Blanche Ring was a star in numerous musicals of the 1920s. She introduced such hits as "In the Good Old Summertime" and "Come, Josephine, in My Flying Machine."

[4] Tom Meighan lived in the Grenewolde section of Great Neck. He was a leading man in silent movies and was married to Blanche Ring's sister.

[5] For lack of room elsewhere, this postscript is typed at the top of page one of this letter.

On 29 October, Perkins wrote suggesting the title *The Love Nest and Other Stories* for the collection in hand of Lardner's short stories.

Great Neck, New York
November 1, 1925.

Dear Max:—

I think your title is all right. It would be better, I believe, to have a straight title like that instead of a trick title, this time.

Have you Scott's up-to-date address? The last I have is 14 rue de Tilsitt, but he said something in his last letter about moving. I hate to write a 1,500-word news letter to him and have it go astray.

R.W.L.

By this time, Lardner was famous enough for a trivial involvement with the law to be newsworthy. On 3 November, the New York *World* carried the following Chicago news, along with Lardner's cavalier response to the threat of Chicago-style legal action:

Speeding Capias Out for Lardner
He Says Not Guilty in Own Court

Chicago, Nov. 3.—Ring Lardner's humor made no appeal to Clyde Dyckman, Inspector of Records in the City Hall. He was reading to-day an ad written by Ring for a big hotel opposite the City Hall. Ring said whenever he returned here he took a room in this hotel "so I can look across the street, view the County Building and see how the other half lives without working."

"I'll fix him the next time he comes," said Dyckman. Then he flashed a record from the office of the Clerk of the Municipal Court wherein was set forth that one Ring W. Lardner had been fined $50 and costs for speeding, June 17, 1919, and had never paid the fine. The court clerk went before Judge George and obtained a capias for the arrest of the writer.

## Ring Says Not Guilty in His Own Night Court

Ring Lardner, holding Night Court in his Great Neck home, pleaded not guilty to the Chicago charge and ordered himself discharged last evening.

"I didn't do it," he said. "It must have been a couple of other fellows. However, I'm ready to take my medicine and begin all over again. If they prove it on me I'll pay the $50. I've never been fined for speeding—Oh, yes, I've been arrested for speeding but never fined. That's different.

"They charge me with speeding in June 1919. I didn't move away from Chicago until the following October. My creditors never wait four months to give me time to leave town."

Lardner then wrote the following letter to Chicago Mayor Dever:

Great Neck, New York
November 4, 1925

Dear Mr. Mayor:—
    I enclose a clipping from the New York World of this morning. The story was in the other New York papers, too. I don't like to have a thing like this against my record in Chicago which was clean, financially, at least. I never, to my knowledge, was fined for speeding in Chicago or elsewhere. I was living in Chicago the entire summer of 1919 and up until October of that year. If the fine was assessed in June, surely I ought to, and could, have been told about it. I certainly was not making any effort to hide.
    I hate to bother you about a trivial thing like this, but I don't know whom else to bother. And I wonder if you could have your secretary or somebody look it up and find out who fined me and why I was kept in ignorance of it. I'll be very grateful.
                    Sincerely,
                    Ring Lardner

The Mayor responded to this "surprising information" by writing to Lardner on 9 November:

   I do not know Mr. Dyckman, whose statement is included in the clipping. I suppose he is an employee of

the Municipal Court, over which we have no jurisdiction whatever.
As you suggest I am having my Secretary look the matter up and have directed him to advise you if he obtains any information serviceable to you.

But Lardner had no success in his struggle with City Hall. The Mayor's secretary replied on 12 November:

> I am writing to inform you that the records of the Clerk of the Municipal Court show that you were arrested by a Lincoln Park Police Officer on June 17, 1919 for speeding: that you appeared before Municipal Judge Stelk on the same date, waived a jury trial and pleaded guilty; that you were fined Fifty Dollars and Six Dollars costs: that you made a motion to vacate judgment, the hearing of which was set for September 30, 1919. As you did not appear in Court on that date the motion to vacate was overruled and a warrant was issued for your arrest.

Sunday, Nov. 8. [1925]

Dear Scott and Darling Zelda:—

I swear to my God I would write to you oftener if you'd stay in one place. Even when you give me an address, you always say you don't expect to be there long.

Max Perkins reports that Gatsby has established you (Scott; not you, dearie) or re-established you or something; that your book of short stories is very good, and that you are at work on another novel. My next book is to come out in March with the title, perhaps, "The Love Nest, and Other Stories."

Ellis, Kate Rice, the Percy Hammonds,[1] my crazy sister and I drove to Princeton yesterday and saw the "Tiger" (Princeton) beat the "Crimson" (H-rv--d) 36 to 0. I won a six dollar pool by predicting a Princeton victory of 30 to 0. But don't get it into your heads that Princeton will have any frolic with Yale. Harvard had the most childish team I every saw representing a big school. A week before they played

---

[1] Percy Hammond was a drama critic from 1908 to 1921 for the Chicago *Tribune*. Then, like Lardner, he moved to New York, where he wrote for the New York *Tribune*. Later, he was one of Lardner's East Hampton neighbors.

William and Mary, winning 14 to 7. Bill McGeehan[1] says it was Mary who scored the touchdown. A week ago, Ellis and I and our sons John and Jim went to Philadelphia and saw Red Grange[2] make a monkey of the "Red and Blue." He is the greatest ball carrier I've seen since Heston.[3]

The other night Heywood and Ruth[4] gave a party at which one of the guests of honor was Rosamond Johnson, the coon, who, as you doubtless know, wrote "Under the Bamboo Tree," "The Maiden with the Dreamy Eyes," and other songs. They asked him to sing the Bamboo Tree song and when he got to the line, "I lika change your name," Ruth, loyal to the Lucy Stoners,[5] hissed. Poor Johnson was what you might call nonplussed.

We are goinq to the opening of the new Charlot Revue Tuesday night. Jack Buchanan, Mundin, Beatrice and Gertrude are all back here with it.[6]

New York is all agog over Michael Arlen and Noel Coward.[7] Heywood, George Nathan and one or two others have taken some awful socks at Mike, but the large majority are mushy over him. Noel I haven't met, but those who have tell me he is—well, you know. I can hardly wait. His "The Vortex" is going big, but "Hay Fever" has flopped. "Hay

---

[1] Bill McGeehan was sports editor of the New York *Herald*. He was chiefly noted for his column "Down the Line."

[2] The so-called "miracle man" of the 1920s, Harold (Red) Grange was perhaps the greatest open-field runner of all time. A three-year All-American halfback/quarterback at the University of Illinois (1923–25), the "Galloping Ghost" later starred for the Chicago Bears in the early days of the National Football League.

[3] William M. (Willie) Heston was the star left halfback of an unbeaten University of Michigan football team from 1902 through 1904.

[4] Ruth Hale was an outspoken supporter of feminist principles and author of several articles on women's rights. She married Heywood Campbell Broun in 1917 but continued to use her maiden name.

[5] Lucy Stoner was an early advocate of sexual equality.

[6] The Charlot Revue of 1926 (it opened on 10 November 1925) starred Beatrice Lillie, Jack Buchanan, Gertrude Lawrence, and Herbert Mundin. It received generally favorable reviews.

[7] *The Vortex* established Noel Coward as a playwright and actor. In 1925, he had five plays running in London. In all he wrote forty-two plays.

Fever," I am told by real people, is much the best thing he has done, but was handicapped by having Laura Hope Crews as lead. As for "The Green Hat," it's a good thing for Mike that Katharine Cornell and Margalo Gilmore are in it. Les Howard is also in it, but it really isn't the right kind of part for him.

I had forgotten what terrible things world's series were so I consented to cover this year's. I got drunk three days before it started in the hope and belief that I would be remorseful and sober by the time I had to go to it. But when I got to Pittsburgh it seemed that I was the only newspaper man in America who had reserved a room; all the others moved in with me and there wasn't a chance to eat, sleep, vork, or do anything but drink. The result was two fairly good stories and seven terrible ones out of a possible nine, including rainy days.

Please don't hold it against me, but I have just written a picture scenario for Tom Meighan.[1] The plot, which has to do with baseball and Florida real estate, was originated by one of the Famous Players' regular men, but they wanted me to elaborate it or something. I didn't want to, so when they said $5,000, I said it wouldn't be worth my while, but I might do it for $7,500. They said that was fine. So I did it, taking four days to the job. They begin making the picture next week. After it's done, I am to write the titles. I suppose some would consider this easy money, but it was a damn bore and unless the picture is very good, I'll be sorry I did it. The reason I said $7,500 is that Tom gets that amount per week, work or no work, and I thought perhaps I could do it in a week and be as well paid as he is.

Speaking, as we were, of Ruth Hale, some of her best friends (closest friends) have nicknamed her country place Halo-itosis.

Did May Preston look you up?

If you give a damn, we are going to Florida in January, coming back here in February and going to California in March.

But I know you are in a fever to hear the latest Buckshot, which is the title I have just thought of for my column of news about the Bucks. Well, Gene, after threatening, for several years, to go into the producing end of the "game," finally bought a play by J.C. Nugent, called "Gunpowder." The thesis was that when an elderly man marries a young

---

[1] This film was *The New Klondike*, for which Lardner wrote the script as a favor to his actor neighbor, Tom Meighan. As the letters to Fitzgerald of 23 February and 10 May 1926 indicate, the titles that finally appeared with the film bore little resemblance to what Lardner had written.

girl, she may some day become a mother at the hands of somebody her own age. The play opened in Washington and ran a week, a record-breaking week. The house for opening night was $300 and for the Saturday night, $8.00. Gene decided something was the matter with the show and took it off to have it rewritten by (you'll never guess) Brandon Tynan,[1] who was also engaged to play the elderly husband's part, replacing Nugent. Well, they opened here in New York on Thursday night and we all got dressed up and went and I wish you could have been there. The audience, trying its best to be decent, laugbed hysterically and uproariously at the saddest parts and when the girl finally announced that she was in a two-family way, there was almost a panic. Two tickets were sold for Saturday night and then Gene took it off.

"I wasn't kiddin' myself," said the young entrepeneur. "I thought I saw somethin' in the play that wasn't there. I thought I read somethin' between the lines, but it wasn't there. But I wasn't kiddin' myself. I said to myself, 'What's the use takin' this troupe to Reading or Stamford and foolin' with it another week? I'll bring it right into New York and see if it's there or not.' That's what I figured. No use wastin' any more money on the troupe if it wasn't there. I wasn't kiddin' myself for a minute. Well, it wasn't there. But it was good experience. And I'll know where I'm at next time. If you got any notion, any comedy notion, just real stuff, you come to me and I'll go through with it. I don't want no great big troupe, but just a homey, real comedy notion. I ain't kiddin' myself."

Well, on top of this debacle, his mother and aunt and five cousins we'd never seen before swooped down on him in rapid succession for long visits, and he hasn't been able to sell the old house and the new one must be a millstone. In the face of which, he and Frank Craven[2] "invested" in some shore front at about $18,000 or $20,000 an acre (five acres of it), making a ten percent payment which, I presume, Frank put up, and are now trying to make "a quick turnover" at $27,500 an acre. I have no doubt it will be worth that in ten years, but meanwhile the interest will just be added to his other burdens. "But it's the relatives that are

---

[1] Brandon Tynan was a well-known actor and playwright. He was the "serious relief" in the Follies from 1923 on. He wrote seven plays and a number of screen treatments.

[2] Frank Craven was an actor, playwright, and director, mostly for John Golden. He wrote dialogue for the Laurel and Hardy movies, and was the original stage manager in *Our Town* (1938).

the poison," he says. "They're what breaks a man's back. I'm glad to own all this real estate; it'll make the kiddies independent some day. But I wish some of my aunts and cousins would lay off, to say nothin' of that sapadola Marguerite married." Also, to say nothing of "Red" and Bucky.

Now, then, we come to my latest theatrical successes. Harry Frazee agreed to put on a revue by me and Jerry Kern if we could land Bill Fields. Bill said it was all right with him and I started to work, only to discover that Bill bad already signed contracts (synchronous contracts) with Goodman, with Ziegfeld and with the Famous Players. He's going to spend the winter in court. Goodman is suing him for $100,000, Ziegfeld has him and he is supposed to be working for Famous Players and getting $6,000 a week.

Well, in August Gene called up and said Ziegfeld was "hot" for the Palm Beach show "we" wrote two or three years ago; he wanted it rewritten into musical comedy form; he "had to have it" to put in the Cosmopolitan theatre to succeed "Louis the Fourteenth," which was slipping. I said it was ridiculous to pretend the show could be fixed up by the first of September (which was the date set by Ziegfeld); besides, I didn't trust him and wouldn't even think about working on it till I saw a check. So then Ziegfeld extended the time limit to October first and gave us $500 apiece, with a written promise to give us $500 apiece more when the completed play was turned over to him, provided it was within the time limit. I got busy and rewrote the play into a musical comedy book; also wrote some lyrics which I thought were not bad. On the first day of October, Ziegfeld had not yet signed a composer, and as you know, it is impossible to turn in a complete book and lyrics these days unless you have a composer with whom to work on the numbers. On the second of October, Ziegfeld engaged Vincent Youmans[1] to write the music. I showed him my lyrics and he didn't seem to care much for them. Neither did Gene. In fact, Gene wanted to write all the lyrics himself, though he didn't say so. Finally I said, "Well, I'm going to write the lyrics of three or four comedy songs and I want them to get a trial anyway." Then I went to the world's series and when I came back, not one tap of work had been done and Gene hadn't even turned over the book to Ziegfeld. Moreover, I think, though I'm not sure, that

---

[1] Vincent Youmans was a composer and producer of musicals. Among his many hit songs were "Tea for Two," and "I Want To Be Happy:" *No, No, Nanette* was his best known musical. He also produced the movie *Flying Down to Rio* (1933), starring Ginger Rogers and Fred Astaire.

Youmans told Ziegfeld he had seen the book and didn't like it. Anyway, both Gene and I got telegrams saying we had broken the contract and I was sick and tired of the whole proceeding that I was glad of it, but Gene said he was going to give Ziegfeld a terrible bawling out. He saw him and Ziegfeld soft-soaped him and said that what he wanted to do was get rid of Youmans and when he did, he would produce the show, probably about the first of the year. So Gene thinks that is what is going to happen, but between you and me, dear Scott and darling Zelda, Ziegfeld is not going to produce the show at any time, whether he wants to or whether he doesn't. And I have written him a letter, to the effect that my stuff was probably known to more people than was that of any of the popular song writers of the day with the possible exception of Irving Berlin and that said stuff never would have got before the public if magazine and newspaper editors had jazz composers engaged to pass on manuscripts. I guess that will make him think, eh, girls?

At present I am Americanizing Offenbach's "Orpheus in the Underworld," which, if I do it well, is supposed to be produced by the Actors' Theater with Otto Kahn's backing and under the direction of Max Reinhardt. I have no confidence that this will come to pass, but I am looking forward to some pleasure in the work because there is no other lyric vriter concerned and the composer is dead.

Ellis and I have bought a farm four miles southeast of here. It is 44 acres.[1] We don't intend to farm, but if possible, to held onto it for five or ten years and sell it at a big profit, the theory being that New York City will grow out to it by that time. We are doing it as a memorial to the kiddies. After I get it all paid for, in two or three years I hope, I'm going to quit saving money and drink in a serious way.

Ed Gallagher of Gallagher and Shean is in an asylum. Not soon enough.

"Sunny," with Marilyn Miller,[2] Jack Donahue,[3] Mary Hay, etc., is a big hit, but it so expensive that they have to take in over $35,000 a week to break even. Mary isn't so

---

[1] Lardner sold this farm at a substantial profit some time before the 1929 stock market crash.

[2] Marilyn Miller came out of the Follies to star in such musicals as *Rosalie* and *Smiles* (the 1930 musical for which Lardner wrote some lyrics).

[3] Jack Donahue began as a dancer in the Follies. His first starring role, as a comedian, was in *Sons o' Guns* (1929). He died suddenly, in 1930, while on tour with the play.

good in it, according to me and other critics. Donahue is wonderful and, in my estimation, the most valuable comedian in America.

A play called "Young Blood," with Norman Trevor[1] and Helen Hayes, opened here in Great Neck Friday night. A young man sleeps with a maid and later on in the show are these lines: "Are you sure?" asks the young man. "Yes," she says. "It's been over six weeks."

Have you heard the story about the Frenchwoman who wanted to go to America just to see the Statue of Liberty and also meet the Bitches, who had all those boys in the American army?

Speaking of Liberty, John Wheeler has been removed as editor. J.M. Patterson of the Chicago Tribune has come to New York to run it and the Daily News. Harvey Deuel, a Chicago newspaper man, will succeed Jack as editor of Liberty. I guess my brother Rex is all right for a while, but if they do anything to him, I'm going to jump to Cosmopolitan.

Do you know that this is about 2,500 words and I'm not getting a nickel for it? You must repay me with love.

Bob Esselstyn.

The following verse to H.L. Mencken suggests that Lardner was now mailing the autographed copies of his books that Mencken had requested six months earlier.[2]

Great Neck, New York
[December 1925]

I will send you in December what you asked in May;
I will send it by the U. S. mails today (the mails today)
Oh, when I have passed away,
Please seek out my pals and say
That I sent you in December what you asked in May.

On 2 December, Perkins sent Lardner a proof of the dust jacket for *The Love Nest and Other Stories*, a royalty check for $1,608.68, and a gift copy of Will James's *The Drifting Cowboy*. Perkins thought that Lardner might enjoy lunch

---

[1] Norman Trevor was an Olympic athlete in 1900 who entered the theater in England in 1907. He made his Broadway debut in 1913 and began making movies in 1924.

[2] See Lardner's letter to Mencken of 25 June 1925.

sometime with James, whose western narratives, all published by Scribner's, remained popular through the 1940s.

Great Neck, New York
December 4, 1925

Dear Max:—
Thanks for the check and the wrap, both of which looked good. I'd like to meet Mr. James, but it will have to be a little later; I've promised to do a stunt for the Actors' Theater and have sworn an oath not to leave this house for immoral purposes till it is completed.
R.W.L.
Ray Long now has my last story—"Rhythm"—which will be in April Cosmopolitan, out March 10.

On the 23rd, Perkins wrote to ask Lardner if he might have another story to lengthen the projected book and to encourage him to write as long a preface as he could without "forcing it."

Great Neck, New York
December 26, 1925.

Dear Max:—
I don't think there is a chance of my writing another sbort story in time for publication before the book comes out. You see, I am now tied up pretty definitely with Cosmopolitan and it is already scheduling the July issue. I'll write as long a preface as I can. When do you have to have it? I can't think of any comments that would go between stories.
We had a merry, though dry, Christmas and hope you did too (not necessarily dry).
Sincerely,
R.W.L.

The following letter refers to another of Lardner's agreements with film companies:

Great Neck, New York
January 12, 1926.

Dear Max:—
I am sorry to trouble you, but the Century Film Corporation which has brought the rights to my "busher" stories, says it is necessary, for the records at Washington, to have the enclosed assignment signed by Scribner's. Will you

be good enough to have it signed and returned to Mr. Siegfried F. Hartman, 120 Broadway, New York?
                        Sincerely,
                        Ring W. Lardner

Lardner wrote a similar letter to Lorimer at the *Saturday Evening Post* on the same day. But though Scribners and the Curtis Publishing Company (publisher of the *Post*) did agree to the contract, the saga of Jack Keefe was never filmed. However, some of Lardner's works did become films. *June Moon* was produced in 1931 and in 1937 (retitled as *Blonde Trouble*). *Elmer the Great* appeared in 1929, in 1931 (retitled as *Fast Company*), and in 1939 (retitled as *The Cowboy Quarterback*).[1] "Alibi Ike" was done in 1935, with Joe E. Brown. After World War II, *The Big Town* (retitled *So This Is New York*), starring Henry Morgan, and "Champion," starring Kirk Douglas, were produced. *Champion* was the most faithfully reproduced of Lardner's works and the most successful. Unfortunately, Lardner had no part in the movie adaptations of any of his fiction.

By 1926 Lardner's popularity was approaching its peak. His weekly column appeared in more than 150 newspapers, and his name was one of the best known in the country. The associated prosperity allowed the family to vacation frequently in the south and the west.

One of Ellis's favorite places in Florida was Belleair Heights. In January 1926, the Rices accompanied them.

Belleair Heights, Florida
January 25, 1926.

Dear Max:—

    Several proofs have been forwarded to me down here. If it is all right with you, I will bring them, together with the preface, when I come up to New York, which will be about February 8. I'm going to be home two or three days and then set out again for New Orleans and California.
                        R.W.L.

To write titles for the recently filmed *The New Klondike*, Lardner interrupted this vacation to return to New York. En route afterward from New York to New Orleans, Lardner

---

[1] See Ring Lardner Jr., pp. 152-53, for an anecdote explaining how Elmer was transformed from a pitcher to a quarterback.

appears to have spent a few days relaxing at the Grove Park Inn health resort in Ashville before Ellis joined him there and they met the Rices again in New Orleans.

Grove Park Inn
Asheville, N. C.
Wednesday.
[February 1926]

Dearest:
　Here are a few more things for you to remember:
　1. Bring along your check book so that you can pay your income tax when the time comes.
　2. Telephone Mr. Kelly (Vanderbilt 6737) and give him our address so he can tell us the amount of the tax.
　3. Mrs. Landis.
　4. Give your trunk check to the man who gets on the train a few stations before Asheville.
　5. Bring along the March American Mercury if it arrives in time.
　In regards to your queries—The weather down here is winter weather, though never getting extremely cold. I haven't seen any of the women (there are about fifteen of them in the hotel) wearing light colored dresses in the daytime, but it has either rained or snowed nearly every day and they may brighten up when the weather does. Most of them dress for dinner, even when the men don't, but their dinner dresses are medium, not startling.
　I started to exercise daily, but ever since Sunday the weather has been impossible. I hope it will be all through misbehaving before you come. Just now it would be ideal for the boys, four inches of snow and plenty of steep hills. I don't know whether you are going to like Asheville at all, but if you don't we can go somewhere else.
　Thanks for sending me the insurance blanks. I have signed them and returned them to Fred Van Ness, who will mail the policies back to Great Neck. Better tell Miss Feldmann[1] to put them away in some drawer when they come.
　My daily schedule is very quiet. I get up about nine-thirty, have breakfast in my room, work, shave and bathe. Go down to lunch about one-thirty, return to my room and uork and read. Go down to dinner at seven-thirty, return to

---

[1] Gusti Feldmann, a trained nurse, had been employed by the Lardners after David's birth in 1919. She remained with the family for most of the next twelve years.

my room, go to bed and read. At odd moments I am busy being inverviewed or refusing invitations to speak.

Tell Bill and Jim that the strip has been sold to the Evening Sun and Globe. They were very curious about it. Also tell them and David that I will write soon and wish they would write to me. Also John.

Love to you and remember me to Miss Feldmann.
                                    Husband.

Grove Park Inn
Asheville, N. C.
Friday.
[ca 1926]

Dearest:

Thanks to you I have been wholeheartedly welcomed into the Asheville aristocracy. A lady called up last night and asked if I was the husband of Ellis Abbott of Goshen and I said yes, so she and her husband and twelve-year-old child came and got me and drove me out to a roadhouse. My hostess was formerly Grace Nisonger and her mother used to be the Abbotts' washerwoman. She knows Frank and Florence better than you, but you will have a chance to get acquainted when you arrive.

I forgot to bring Volume 4 of the war history and I wish you'd bring it if you have room. I'm nearly out of reading matter.

The snow is practically gone and warmer weather is predicted. I've been out only once since Sunday and that was on Grace's party.

This will be my last letter to you, as the mail service between here and Great Neck doesn't seem very swift. I will certainly be glad to see you Thursday as I am very lonesome.
                                    Husband.

While in New Orleans, Lardner got together with fellow author Sherwood Anderson for a memorable evening that Anderson later descrbed in an essay "On Meeting Ring Lardner":

> Ring Lardner did often escape. He had a marvelous technique. He could always get behind the mask, and then, too, he must always have had a great deal of what he was getting that night at dinner; that is to say, warm affection from many people. We poured it over him as we poured the wine down our throats. We

loved him. I cannot help thinking it was a rich and rare evening in his life. He laughed. He talked. He drank the wine. He told stories. It was a good evening for him. It was something more than that for the rest of us.

From New Orleans, the Lardners and the Rices next traveled to California.

Hotel Del Coronado
Coronado Beach, California
Feb. 23, 1926.

Heap Big Zelda and Scott:—
I am in the Indian and Mexican country and am learning the language rapidly.

The elegant picture, "The Fitzgeralds' Christmas," was forwarded to us here and we really did and do like it. We agree that Scotty is the second best looking one in the outfit, or shebang, to use the colloquial.

We and the Rices, including their daughter, went to Belleair, Florida, the first week in January and staid there three weeks. Then I had to go home for a few days and view a Tommie Meighan picture, to which I was engaged to write the titles. The picture, I believe, will be the worst ever seen on land or sea, and the titles are excruciatingly terrible. They will look as if Jack Hazzard[1] had written them.

On the tenth of February, if you are still interested, we set out for New Orleans, stopping fifteen minutes in Montgomery, where we shed a tear. (But I almost forgot to say that while in New York, Ellis and I saw "The Great Gatsby." It was a matinee on a day of the worst weather ever seen in the city or anywhere else; yet the house was over three-quarters full. The blizzard was so bad that all the schools were closed and the commuters had a terrible time getting to New York at all. The man who plays Buchanan lives on Long Island and arrived during Act 2. But we thought the show was great and that Rennie[2] was just about perfect. I regretted that they left out the drunken apartment

---

[1] An actor neighbor in Great Neck, John E. Hazzard played the lead in *The Good Fellow* (1926), George S. Kaufman and Herman Mankiewicz's unsuccessful play.

[2] James Rennie played Gatsby. He was a star of the London stage and on Broadway. He made a number of movies, several with Dorothy Gish, whom he married in 1920. They were divorced in 1935.

scene, but I presume Davis[1] figured that one party scene was enough. Every now and then one of Scott's lines would pop out and hit you in the face and make you wish he had done the dramatization himself.

Well, anyway, we got to New Orleans for the Mardi Gras and were rushed by a bunch of morons and I couldn't stand it and fell off the wagon and we all got the flu and had a very sick trip from New Orleans to this place, where we are resting. From here we go to Los Angeles (including Hollywood), Monterey and San Francisco; then home, arriving there the first week in April. The Rices have been with us right along and we are still all speaking.

Write soon, both of you. You, Zelda, come home and show up the Charleston dancers. You, Scott, also come home and write a play.

And Oh, yes, we had two long and entertaining sessions with Sherwood Anderson and wife in New Orleans. We took them along with us to one of the dinners given, for no reason, in our honor and Sherwood was very frank in stating his opinion of the host and local guests.

Tallulah.

The following is the first of several surviving letters written over the next few years to Burton Rascoe, Lardner's old colleague on the *Tribune*, who was now also a New York newspaperman, the author of a syndicated column, "The Daybook of a New Yorker."

Great Neck, New York
Monday, May 10.

Dear Burton: —

Ellis and I traveled constantly from the first of January to the first of April and have no intention of leaving Great Neck again for months and months. So it is up to you and Hazel to come out here. Can you endure waiting till our alterations are completed? Ellis is taking my room and I am taking hers, but of course she couldn't live in a room that looked like a man's room and vice versa; hence the alterations, which, they promise will be done in three weeks. When they are, I will write to you and you must bring your overnight bag. Allow me, as an expert on ferries, to advise

---

[1] Owen Davis's dramatization of *The Great Gatsby* had opened in New York on 2 February 1926. In his lifetime, Davis was the author of over two hundred plays, including *Icebound* (1923), for which he won a Pulitzer Prize.

against the Greenwich line, which runs infrequently and lands you way out at Oyster Bay, and to recommend the Clason Point–College Point line, which is a municipal institution, runs every forty minutes, brings you from the Bronx to Flushing and costs you about forty cents, car and all.

Love to Hazel.<br>R.W.L.

The reference to the Lardner's arrangement of separate bedrooms is an interesting revelation on which Ring Lardner Jr. comments.[1] While Lardner was serving as a war correspondent in France, Ellis arranged separate bedrooms in their just-rented Evanston house. It may or may not have been a shock to Lardner when he returned to find his things moved to another room, but one should not misinterpret such information. Separate bedrooms was a common convention in the 1920s for married couples.

Monday, May 10, 1926.

Dear Scott and Darling Zelda:—

I just got through reading the current Bookman and it certainly gave me the impression that you, Scott (or Fitz), are having a violent affair with Johnnie Farrar.[2] I was touched particularly by his assertion that he was glad you were coming back this fall, though you and he quarreled a great deal.

Ellis and I are exceedingly grateful to you, Scott, not you, Zelda, for dedicating "All The Sad Young Men" to us. I had read all of it except the first story, which, I think, is the best story. I think also that you were a sap not to have made a novel of it.

"Gatsby," I see by the papers, closed Saturday night owing to Rennie's impending trip to England. It's too bad it couldn't have run on, but it would have been a mistake to continue it with somebody else in the lead. If there was ever a man that fitted a part and vice versa, etc.

In case you haven't heard of the Pulitzer awards— George Kelly got first prize for his play, Craig's Wife." Aleck Woollcott said he would have given it to Marc

---

[1] Ring Lardner Jr. pp. 75-76.

[2] In 1926, John Farrar, later to be a successful book publisher, was editor of *The Bookman*. The reference here is to Farrar's review of *All the Sad Young Men*, which he termed the "very best" of Fitzgerald's short stories.

Connolly's "The Wisdom Tooth," which is a damn good play, and Percy said he would have placed both "Gatsby" and "The Wisdom Tooth" ahead of the winner. The fact that Owen Davis was on the committee may have ruined "Gatsby's" chance. It's too bad you couldn't have seen "Gatsby." I think you'd have been pleased. Red Lewis got the book prize with "Arrowsmith" and turned it down. I can see his point. I am against all that kind of stuff, meaning the Pulitzer awards and the All America football team and "The Best Short Stories of so-and-so," even when Mr. O'Brien honors me with a place or three or four stars in the last named.[1]

Reviews of "The Love Nest" have been perfectly elegant. I don't know whether you've seen the book, but I had an introduction to it written as if I were dead. The Sunday Times ran a long review and played up the introduction strong, saying it was too bad I had died so young, etc. and the result was that Ellis was kept busy on the telephone all that Sunday evening assuring friends and reporters that I was alive and well. It just happened that I was at home and cold sober; if I'd been out, she might have worried a little. Or maybe not.

Max Perkins tells me you have sold "Gatsby" to the movies. It ought to make a great picture and it would be a knock-out if they got Rennie to play in it.

Speaking of pictures, I rewrote a lousy baseball-Florida real estate story for Tom Meighan, some one else having written it first, and I also wrote the titles after seeing the uncut film. When the picture came out, it was a complete surprise to me and one of the worst pictures I ever saw. But it seems to be going all right and I am told that it compares very favorably with most of Tom's recent releases.

I can't remember when I wrote to you last, so I may be telling you old stuff. (Stop me if you have heard this one). Ellis and I toured California with the Grantland Rices and their daughter. I'd have had a much better time in Hollywood if I'd been drinking. Anyway, Charlie Chaplin had us out to dinner and was more or less amusing and we met all the nuts.

Gene and Helen spent six weeks in Palm Beach while Gene was working on Ziegfeld's "Palm Beach Nights," a girl show which Flo put on down there with somebody else's money and which proved a dismal flop. However, Gene and

---

[1] From 1919 through 1941, Edward J. O'Brien annually edited a volume of of the year's best short stories, with an index in which one, two, or three asterisks were prefixed to the titles to indicate distinction. Three asterisks meant that the story was listed in the "Roll of Honor."

Jimmy Hanley had a good song in it— "No Foolin'" —and I think he (Gene] will make some money out of the song. He has bought a Lincoln "town car," but the old homestead is still on the market. I suggest that you two take it off his hands when you come back. Anyway, I insist on your living somewhere in Great Neck. You have no idea how I miss you, Zelda, not you, Scott.

Tom and Peggy Boyd are expected in New York soon and will be invited out here to dinner.

Burton and Hazel are also threatening to visit us. I think Burton is doing pretty well, writing a daily syndicate letter for Johnson Features and also acting as editor for the concern's other features.

Harry Hansen has quit the Chicago News and taken Laurence Stallings' place on the World.

Max Perkins gave me your address over the telephone and I hope I got it approximately right.

Write and tell me your plans. If you want me to be looking up a house in Great Neck, let me know and I'll be glad to serve.

I went on the wagon April 18, theoretically for a year, but I might get a week off when you come back.

Gil Boag

The following letter is to Bob Davis, a well-known writer and photographer of the 1920s, who had just published *Ruby Robert*, a book on Bob Fitzsimmons, former heavyweight boxing champion:

Great Neck, New York
June 15, 1926.

Dear Bob:—

Though the defeat of Corbett in 1897 broke my young heart, I was always interested in his conqueror, curious about his offstage personality, character, habits, etc. Fitz, it seemed to me, must have been one of the most diverting of the champs, but until you came across with "Ruby Robert" there was no first hand dope on him available. It's an entertaining, readable book, Mr. Davis and fills a l.f.w.
Sincerely,<br>Ring W. Lardner

Between you and me, Bob, I was intrigued by some of the disagreements as to fact between your book and Corbett's "The Roar of the Crowd." I copied off a few for G. Rice, who said he might use them in his column. If he does, it won't hurt the sale of either book.

# Years of Adversity
## 1926–1933

In the summer of 1926, Lardner discovered during a routine checkup that he had tuberculosis, the disease that, coupled with his alcoholism, was gradually to destroy his health in the following years. Characteristically, Lardner kept this news as much as possible to himself and did not mention it in his letters.

The following letter to Ellis's older sister indicates clearly Lardner's disgust with the outcome of the 1926 Dempsey-Tunney fight, which Tunney had won by a judges' decision. Though Lardner was not alone in suspecting that the fight was fixed, the allegation has never been proved. Lardner knew Dempsey and had bet heavily on him.

Great Neck, New York
October fourth. [1926]

Dear Rube:—

I have never talked on a radio and it is my ambition to keep that record spotless.

I don't know how much of my story got into your paper. About a third of it missed the New York World and most of the other papers because of wire trouble. However, the readers are probably just as well off.

None of us could write what we (Eighty percent of us, at least) really thought—that the fight was "one of those things"; a paper printing such a story would lay itself open to a libel suit, and about the only way a boxing match can be proved a fake is to have one of the parties confess. I don't blame Jack much—He needed money; he figured everybody was trying to fleece him; if he won, there was no other fight in sight, and whatever he got for "laying down" was money that the income tax collectors won't know anything about.

Otherwise, everybody here is well. The absent John is evidently homesick and I think Ellis will have to pay him a visit. Love to Robin and the kids.
R.W.L.

In the following letter, Lardner corrects Burton Rascoe's account of how Lardner's busher stories were first accepted by the *Post*:

Great Neck, New York
October 7, 1926.

Dear Burton:—
    It isn't often I care what the boys and girls say about me in print,
    (Author's note: That's a dirty lie!)
                        but honestly, Burton, that stuff you wrote under date of October 2, well, you must have got the information from Willie Stevens.[1] The first "busher" story was never sent back by the Post; it was accepted promptly by Mr. Lorimer himself. I didn't show it to Hugh Fullerton or Charlie Van Loan first; I sent it to Mr. Lorimer at the Post's office, not to his residence; I didn't write "Personal" on the envelope in even one place; I didn't write any preliminary, special delivery, warning letter to Mr. Lorimer; no sub-editor ever asked me to correct the spelling and grammar, and I never sent any sub-editor or anyone else a bundle of letters I had received from ball players. Otherwise—
    Ellis' mother died in July and we have had a quiet summer. But we do want you and Hazel to come out some time. Love to her.
                        R.W.L.

The following letter is perhaps most remarkable for its tone of boredom and cynicism. Outside baseball, Lardner had two passions in sports—Notre Dame and Jack Dempsey, both of whom he regarded as representatives of the midwest. The bitterness of the assertion that Dempsey had thrown his first championship fight with Tunney is intensified by the stoical comment at the beginning of the letter that "nothing happens." The tone may also reflect Lardner's awareness that he was ill. For that reason and because he was tired of writing his weekly Bell Syndicate column, he gave up the column in March of the following year to concentrate on magazine pieces, short stories, and plays.

---

[1] Willie Stevens was an eccentric figure in the Hall–Mills murder case.

October 13, 1926.

Fitzgeralds one and all:—

I have said to myself a hundred times, "Ring, you just must write to those sweet Fitzgeralds," and then I have added (to myself, mind you), "Better wait, perhaps, until there is something to write about." But the days come and the days go and nothing happens—nothing may ever happen. Best not delay any longer.

Very, very glad to hear you are returning soon to God's Country and the Woman. Don't you dare live anywhere but Great Neck, but if I were you, I'd rent awhile before I thought of buying. If you want me to, I will be on the lookout for a suitable furnished house.

Ellis had two babies this summer. They are both girls, giving us two girls and four boys, an ideal combination, we think.

On a party with the Rices, at the Sidney Fishes'[1] in East Hampton, we ran into Esther Murphy and her father and mother. I had an interesting talk with Miss Murphy (Interesting to me, mind you).

The Ziegfeld show (Gene's) didn't do well in New York, but is going better (they say) on the road.

I was in deadly earnest when I said I liked "The Peasants." I knew damn well it would be over your head (Not yours, Zelda).

May Preston reports that she saw you (not you, Zelda) on your way to the hospital, in Paris, and that you were carrying a bouquet of corsets to give your wife.

I enclose a copy (nearly complete) of the story I wrote about the "fight" in Philadelphia. Heywood Broun refused, at the last moment, to cover it and as a favor to Herbert, and to my syndicate, I said I would do it. We had terrible wire trouble on account of the rain and only about half my story got into the World. It broke off (the story) in such a manner that people must have said to themselves that I was very drunk. It made me so mad that I am going to quit newspapers as soon as the last of my present contracts expires, which will be in six months. After that I am going to try to work half as hard and make the same amount of money, a feat which I believe can be done. I bet $500 on Dempsey, giving 2 to 1. The odds ought to have been 7 to 1. Tunney couldn't lick David if David was trying. The thing was a very well done fake, which lots of us would like to say in print, but you know what newspapers are where possible libel suits are concerned. As usual, I did my heavy

---

[1] Sidney Fish was a prominent attorney from an old New York family.

thinking too late; otherwise I would have bet the other way. The championship wasn't worth a dime to Jack; there was nobody else for him to fight and he had made all there was to be made (by him) out of vaudeville and pictures. The average odds were 3 to 1 and the money he made by losing was money that the income tax collectors will know nothing about.

You ought to meet this guy Tunney. We had lunch with him a few weeks before the fight and among a great many other things, he said he thought the New York State boxing commission was "imbecilic" and that he hoped Dempsey would not think his (Tunney's) experience in pictures had "cosmeticized" him.

I think now (if you care what I think) that the Gibbons–Tunney fight was fixed and that the Dempsey–Gibbons fight was fixed, to let Gibbons stay, and that it was all leading up to this climax—to gave the public a popular war hero for champion. Well, he's about as popular as my plays.

We have just had a world's series that neither club had any right to be in, let alone win, and that is all I will say about sports, excepting that Heywood, who has become quite a Negrophile, wrote column after column on the fistic prowess of Harry Wills and the dread that he was held in by Dempsey et al. and how unfair it was not to give Harry a chance, and—Well, last night Wills deliberately fouled Jack Sharkey in the 13th round after Sharkey (who isn't even as good as Tunney) had beaten the life out of him from the very beginning.

I have been on the wagon since early in July, when Ellis' mother died. Before that I had a spree that broke a few records for longevity and dullness.

A couple of months ago, the Metro-Goldwyn people asked me to write a baseball picture for Karl Dane, the man who made such a hit as "Slim," one of the doughboys in "The Big Parade." We talked matters over several times and finally the man asked me how much I would want. I told him I didn't know what authors were getting. He said, "Well, we are giving Johnnie Weaver $7,500 and Marc Connelly the same," so he asked me again what I wanted and I said $40,000 and he threw up his hands and exclaimed, "Excuse me, Mr. Lardner, for wasting your *valuable* time!" Maybe I told you that before; I have no idea how long ago it was I wrote to you.

It may not be very lively for you, but why not come and stay with us awhile before or after you go to Montgomery.

Keep me posted on your plans and accept the undying love of the madam and

I.

When Rascoe informed Lardner that he had published a correction of his earlier story, Lardner replied:

Great Neck, New York
October 29, 1926

Dear Burton: —
The clipping bureau[1] hasn't come across with the second story, but probably will in its own good time. However, so long as you made the correction, it doesn't matter. I don't like to have the impression spread, more than it has, that it is hard for new writers to break in, when the fact is, as you know, that editors are tickled to death to get anything printable, even if it is written by a day-old child. The false impression impels countless young writers to send their stuff to veteran writers with the request that they (the vets) use their "influence" with editors to have it read, approved and published.

What I probably told you was that I talked over the idea of the busher letters with Charlie Van Loan, and that he liked it and said he would write to Lorimer to be on the look-out for the first batch. That was when he was merely a Post author; long before he was an ascociate editor or scout.

Are you reading Stagg's[2] memoirs? I wish he had written them himself.
                                    R.W.L.

The following fragment of a letter to the Fitzgeralds, containing the news of the Chaplin–Davies–Hearst scandal, was probably written shortly before 10 December 1926, when the Fitzgeralds returned to the United States, after two and a half years abroad:

Great Neck, New York

Anyway, the "low down" as Gene calls it is that Hearst found out that Chaplin was giving Marion the "run around" as Gene calls it and Hearst closed the Davies studio

---

[1] Paradoxically, though Lardner did not keep copies of his work, he did from the early twenties subscribe to a clipping service. The clippings that he regularly received have now been donated to the Newberry Library by Ring Lardner Jr.

[2] Amos Alonzo Stagg was the famous coach of the University of Chicago football team. He had a high opinion of Lardner as a football reporter, and Lardner respected him as a coach.

and leased the Cosmopolitan theater, where Marion's releases were wont to be released, to Ziegfeld because he, Hearst, had been given the "air" as Gene calls it by Marion, and he also ordered his papers to cease mentioning her name. And poor old W.R. as Gene calls him is alone on his ranch in California and doesn't dare come to New York because Fallon is laying for him to serve papers in a libel suit and Fallon is the boy who has the birth certificates of the W.R.–Marion offspring. Chaplin and Marion are, of course, obliged to live out of wedlock as I call it on account of the new Mrs. Chaplin who certainly made a monkey out of Charley. "With all his money, there's two things W.R. can't buy—One is Marion's love and the other is Bill Fallon. There's one square fella (Fallon) and he can't be bought!" (Well, Zelda, you know yourself what a nice, straight, clean-cut, decent fella Fallon must be. But a Catholic.) "W.R. wanted the worst way to marry Marion, but Mrs. Hearst wouldn't divorce him. She was too smart, see? She was too smart. Mrs. Hearst was too smart. She wouldn't divorce him. She was too smart. And now Marion gets stuck on Chaplin and Chaplin gives her a $25,000 stone (diamond not gall) and W.R. hears about it. Can you imagine! Where is the damn fool Chaplin goin' to fit if the Hearst papers gets after him? Can you imagine! That's the low down."

I think you've stayed away long enough for all the scandal to blow over and if you'll come home I'll fall off the wagon for a week or as long as you think necessary.

There's a new paper in Great Neck—a tabloid affair called the News. Jack Hazzard runs a funny column on it; Funny ain't the word for it.

Here is some more "low down:" Some of the Algonquin bunch was sort of riding Michael Arlen, I don't know why. Anyway, when Edna Ferber was introduced to him, she said: "Why, Mr. Arlen, you look almost like a woman!" "So do you, Miss Ferber," was Michael's reply.

Mrs. Nell.

That Christmas, Ring sent some postcard verse to the Rices:

We haven't heard from you in three long years;
Christmas just comes, and Christmas disappears,
But little's came from you in Yuletides recent.
For God's sakes, sweet, start sending something decent!

Perkins, who realized that Lardner's mock autobiography, *The Story of a Wonder Man*, which Scribners was about to publish, was merely a potboiler, was pressing Lardner at this time to do a longer fictional work:

> I wish though, that for the next book of stories, we could have one long one, and the longer the better. I know that while you are writing for the Cosmopolitan, this is impossible for periodical use but couldn't you do one long one just for a book? If it were twenty or twenty-five thousand words, we would have something entirely new, and we could make ever so much of it, and we might be able to even get a financial return that would warrant the sacrifice of magazine publication.

When Lardner did not respond to the urging, Perkins tried again:

Jan. 18, 1927

Dear Ring:
    Why don't you write about the boy who believed the 'ads'; read up on all the highbrow stuff and tried it on the gals!!—And the boy who didn't.
                            Yours,

Great Neck, New York
January 19.

Dear Max:—
    That sounds like a good idea and I'll see some time what I can do with it. Thanks.
                            Sincerely,
                            R.W. L.

In the following letter to Burton Rascoe, Lardner refers to an article he had written at the request of John Siddall, editor of *American Magazine*. He refused to write the standard success story for which the magazine was famous. Instead, he wrote an account of his career as a songwriter. Siddall rejected the article.

Great Neck, New York
March 30, 1927.

Dear Burton: —
   The article was on "How I Won Success as a Song Writer" and I wrote it more to kid John Siddall than anything else. I destroyed it long ago.
   I am glad to hear you are going to have "The Bookman." I think it is just the spot for you and you ought to make it a wow, as the boys say.
   Love to Hazel.
                              Sincerely,
                              R.W.L.

   The following letter is addressed to "Mrs. Grantland Rice, East Hampton." Lardner had given up writing "Ring Lardner's Weekly Letter" for the Bell Syndicate at the end of March, and the Lardners vacationed in the summer of 1927 at Lake Placid, in hopes that the air would be beneficial to Lardner's health.

[Lake Placid, New York]
Sunday afternoon.
[25 July 1927]

Dear Mrs. Rice: —
   I enclose a note from your hero.
   Who should be in our car Friday night but Karl and Sylvia and two boys, one of them named Parsons, who looked like Fred Godwin and said he knew Floncey.[1] Sylvia's chin and eyes reminded me so much of Sharkey that I nearly fouled her.
   We spent Saturday with the Conways, meeting all the children and accessories. I played the piano to accompany Sylvia's violin and wish to state that her violin playing is at least as good as my piano playing. In plain words, it is excellent.
   Well, what I started to say was that on Friday afternoon, I had to go way downtown to buy an algebra book for John, and I came uptown on a bus. I sat on the roof and a lady sat down beside me. Her costume looked as if it had been cut out of a wash cloth. She said: "What time is it?" I said. "It is half past three." She said: "Oh, I thought you were a Mexican."

---

[1] Grantland and Kate Rice's daughter Florence.

> Conversations like that can never be explained.
> Tomorrow I am going under the knife. The doctor's name is Trembley, and so am I.
> Salami I Salute You.

The non-sequitur dialogue in the above letter is a beautiful example of human inattention to what others have to say, and it may have inspired "Dinner Bridge," another of Lardner's nonsense plays, which he wrote for a Dutch Treat show in 1927, and which Edmund Wilson published in *The New Republic*, to the chagrin of H.L. Mencken, who would have published it in *American Mercury*. When Mencken wrote to Lardner about it, Lardner replied:

August 2.

Dear Mencken:
The thing in "The New Republic" was written for the Dutch Treat show. Bunny Wilson wanted to print it so I gave it to him. Next time I have anything of the sort, I will think of you.
Meanwhile—
I'll pardon your calling the Comstockers "wowsers,"
But not your attiring yourself in red trousers.
Dr. Lardner

The following is the only surviving page of a letter Lardner wrote to the Fitzgeralds at Ellerslie, the old mansion outside Wilmington, Delaware, to which the Fitzgeralds had moved after an unhappy stay in Hollywood:

Sunday, Sept. 25.

Dear Sir and Madam:—
Our son Jimmie has joined our son John at Andover, and Jimmie is pretty homesick, so Ellis is going up there to spend next week-end with him. If she broke that engagement, he would die. So, you see, we can't visit you and we are both sorry. I hope you are, too.
If you care to know anything about my affairs, I had quite a wet summer, but have now been on the wagon since the 22nd. of August. During the dry intermissions, I wrote a

baseball play¹ which George Cohan accepted. He says he is going to put it on this fall, but you know these d—d producers. If he does, and if he should happen to try it out at Atlantic City, I'd expect the Fitzgeralds to be in attendance as a belated reward for the Lardners' sacrifice of time and money in 1924 or whatever year "The Vegetable" was staged.

I have written three short stories this month in an effort to ease the financial situation brought about by weeks of idleness and weeks of work on the play. To make that situation a little more desperate, the Pittsburgh ball club seems ready to lose the National League pennant and finish behind the Giants. Last spring I bet $800 to $2400 that Pittsburgh would win the pennant and $800 to $800 that it would beat out New York. A week ago, it looked as if I could begin spending my $3200 winnings, but now, with New York having all the best of the remaining schedule, I appear to be sunk.² To offset that, I am thinking of covering the world's series for Jack Wheeler. Two years ago I swore I would never work on another one, but when poverty . . . .

On 11 October, after visiting the Fitzgeralds, Perkins wrote expressing his fears to Lardner about Fitzgerald's health. Lardner replied:

Great Neck, New York
Thursday, Oct. 13, 1927

Dear Max:—
I am sorry to hear that Scott isn't well. I wouldn't recommend Muldoon's as a cure for nerves, especially Scott's kind of nerves. From what I have always heard, it is

---

[1] *Elmer the Great*, a three-act play, in collaboration with George M. Cohan, based on Lardner's story "Hurry Kane." The story of a baseball pitcher who, captivated by a chorus girl, momentarily agrees to throw a game (he later changes his mind), it was not to be a success. After opening in Boston and Chicago, with Walter Huston in the leading role, it ran for only forty performances at the Lyceum in the fall of 1928. Cohan and Lardner were ill-matched as co-authors, since Cohan was not sensitive to Lardner's subtle humor and deleted most of it, so that the play became a melodrama, and Elmer became the "honest-Abe" savior of the game. "Hurry Kane" is not one of Lardner's better stories, though it is indicative of his deepening pessimism towards baseball.

[2] Pittsburgh did win the pennant, by 1 1/2 games over St. Louis and 2 games over New York. The Pirates then proceeded to lose the Series in four straight games to the Yankees.

so strenuous that when a person is released, he is inclined to go on a bat to make up for it. I don't believe I have any influence over Scott, but I'll try to see him some time soon, either down there or here.

The play isn't finished. I have done it through the first time, but it is still to be torn to shreds by Cohan and done over again by him and me.

Cosmopolitan has enough stories, already printed or to be printed, to fill a book, but only about two of them are worth putting in a book. I'd rather wait until there are enough decent ones or until I've done something "different." If ever.

R.W.L.

GREATNECK NY
1927 OCT 14 AM 11 52
H L MENCKEN.
1524 HOLLINS ST BALTIMORE MD.
A PLAY CALLED OLD HONEY OPENS IN BALTIMORE NEXT MONDAY NIGHT FOR A WEEKS RUN THE AUTHOR SOPHIE TREADWELL[1] WOULD LIKE TO HAVE YOU SEE IT IF YOU WISH TO PLEASE WIRE ME WHAT NIGHT YOU CAN ATTEND AND SHE WILL MAIL YOU SOME TICKETS.

RING LARDNER.

Perkins next wrote to ask Lardner's permission to publish the play that Robert Sherwood had adapted from "The Love Nest." This play would not be a stage success; it would run only three weeks, beginning on 22 December 1927, though June Walker was to receive good reviews as the dipsomaniac wife. The play was faithful to the short story, with the exception of the resolution. In the play, Mrs. Gregg leaves her husband and elopes with the butler.

Great Neck, New York
December 17, 1927.

Dear Max:—
I honestly haven't the slightest objection to your publishing "The Love Nest."

Some time this winter I may write one decent short story and if I do, we can talk about a book for next fall.

---

[1] Sophie Treadwell was married to William McGeehan in San Francisco in 1910. She had a long and active career as a dramatist.

> I thought Hemingway's book was great and am glad it went, and is going, well. Also that Scott is in better shape.
> R.W.L.

At Christmastime, Lardner sent his annual postcard of printed verse to several of his friends, including H.L. Mencken and the Fitzgeralds:

[20 December 1927]

We combed Fifth Avenue this last month
A hundred times if we combed it onth,
In search of something we thought would do
To give to a person as nice as you.

We had no trouble selecting gifts
For the Ogden Armours and Louie Swifts,
The Otto Kahns and the George E. Bakers,
The Munns and the Rodman Wanamakers.[1]

It's a simple matter to pick things out
For people one isn't so wild about.
But you, you wonderful pal and friend, you!
We couldn't find anything fit to send you.
                   The Ring Lardners

Fitzgerald replied in kind the following Christmas:

> To the Ring Lardners
> You combed Third Avenue last year
>    For some small gift that was not too dear
> —Like a candy cane or a worn out truss—
>    To give to a loving friend like us
> You'd found gold eggs for such wealthy hicks
>    As the Edsell Fords and the Pittsburgh Fricks
> The Andy Mellons, the Teddy Shonts
>    The Coleman T. and Pierre duPonts[2]
> But not one gift to brighten our hoem
> —So I'm sending you back your God damn poem.

---

[1] All these people were prominent socialites in Chicago and New York.

[2] Fitzgerald is supplying his own list of prominent people, in response to Lardner's references.

Great Neck, New York
December 21. [1927]

Dear Scott and Zelda:—
 Thanks for your telegram, which arrived this morning. This ain't my play, though of course I will share in the receipts (There won't be many). I saw a dress rehearsal last night. Bob has done some very clever writing and the second act is quite strong, with June Walker great as a drunk. But I'm afraid most of it will be over peoples' heads. This, of course, is under your hat (to use a slang expression).
 Gene has another of those things, I fear.
 Scott, Lynne Overman[1] said he had written to you in regard to a dramatization of "The Jelly Bean" and you had named your terms. He wanted my advice as to whom to get to collaborate with him and I suggested that he get you yourself. His knowledge of stage tricks and your lines would make a good combination. He's a pretty good actor. He is about to appear in a Shubert musical, which he thinks is bad but will be successful, so there is no immediate hurry. However, he would like to hear from you. In care of the Lambs will get him.
 My thing with Cohan is supposed to go into rehearsal in February, but you never can tell. Walter Huston is to be our star. You will be notified in plenty of time for that opening and you've got to attend it.
 John and Jim are home from Andover. John "made" the Phillipian (the semi-weekly paper) board, being rated No. 1 among the contestants.
 I have been on the wagon since August 22 and haven't smoked since October 31. All I know about you is that a novel is near completion. What is its title and what is it about?
 And you, Zelda, my queel, are you as beautiful as customary?
 Write me a decent letter and tell me your news.
 Ellis sends love.
                    F. Farmer Fox.

The "thing with Cohan" was *Elmer the Great,* an unfortunate rewrite of "Hurry Kane" as a comedy. Had Cohan not removed most of Lardner's humor, the play might have been better, but no audience recalling the 1919 Black Sox Scandal

---

[1] Lynne Overman was a character actor in more than fifty films. He played in burlesque, in vaudeville, and as a minstrel man between dramatic engagements.

was going to take Elmer seriously as a baseball hero, no matter how dramatically Walter Huston might portray his transformation, because Elmer had originally agreed to throw a game.

The reference to abstinence from smoking recalls that Lardner apparently had almost as much difficulty avoiding smoking as he did drinking. On one occasion, Lardner prefaced his return from a trip with a telegram to Ellis: "I DON'T SMOKE," but when he arrived, he had a cigarette in hand.[1]

The following letter was written to Burton Rascoe probably in the spring of 1928:

Great Neck, New York
Thursday.

Dear Burton:—

Miss Feldmann had your notebook all wrapped up and ready to address when I got downstairs Monday, so I didn't have a chance to read it.

I think the French would be mystified by a translation of my book, but I have no objection to your sending a copy to whoever M. Galantiere is. If he is interested, he can take the matter up with Charley Scribner's boys.

We are leaving for Cleveland and points west Sunday evening, to be gone until the twenty-second. If I live through the trip, we'll be glad to see you in the city.

I still maintain that Great Neck is the proper place for you and Hazel to live. Also that you are criminally insane not to save the Day Book.[2]

R.W.L.

In the spring of 1928, the Lardners and the Grantland Rices bought adjoining tracts of land in East Hampton, about ninety miles east of Great Neck, where they built neighboring houses fronting on the ocean. The move reflected Lardner's desire to remove himself from the excessive social demands of Great Neck to a more peaceful location. Lardner called this new home "Still Pond"—"no more moving."[3] Associated with the move was a reduction of time spent in New York; a

---

[1] Elder, p. 199.

[2] Rascoe had written a syndicated column, "The Daybook of a New Yorker," from 1924 through early 1928.

[3] Elder, p. 306.

concentration on writing plays, songs, and stories instead of newspaper articles; and a confining, at first, of his socializing to a circle of such close friends as the Rices, the Percy Hammonds, the James Prestons,[1] and the John Wheelers.

At this time, Perkins began putting together a collection of 35 of Lardner's short stories, later to be titled *Round Up*, containing 16 new stories plus all the stories collected previously in *How to Write Short Stories* and *The Love Nest*. Most of the new stories had been written in the interval between his temporary retirement from newspaper work and his return to write for the New York *Morning Telegraph* in December 1928. *Round Up*, which was selected by the Literary Guild as one of its monthly offerings, had the aura of a contemporary classic and solidified Lardner's position as one of the outstanding fictionists of his day.

The new stories are mostly variations of earlier stories and themes, though they are more heavily satiric in their commentary on American life and character types. In "Contract," for instance, Lardner's voice is evident in Shelton's disgust about the "education complex" of bridge players:

> It's a conviction of most bridge players, and some golf players, that God sent them into the world to teach. At that, what they tell you isn't intended for your edification and future good. It's just a way of announcing "I'm smart and you're a lunkhead." And to my mind it's a revelation of bad manners and bad sportsmanship.

In "Nora," Hazlett, the writer of a musical comedy, endures the destruction of his play by a philistinic producer and his staff who change the Irish heroine's nationality because they have a Spanish actress idle under contract, and who rewrite the script to insert various tunes they have composed. These damning caricatures probably reflect Lardner's frustrations in theater ventures with Florenz Ziegfeld and George M. Cohan. Lardner's reaction must have been similar to Hazlett's:

---

[1] James Moore Preston was an artist and illustrator who made his first impact in the Armory Show of 1913. He had one-man shows in New York and London, as well as in East Hampton.

Hazlett said good-by to his producer and collaborators, went home by taxi and called up his bootlegger.

"Harry," he said, "what kind of whiskey have you got?"

"Well, Mr. Hazlett, I can sell you some good Scotch, but I ain't so sure of the rye. In fact, I'm kind of scared of it."

"How soon can you bring me a case?"

"Right off quick. It's the Scotch you want, ain't it?"

"No," said Hazlett. "I want the rye."

Among the better new stories is "I Can't Breathe," the often-anthologized diary of a predatory young female flirt, in which Lardner captures masterfully her adolescent hyperbole as she recounts her romances with four young men. Another is "Liberty Hall," about a writer of musicals who, with his sympathetic wife, must during a weekend in the country endure hosts who insist on imposing their tastes upon their visitors. Ben Drake is forced to drink coffee with cream; he must smoke a cigarette brand he dislikes; and he cannot play the piano because he is there for a rest. Drake finally resorts to faking a telegram calling him back to work. In contrast, "Ex Parte" deals with a marriage in which there is no real bond or understanding. The narrator is a bridegroom with conventional tastes, but his wife prefers Early American antiques. When they visit some friends living in a renovated barn, she admires their furnishings extravagantly, with the clear implication that she regards her groom's furnished house as vulgar and common. Her husband resentfully gets drunk on "Early American rye" and tries to "antique" their new house by applying a blowtorch and an axe to the dining room table. The "traffic policeman story" is "There Are Smiles," a rather sentimental treatment of a semi-literate, good-natured traffic cop who becomes infatuated with an attractive female speeder. Because the policeman's life and marriage lack direction and communication, the speeder, who is amused by his trite jokes, represents a romantic escape. When he reads of the woman's death in a traffic accident, the reader pities him in his wonderment: "I can't feel as bad as I think I do. I only seen her four or five times. I can't really feel this bad."

The best of the new stories is "The Maysville Minstrel," which also depicts the entrapped common man for whom escape is illusory. Stephen Gale is a small-town bookkeeper for the Maysville gas company who admires the poetry of Amy Lowell and Edgar A. Guest[1] and writes his own verse, on the order of the following "classic":

> The Lackawanna Railroad where does it go?
> It goes from Jersey City to Buffalo.
> Some of the trains stop at Maysville but they are few
> Most of them go right through
> Except the 8:22
> Going west but the 10:12 bound for Jersey City
> That is the train we like the best
> As it takes you to Jersey City
> Where you can take a ferry or tube for New York City.

Stephen quits his job because a water-heater salesman convinces him that he can sell his poems for a dollar a line, but eventually he realizes that he has been tricked and that he cannot escape from the mundane existence to which not only his poverty but his own natural limitations condemn him. Unlike "Haircut," this story entails no possibility for revenge. In the last line of the story, "Stephen realized there was nothing he could do about it." "The Maysville Minstrel" is at once the most poignant and the bleakest of Lardner's stories.

It is the projected preface for *Round Up* to which Lardner refers below:

East Hampton, Long Island
June 3.

Dear Max:—
 Sure I'll do a preface if you don't want it too soon. I am still trying to think of a title. I believe the traffic policeman story, which people seem to think is best, ought to have a good position.
                                    R.W.L.

East Hampton, Long Island
July 9, 1928.

Dear Burton:—
 I didn't do any work whatever between February and the first of June and as a result, I won't be able to catch up

---

[1] Lardner deplored equally the works of Lowell and Guest.

with myself for months. So will you please excuse me from the Almanack.

I hope that what I heard in Chicago (from Maude Evers Ellis or somebody) is true—that the Rascoe family struck oil and is growing filthy rich.

Love to Hazel.

The following letter is to Edward H. ("Ted") Coy, former Yale University fullback (1907-1909) and twice All-American (1908-1909). Coy, a New York stockbroker in August 1928, had just married his third wife, Lottie Bruhn, in El Paso, where they were probably still staying when Lardner wrote to him. During the 1912 baseball spring training season, when Lardner was traveling with the White Sox, the club had spent some time in El Paso.

12 East 86th Street
America's Pre-Eminent Apartment Hotel[1]
New York City
October 23, 1928.

Dear Ted:—

Your letter finally caught up with me here.

It is all right for Grant to send you his picture; he has looks. But I am not going to send you mine as the physical distress it would cause your wife might spoil the honeymoon. I will ship you a book as soon as I can get downtown and buy one. My madam does not allow them in the house.

You are living in my favorite town, but I hope you can tear away from it and come east soon so I can hear the piano played all night—and I'm on the wagon at that.

Sincerely,
Ring Lardner

In December 1928, Lardner for financial reasons returned briefly to newspaper work as a columnist on the New York *Morning Telegraph*, which had offered him $50,000 a year to write four articles a week on any subject he wished. However, the column, "Ring's Side," lasted only two months before the paper's financial problems forced a termination of the agreement.

The following letter was to Mrs. Mildred Luthy, the sister of Kate Hollis Rice (Mrs. Grantland Rice). Through the

---

[1] The New York Croydon.

Grantland Rices, the Lardners had come to know both Mrs. Luthy and Mrs. Elizabeth ("Myrt") Vereen, another of Kate Rice's sisters.

12 East 86th Street
New York City
January twelfth. [1929]

Dear Millie: —
    Granny has gone to Alabam' to shoot mules and Ellis and I have advised Kate to take the telephone receiver off the hook during his absence but she is a Hollis and stubborn.
    If you and Myrt are going to quarrel over my letters, there is only one thing I can do—use a carbon and send a copy of one letter to each of you. But please try to get hold of yourselves. I am quite nice, but not as nice as you think.
    You can't expect me not to sympathize with Jane over her attitude toward your absences from home. If you left me for an evening, I'd cry, too. In fact, I've cried every evening since September. And most mornings.
    Honestly I don't think you ought to treat Myrt the way you do in the matter of food. She is growing and building up tissue, and besides, she is by nature a great big eater. I recall one evening I took her and the Rices to the theater, and before the theater we went to dinner somewhere and I kind of hoped that inasmuch as I was paying for the theater tickets, Granny would settle for the meal, but as usual on such occasions, he was writing poetry when the check came, so it was brought to me, and it amounted to $24.00 of which the Rices and Ellis and I had eaten four and a half dollars' worth. You can't cut a woman like that down to a plate of beans in one day.
    I ought to have spent this whole day working and I guess it's just as well I am not on corresponding terms with Mrs. Hand, Mrs. Lanier and Mrs. Crisp.
                              Ringgold.

    A title for the collection of short stories was again a problem. The one chosen, *Round Up*, was Perkins' idea. Other titles considered were "Our Kind," "Some of Ours," "Such as We," and "Sorts and Conditions." Perkins anticipated the criticism that the title was "especially western" and argued that "it is now used about almost every sort of gathering together,—even that of crooks." In fact, the title is inappropriate, though its cowboy connotations may have enhanced sales. When Lardner offered a better title, it was too late:

NASSAU
1929 FEB. 9 PM 11 27

MAXWELL PERKINS=
  CHARLES SCRIBNERS SONS FIFTH AVE NEW-
YORK (NY)=
I PREFER ENSEMBLE TO ROUND UP DONT YOU.
       RING LARDNER.

In addition to printing 20,000 copies of *Round Up*, Scribner's also printed an additional 70,000 (with an alternate cover) for the Literary Guild, whose selection committee of Carl Van Doren, Hendrik Willem Van Loon, Elinor Wylie, Joseph Wood Krutch, and Burton Rascoe had chosen Lardner's book for one of the Guild monthly selections. The choice reflected Lardner's stature as a writer of fiction, and Perkins wrote to say: "We have never thought that you have had the sale your books are entitled to, and we are going to try to get it now, and to build for the future."

In fact, *Round Up* had a combined sale of over 80,000 copies in its first year, and Lardner's royalties for 1929 alone amounted to $11,873.21. His status was further assured by unanimously positive reviews. The *Times* review, by John Chamberlain, was typical: "'Round Up' gives the full measure of his talent—a talent that is mature and sure-footed." Lewis Mumford, in the New York *Herald Tribune*, asserted that "the short stories brought together in 'Round Up' must be counted among the few that will be readable twenty years hence."

The following letter, to a director of the Bread Loaf Conference, a writers' summer conference in upper New York state, reiterates Lardner's distaste for public speaking:

New York, New York
May 2, 1929.

Dear Mr. Davison:—
  I am sorry to say I cannot possibly come to the Bread loaf Conference this summer. It is not a question of money, but I am utterly incapable of talking, even to a small audience. It is something I tried years ago and "swore off."
              Sincerely,
              Ring Lardner

East Hampton, Long Island
June 19, 1929.

Dear Max:
I had a letter from Mr. Bennet,[1] whom (it seems) I met in Waco, Texas, years ago. He said he hadn't been able to peddle any of the "Round Up" stories to the talkie people. I am not tied up for movie rights and would be glad if Scribner's could sell some of the st ories.
"Show business" has kept me so busy that I haven't even considered the novelette. But show business is slow on financial returns and maybe I'll be asking you for some advance soon.
I haven't heard a word of Scott. Hasn't he ever finished the novel?[2]
Sincerely,
R.W.L.

After the great success of *Round Up*, Lardner turned again to drama and popular music. During much of 1929, he collaborated with George Kaufman on their play, *June Moon*, which was presented in the fall of 1929. It also was a great success, running for 273 performances in New York. The reviews wore favorable, and Burns Mantle included the play in his volume *Best Plays of 1929-30*. Two songs from the play, "June Moon" and "Montana Moon," also achieved some popularity.
Consequently, Perkins wrote:

I am delighted with the reviews of your play. Don't you think we ought to publish it?—if it's to be the success it looks like, we should for there should be sufficient sale, at least.
I have much better news about Scott. He is getting on well.

---

[1] Bennet was an agent to whom Perkins had given a copy of *Round Up*, in hopes of negotiating film adaptations with movie producers. The advent of talkies in this year seemed to offer considerable opportunity for the presentation of Lardner's fictional world.

[2] Fitzgerald had dropped the matricide novel on which he had been working for so long, in favor of "The Drunkard's Holiday," a new novel that by 1934 would evolve into *Tender Is the Night*.

During much of September 1929, Fitzgerald had worked hard on the new novel (though he would not finish it until 1934).

The stock market crash that ushered in the Great Depression of the 1930s began on October 24, though ominous price fluctuations of shares had occured during the previous week. On the 24th, heavy panic selling by small shareholders threatened to create a "no-bid" situation on the floor of the New York Stock Exchange. The following "black" Tuesday, an incredible 16,338,000 shares were dumped for pitifully low bids. A subsequent wave of bankruptcies and suicides signified that the economic joyride of the 1920s was over.

Curiously, in the surviving letters at least, Lardner does not allude immediately to this national economic disaster.

The Croydon
12 East 86th Street
New York City
December 31, 1929.

Dear Max:—
George Kaufman is trying to get a script into shape for publication, but it is such a mess now that it may take a little time.
Have you seen Scott since he came back, or is he back? I haven't heard a word from him.
Sincerely,
R.W.L.

The next letter was to Lardner's eldest son John, who was a freshman at Harvard:

The Croydon
12 East 86th-Street
New York City
January 17, 1930.

Dear John:—
You haven't written to me, but I am without pride and will write to you just the same. You are cordially invited to spend your off-week at the Croydon and your mother, the financier, encloses a check to pay for your trip and extraneous expenses. Please wire or write us what train you will come on, and if it is a train that stops at 125th. Street, get off there, informing us in your telegram or letter just where you are going to get off and when.
R.W.L.

New York, New York.
January 22, 1930.

Dear Scott:—

Mrs. Mabel Johns, a friend of mine (as who isn't?) will be in Paris in a month or so and she doesn't know a soul there. She will mail you this letter from wherever she happens to be at whatever time she wants to mail it, and your job is to reply to her in care of the American Express Company, tell her where she can find you, and then advise her where to go and what to see.

I hear from Max Perkins that your book is nearly finished. What are you calling it, the Encyclopedia Brittanica? (That seems to be spelled wrong).

I won't write any more because you owe me a letter. Love to Zelda.

R.W.L.

The following note appears at the bottom of the above letter:

> I certainly hope to meet you in Paris because Ring said you are *wonderful*.
> Mabel Johns.
> Will be in Paris about Mar. 20–Feb. 28.

The Croydon
12 East 86th Street
New York City.
February 27, 1930.

Dear Scott:—

I've forgotten who owes whom a letter. Anyway there is a girl (three or four years younger than I) who expects to be in Paris, at the Continental, on or about March 19—it is her first trip abroad and she asked me to pick on a friend or two in each port to look her up so she would not be entirely unacquainted. Her name is Mrs. Mabel A. Johns: she is divorced; I met her twenty years ago; she used to be from St. Louis, but now lives in Long Beach, California. If you and Zelda could call her up or write to her and give her part of a day, or night, you would put me in a fever of gratitude.

I hear (from Max Perkins) that your book is nearly done and (from Walter Winchell) that you have sold the serial rights to Liberty for an unheard of sum. I hope this is true and that you will see fit to pay us a visit soon.

"June Moon," the play I wrote with George Kaufman, will run about six more weeks here, I think; then will play

Philadelphia, Boston and perhaps Pittsburgh before folding up. It is still doing all right, but nearly everyone will have seen it in a little while. We have no kick coming; it opened in New York on Oct. 9 and, until the first of the year, broke all records for a non-musical show. We put out a second company, which played a week in Cleveland and is now in Cincinnati, after ten weeks in Chicago, where it did well. It will play a week each in Milwaukee, St. Louis and Kansas City and then go to the Coast. The notices, here and in the other towns, were grand. George and I worked on the play nearly all last spring and summer and when the New York opening was over, I went on a bat that lasted nearly three months and haven't been able to work since, so it's a good thing that the play paid dividends. I wish you had had George to collaborate with you on, or to direct, "The Vegetable," and not Sam Forrest, who, to me, is one of the mysteries of show business.

I'd like to hear first hand what your plans are and news of a personal nature; and I'm anxious to know all there is to tell about the premiere danseuse and her daughter, to both of whom I send love.

R.W.L.

Unlike the earlier George M. Cohan collaboration, Lardner's work with George Kaufman was a profitable venture by two compatible writers. The difference was that Kaufman understood Lardner's humor and satire. Lardner wrote most of the play, and Kaufman revised it mainly to provide a stronger dramatic structure. Lardner's finances were improved considerably by the successes of *Round Up* and *June Moon*—a fortunate development, because he became increasingly ill in 1930 and spent considerable time in hospitals for treatment of tuberculosis and heart trouble.

The following letter must have been written on older stationery, because the move to East Hampton had occurred over two years previously. Rascoe was interested in publishing one of Lardner's "nonsense" plays. Lardner's reply indicates that he seems not even to have kept copies of his books!

Great Neck, New York
July 25, 1930.

Dear Burton:—

You are welcome to I Gaspiri (if Scribner's says so). I think it was in a book called "What Of It?" and I have no copy.

R.W.L.

Letters to Lardner's sons occur more frequently now. In the fall of 1930, when the Depression was adversely affecting so many other people, the Lardners were still enjoying the benefits of a highly successful book and a play in the previous year. After his freshman year at Harvard, John had persuaded his parents to allow him to go to France that fall, to study French at the Sorbonne, because he felt a knowledge of the language would further his newspaper career.[1]

Jim and Ring Jr. ("Bill") were now both at the Phillips Academy, a preparatory school located in Andover, Massachusetts. David had been enrolled (as a boarder) in the seventh grade at the Riverdale Country School in upper New York City.

Sunday, September 28.

Dear Jim: —
　　I am afraid you will have to wait years for your share of the royalties. The producers say that times are too hard to risk an expensive musical play. It is just possible that the real reason for their shyness is that they don't appreciate what we have written.
　　John is going to Philadelphia for the first two games (at least) of the world's series, and he sails for France on the 17th of October, aboard The France itself. It seems to me you have a very tough schedule and I don't see how you are going to have time for the Phillipian, football and sleep.
　　I subscribed for the Phillipian, but told King Howard not to start sending it until we know where we will live this fall and winter.
　　You might as well reserve two rooms (if you can) for commencement. Your mother will write to you in detail about it.
　　Let me know if you and Bill fail to receive The New Yorker, and write again soon.
　　　　　　　　　　　　　　Buddy Beale.

Later that fall, Lardner wrote to John in Paris:[2]

　　The thing that took me to Boston and gave me a chance to visit Andover, and the Kitchells at South Byfield, was a

---

[1] Ring Lardner Jr., p. 199.

[2] Elder, pp. 265-67. Fortunately, Donald Elder quotes extensively from this otherwise unlocated letter. The words in brackets are Elder's.

summons from Ziegfeld to "help out" with the lyrics of the Marilyn Miller–Astaires show, "Smiles." While the company was still in rehearsal here in New York, the Astaires threatened to walk out because they didn't have a single song together and demanded two. I wrote them two, to Vincent Youmans' music, for a flat price, and thereby got myself into a world of trouble because one of the two was so very comical that, on opening night in Boston, it stopped the show. This was too much for Marilyn's temperament and she told Ziegfeld she would walk out unless I wrote her a comical one (she being as well equipped to sing a "funny" as Miss Feldmann). Ziegfeld called me up from Boston and asked me to come there and write a song for Marilyn and rewrite three other lyrics that were not so good. I, knowing him well, asked for an unheard of advance royalty. He accepted my terms and I went to Boston and wrote eight songs instead of four, and have written two more since I came home (Youmans singing me his tunes over the long distance telephone). Your knowledge of mathematics will tell you that I have written twelve songs altogether (three of them purely production numbers), but there isn't a chance that more than seven of them will be used because there won't be room for even that many. My work in Boston was rendered quite feverish owing to the fact that it was next to impossible to get Youmans (who was quarreling with Ziegfeld) out of bed and to the piano.

The book of the show, by William Anthony McGuire, was unbelievably terrible as I saw it in Boston, but it may be better when it opens here next Tuesday night. I will send you my songs when, and if, they are published.

[The book of the show concerned four American Army buddies who adopt a French orphan girl and bring her back to the United States where she is brought up as a Salvation Army lassie.]

. . . Paul [Lannin] resigned his job as musical director at Youmans' suggestion (everybody knew there was something the matter with the show and picked on Paul, who was not at fault) but I gather from latest reports that he is reinstated and that some of the quarrels have been patched up. The real trouble is the book and the fact that the three stars are cutting one another's throats and each trying to help him- or herself instead of the production. For example, the best of my contributions, a duet and ensemble for the opening of the first act, will be left out through the protests of Fred Astaire—the number calls for the presence of some Park Avenue women in evening dress and he doesn't want anybody to appear dressed up before his own entrance.

All and all my trip to Boston was kind of wearing, but I wouldn't have missed it because it was so ludicrous. I got two hours of sleep out of each twenty-four and spent the rest of the time coaching Youmans to the piano. One morning when I was retiring at four o'clock, Harland Dixon, who was directing some of the dances, came into my room and said, "I'm drunk and I'm going to tell you some tragic incidents in my life, though I know I'll regret it tomorrow. "I said, " I know I will, too," but that didn't stop him and he went on relating tragic incidents until suddenly I had a bright idea— I drank some paraldehyde and went to sleep with him still standing there with his incidents.

Hotel Elysée
New York City
Sunday, November ninth.

[To Jeannette Abbott Kitchell]
Dear Jane:—
  This is a belated bread and butter (or rather, chicken and jello) note. Thanks for the only meal I had in New England. And please tell Kitch that the three-lettered Cornell man I tried to think of was Kaw.
  It would take me years to relate the incredible things that happened after I got back to Boston, and since I have got home. Here is the barest synopsis: I finished the "happy" lyric on the train from Newburyport. It was acceptable (though terrible). Then Flo, on Sunday evening, told me what I and everyone else had been telling him for weeks— that Marilyn's first dance with Fred (to the tune of "Young Man of Manhattan") took her entirely out of her character and, besides, was too hot for her. I must get together with Vince and write a "light" duet that would give the pair a chance to do a dance that she *could* do. Also, I must get Vince to write a tune to which I could set a lyric, a "smart" lyric, with which to open the first act, in place of that remarkable "East River Flows" number where the girls appeared with tail feathers or something. Vince was still in his room, where he had been since Friday, in pajamas. From seven till ten Sunday evening, I struggled to get him at the piano, and the instant I got him there, an explosion in a cleaning and dyeing establishment across LaGrange Street, right outside his window, knocked both of us off our chairs. Before we could get to the window to see what had happened, the dyeing establishment was a mass of flames. We had a beautiful place from which to watch a big fire, and of course there was no hope of getting back to work till it was all over. Vince got statistical and counted over thirty pieces of fire apparatus. It was cold leaning out the window and I had to be his nurse and force a bathrobe and overcoat on him.

After midnight, I succeeded in interesting him in music and was about to accomplish something when several girls and the nutty dance director came in and made it a party. I gave up at two o'clock and went to my room and to bed.

On Monday I made him get up before noon and dress. Then he went to the theater and rearranged the first act finale. Flo told me to forget the duet for Marilyn and Fred and concentrate on the opening. I wrote a lyric that would go to the old "Bambatina" rhythm and tried to make the lyric good enough so that the tune wouldn't matter. Between five and nine I got a tune out of Vince; then I went to the show. Paul Lannin had forgotten the rearrangement of the first act finale. The curtain came down on confusion and I went back stage and found the three stars in hysterics. Flo naturally called Vince up about Paul's mistake and Vince made Paul write a letter of resignation for his own (Paul's) sake, so Vince said. I don't know yet whether Vince was double-crossing Paul. Anyway I felt kind of low about Paul and decided to take some paraldehyde to make me sleep (it works instantly). I asked a boy to get me some orange juice to mix with the paraldehyde, which is terrible tasting stuff. There was a knock at my door and I said, "Come in," thinking it was the boy with the orange juice. Instead, it was the dance director with a confidential, weeping jag. He said: "I'm going to tell you some tragic incidents in my life, and tomorrow I know I'll be sorry I told them to you." I said: "I know I will, too," but that didn't stop him and he went on for an hour. The boy came with the orange juice and I got into bed and drank the paraldehyde and fell asleep with the dance director still telling me tragic incidents.

    I wrote another lyric Tuesday and finally got out of town Tuesday midnight. I had been home less than three hours when Flo called up from Boston and said he wanted the Fred–Marilyn duet after all. Fortunately Vince had an old tune in his New York office and I got it. Flo called up again at half past one Thursday morning. I was asleep and Ellis refused to arouse me. He asked her if she would allow me to come back to Boston. She said I wasn't feeling so good, but maybe I would come if it was necessary. He called me up Thursday forenoon and said Marilyn was going to quit the show unless she got a song to sing in place of "Carry On, Keep Smiling." Would I write a lyric? I said, yes, but I must have a tune. Flo said Vince was mailing me a tune. The tune didn't come and Flo asked me to come up to Boston and make Vince write it. I got reservations on the five o'clock Saturday afternoon train, but at noon Saturday, Vince called up (from Boston, of course) and sang me the tune, with some dummy words. I stayed here and did the best I could with it and mailed it to Flo last night. He has mercifully let me alone today, but I have a hunch I'll be back in Boston for a few hours later in the week.

And did I tell you that Fred Astaire pouted over my opening ensemble idea because it required the presence of some Park Avenue women on one side of the stage and he didn't want anybody to appear dressed up before his entrance? And I wrote a lyric for Eddie Foy to sing in place of that dismal thing the girl sings in front of the curtain just ahead of the marvelous bedroom scene. I have written eleven numbers instead of the six I was asked [to] write, and they can't possibly get more than seven of them in, and I have written you the longest letter (about tragic incidents in my life) I ever wrote to any Abbott girl excepting Ellis.
Love to the boys, who seem quite nice.
A Refugee.

The two letters above are ominous for their references to Lardner's taking of paraldehyde to overcome the insomnia that increasingly troubled him during his last years. Also portentous is an observation by Ellis in a letter she wrote to John on 14 December 1930 while John was still in Paris: "Dad is not very well. I get so discouraged about him. He is eating and trying to take care of himself but the results are not what they should be."

New York
February 11, 1931

[To H. L. Mencken]
Gent:
It is too late to congratulate you on your wedding, so let's just forget all about it.
When I was in my nonage I "went with" a Jewish girl. Now she is writing verse and will probably send you some. Will you please read it? I read it myself and know just as much about poetry as I did before.
Sincerely,
Ring Lardner.
Her name is Ethel Miriam Pick.

Tuberculosis, heart trouble, and alcoholism were by early 1931 depleting Lardner's physical and creative energies:

The Vanderbilt Hotel
Thirty-Fourth Street East at Park Avenue
New York
February 13, 1931.

Dear Max: —
 My health hasn't been so good. I guess I am paying for my past—and I'm not averaging more than four short stories a year. None of the recent ones has been anything to boast of and I'm afraid there won't be enough decent ones to print by fall. Maybe I'll get more energetic or inspired or something in the next few months.
 This is just a temporary address. You can always reach me in care of the Bell Syndicate, 63 Park Row.
Sincerely,<br>Ring Lardner

That February, after returning from their usual Florida vacation with the Rices, Lardner agreed in spite of his declining health to do a short daily Bell Syndicate piece, in association with the Chicago *Tribune* and the New York *Daily News* (circulated by wire service), titled "A Night Letter from Ring Lardner;" for $750 a week. It was an unsuccessful effort and was terminated in April. In addition to his illness, Lardner was laboring under the difficulties of not being up to date on current events and of trying to be funny in the darker days of the Depression.

 He began writing the "Night Letter" from his and Ellis's suite at the Vanderbilt Hotel, to which they had been forced by a severe Atlantic storm that had washed away nearly two hundred feet of beach and seriously damaged the foundation of their East Hampton house. A few weeks later, Ellis wrote describing the damage to John in Paris:

> There is some malign power that keeps me from writing to you. This time it took shape as the Atlantic ocean which rose up in two terrific storms and washed away practically all of our dune leaving over half the house hanging out over the ocean and taking most of the basement foundation out to feed the fishes. We had props put under her but she will either have to be moved at great expense or left to float out to sea.

In New York                          The Vanderbilt Hotel
3 am. Sunday, Feb. 15, 1931          Park Avenue at Thirty-fourth
8 am. the same day in Paris          Street
                                     New York

Dear John—
Keep a hold of this letter
For fear you won't get anything better.
It is written in the "wee small" hours of the morning
Without an instant's warning;
I just suddenly took a notion,
Having sworn off the nightly self-administration of
 a sleeping potion,
To get out of bed and use my Underwood portable
Rather than go out and walk the streets and perhaps
 court a belle.
We are back from the South and stopping at the
 Hotel Vnde–b—t,
A place that some goose or gander built.
The food here would annoy you and pain you
More than that procurable at the Pennsylvania,
And my opinion, which is seldom wrong,
Is that we won't be stopping here long.
If you should care to write us, through a sense of
 duty or pity,
Address us in care of the Bell Syndicate, 63 Park
 Row, N.Y. City,
Which, in association with the Chicago Tribune and
 New York Daily News,
Both of whom have plenty of money to lose,
Has engaged me to write a daily wire a la Will Rogers,
Designed to entertain young folks and old codgers.
I am supposed to write a hundred words or less per day
On timely topics, at very fair pay,
Though you are safe in betting
That I am not getting as much as Mr. Rogers is getting;
However, it keeps the wolf from the door
And while I may not be getting so much now, some day
 I might be getting more.
The reason I accepted this position
Was that my food was not giving me proper nutrition
And I seemed to lack the strength
To write short stories or plays or other works of
 any length.
When I am feeling fit again and everything is nice
 and tidy,
I intend to write the book of a musical show with a
 brand new idea.
A while ago I received a letter from a young man who,
 I am sure,

Had recently seen my own elegant signature,
And some time last autumn, ere the leaves were off
   the limb,
You had written my autograph and sent it to him;
He sent this autograph back and said he didn't
   want it;
By the vicious words of his accompanying letter I am
   still grieved and haunted.
David and your mother are in the next room,
Sleeping soundly, I trust, through the inexorable gloom.
The little one came in from school yesterday to meet us
And greet us with an advanced case of tonsilitis.
His throat is so sore that it irks him to swallow,
And if the ailment were to continue eight or ten years,
   his insides would become hollow.
Yesterday afternoon, your mother and I went to a matinee:
"America's Sweetheart," the new Fields, Rodgers and
   Hart musical play.
Gus Shy, John Sheehan, Jeanne Aubert and Inez Courtney
   are in it
And some of the songs are pretty enough to take home
   and play on your spinnet;
In fact, it is the best Rodgers score I have heard
   for a long time
And I'll send you the three best numbers when I
   think it is song time.
I thought you very deftly and wittily
Described your visit to s——y Italy.
This spring, if you have another holiday,
I wish you would spend it in Montpellier
Where my mother's niece Amy Serre
Lived unless she has moved from there.
She is a widow about seventy and has a daughter
Who grew old before a suitor caught her.
But they are nice and the daughter is a musician
Who prefers playing the pianoforte to going fishing.
I shall find out whether they're still there, yes or no;
Meanwhile, you inform me whether you'd like to go.
At Miami Beach, I saw very
Much of Paul Waner and Max Carey.
Paul is holding out for a larger salary
And poor Max is about through playing for a baseball
   gallery.
He is a free agent and would make a swell coach;
Barney Dreyfuss would keep him if he (Barney) were not
   a roach.
"June Moon" closed in Boston a week ago
After making quite a lot of money for such a small show.
I still think they were rather silly

To let it play four weeks in Philly,
But we beat Holiday records in Detroit,
Greatly to the stockholders' delight.
My experience with "Smiles" is too funny and too long
    to put in a letter;
When I see you I can tell you better.
And now when you think it isn't too much bother,
You might write a letter to sincerely your father.

In spite of his distaste for Florenz Ziegfeld, Lardner had written several lyrics for Marilyn Miller and Fred and Adele Astaire, six of which finally remained in the show *Smiles.* But this activity too was cut short by his doctor's recommendation that Lardner spend some time at the Desert Sanitarium in Tucson, Arizona. Ellis had to stay in New York, to oversee the moving and repair of the East Hampton house.

The Vanderbilt Hotel
New York
Feb. 23. [1931]

[To James Lardner]
Son whom I esteem nearly the best:
I am about to venture into the far-flung West;
They are about to turn your father loose on
The desert in Arizona near Tucson,
In the hope that he will regain that manly vigor
So noticeable in the liver-lipped nigger
Beloved by Shakespeare's heroine, Desdemona.
My address will be the Desert Sanitarium, Tucson, Arizona;
Not that that makes any difference to you.
I might as well be in Timbuctoo
So far as is concerned the reading of your letters,
Which are probably written to those you consider my
    betters.
As you may have heard from the mouths of birds,
I am now writing a daily sixty or seventy words
(A sort of Will Rogers message it is,
Though doubtless not as good as his);
It appears in papers from Portland to Austin,
And I think the Globe carries it in Boston;
At least, the Globe has always bought my stuff,
Throwing the Post and Herald into a rip-roaring huff.
Speaking of rip, has Dartmouth accepted you
Or have you changed your "mind" and decided on the
    Blue?
David cane home last week with an attack of tonsilitis.

Even milk was hard to swallow, and you know how tough
    meat is.
His sore throat is now nearly gone;
The only time it hurts is when he has to yawn.
The only time he yawns is when anyone speaks French
    around the house,
Which, as you can readily fathom, makes me quiet as a
    louse.
It is now time to superintend the packing of my trunk;
It will be a big job owing to my last-minute decision to
    take along a skunk.
Write soon and often to the Desert Sanitarium, Tucson,
    Arizona,
And if I ever wake up in the night particularly lonesome,
    I will phone you.
      Father in Heaven.

The Desert Sanitorium
Tucson, Arizona
March 6, 1931.

[To Ring Lardner Jr.]
Bravado:—

 A telegram from you and Jim, congratulating me on my twentieth birthday, iust arrived. I congratulate you for remembering the date; also for being chosen in the upper bracket of the Means contest.
 I hope your essay
 Is not too messay.
 There was a night letter from your mother, too, telling me about our houseboat in East Hampton and hinting that she was going to Andover to hear your oration. I wish I might hear it, but as I can't, you would please me by writing about it or sending me a Phillipian containing a report of same.
 This joint is 2,500 feet up in the air and surrounded by mountains that are close to a mile high. It is in the middle of the desert and has queer flora and fauna. Among the latter are coyotes and the funniest looking rabbits I ever saw. The full grown ones are as big as ponies and have ears that are at least half a foot long. They say that one of the female patients saw one and thought it was a deer.
 I received a letter from an inmate of the Arizona state prison, saying he had met me several times when he was one of the hangers-on of Jack Dempsey and Jack Kearns years ago. All he wants now is money with which to buy himself an artificial leg. I could better afford to give him one of my own.

On the train coming down, a Dartmouth alumnus introduced himself and when I told him one of my sons was probably going there next year, he said, "There's no place like it," which I don't doubt a bit.
Write soon and often and keep out of the infirmary.
Uncle Henry.

The Desert Sanatorium
Tucson, Arizona

Dear Jim or his brother: —
The spouse of your mother
Thanks you for the books,
Which, to iudge from their looks,
Will furnish qood reading,
A thing I've been needing.

The following letter is to Mrs. Mildred Luthy:

[The Desert Sanatorium
Tucson, Arizona]
Wednesday, March 11 [1931]

Dear Millie: —
You are a nice girl to take time from your gardening and your games with Jane to write to me. Most of the letters I get are from lawyers or income tax agents who seem to think I am a born embezzler. Yours (your letters, I mean) take the curse off the others.
You had better not offer your services as nurse unless you are in earnest. I would give a fabulous sum (if I had it) for one like you, even though I know you would try to force those funny drinks on me. The nurses here are a hard-boiled lot and evidently selected for their ugliness. There is only one pretty one and she, strange to say, is from Georgia. Stranger to say, she is incompetent.
Something tells me I am not going to linger here long. The doctors know their business and the weather is perfect, but the Lord didn't intend me for sanatorium life two thousand miles from home. What I'd like and hope to find is a suitable place within easy telephoning and visiting distance of New York. I suppose it would be sensible to obey orders and stay here six months, but I'm just not sensible.
Ellis and I would have come to Americus and stayed there until we were driven out if Sister Kate hadn't obiected to the idea so strenuously. I guess she wanted all the

attention herself. We will come at a time when there is no danger of stealing the spotlight from anybody.
Love to you and your mother and all the other Hollises.
R.

[The Desert Sanatorium
Tucson, Arizona]
Sunday, March 15 [1931]

Dear John:—
Believe it or not, your letters are much better reading than the Arizona Star or the Tucson Daily Citizen. I have learned from the latter, however, that Old Homme Seine is running amuck and, perhaps by this time your dormitory has become a house boat like the Lardners' hovel in East Hampton . . .

My wardens, not knowing I am a born rover, think I intend to stay here all spring and most of the summer, but right after the middle of April les Etats Unis will be placarded with announcements that I have escaped. As Lincoln said, you can stand Arizona part of the time, you can even stand Arizona some of the time, but you can't etc.

My daily "night letter" is not in as many papers as it is out of. It would be more readable if I weren't always four or five days behind the news, but I do think it's as good as Bill Rogers' or Coolidge's stuff.

All my neighbors have radios (a recent invention) and just as I get ready for my sleeping potion at nine P. M. (Mountain Time) they turn on Amos and Andy, who, as you may not know, are now broadcasting twice per night. I can't hear them distinctly and wouldn't mind if I could, but what wrecks me is the kind of laughter with which one of said neighbors greets their gags. It is like the bleat of the coyotes in the surrounding mountains and keeps me awake long after it is hushed for the night . . . .

Write whether you feel like it or not and keep going to them concerts.

A Vagabond[1]

---

[1] This letter quoted by Elder, pp. 325-26. Unlocated elsewhere.

The Desert Sanatorium
Tucson, Arizona
April Fool. [1931]

[To John Golden]
Dear John:—
 After a careful examination of the list of productions at the bottom of your stationery I am constrained to ask, "W'at about 'The W'eel'"?
 Mrs. "Sid" is in the arthritis section of this jail and I have had a couple of pleasant visits with her. She is a lot worse off than I am because she suffers physically. My suffering is entirely mental and mostly, I guess, ridiculous; besides, can have it stopped promptly by hollering for my "personal physician" who is sufficiently understanding and sensible to know that a shot in the arm is less harmful than the heebie jeebies. If it weren't for the pain, I think Jean Siddall would enjoy it here—She likes company and there are lots of congenial women in her part of the asylum. As for me, I have been anti-social for a long, long time and wondered why. It is, they tell me, a characteristic of the ailment in a good many cases.
 Do I seem to be answering your letter? A thousand times No. Well, then, I think it was mighty nice of you to relay Mr. French's[1] message and to volunteer your services as agent. The trouble is that Mr. French must be thinking of four or five other fellows. I never wrote a one-act play. I have an idea for one act *of* a play and only need ideas for the other two acts. I have written short sketches for gambols and Dutch Treat shows and the like, but I have no copies of them and they are way out of date and weren't so hot in the first place. Also I have had short things, in play form, published in newspapers and magazines, but they were absolutely unplayable and never intended for the stage. Will you be good enough to convey this information to Mr. French?
 Give my love to May. And thanks for writing. You are excused from writing again because willy-nilly, I am coming home in a very short time. I can't do daily syndicate work in this joint, where news arrives by pack mule about two weeks after it is news.
                                     Sincerely,
                                     R.W.L.

---

[1] Samuel French was a prolific publisher of plays for production by amateur or community theaters.

The following letter to Ring Jr. ("Bill,") comments on the injuries (a fractured pelvis and shoulder) he had sustained from a fall from the ledge of a fourth-floor dormitory window at Andover while attempting to crawl to the window of the next room. Ring Jr. was then recuperating at the Phillips House hospital in Boston, while his father, having returned in mid-April from Tucson, was at Doctors Hospital in New York.

[Doctors Hospital
New York]
Monday night, April 27 [1931]

Dear Bill: —
 I don't intend to allow a son of mine to show me up. If you can live in a hospital, so can I. I *would* like to trade ailments with you, for I have no excuse not to write letters; you have, which means that I shall hear from you almost as often as before.
 I am on the ninth floor of this structure so that if I ever take a notion to step out of the windov and stroll along the walls, the X-rays are likely to show a couple of fractured fingernails as well as the conventional arm and leg breaks.
 Out in Arizona, the gent in charge of me said I mustn't do any work for six months at least, and preferably for a year. I had hoped for an order like that, from a competent physician, for a long, long while, but I didn't like it so well when it was actually issued. So I said I wouldn't do anything excepting for a daily syndicate "feature" of about one hundred words; it was no strain, paid very well and couldn't really be classed as work. He said anything I had to think of every day was sure to be a strain and a handicap. I said maybe that was true, but I intended to keep it up. Well, you can imagine my blushes when I got back to this city (New York) and discovered that the various newspapers throughout the country were in thorough agreement with my Arizona doctor; not only did they feel that I mustn't do any work, but also they doubted that I had been doing any. The only reason I can think of is that readers of the few papers to which my stuff had been sold were dying with laughter in such numbers that the editors were afraid the entire circulation would soon be in the col', col' ground. Anyway, massa is temporarily amongst the unemployed and awaiting offers from magazine editors. I presume I shall have to ask for a squad of mounted police to keep them in line at the door.
 A very unfortunate thing just happened to you. Your mother called up and reported that she had received a letter

from you, written on a one-armed typewriter. If you can write to one parent, etc. But don't do it if it tires you.

Sr.

Doctors Hospital
Tuesday evening
[May 1931]

[To Mrs. Mildred Luthy]
Dear Mildred:

A Mr. and Mrs. Lanier called on me yesterday morning. Mrs. Lanier claimed to be one of the Hollis family of Americus, but I couldn't quite believe it because I never saw anyone from Americus, least of all a Hollis, move so fast. Before I had a chance to say hello, they were saying goodbye and were gone. They seemed to be very nice people and I would have enjoyed a longer visit with them, but they evidently were under the impression that they were disturbing me. The only thing about a Hollis that can disturb me is its obstinacy. I have never met one I wanted to say good-bye to. If they are really relatives of yours, I wish you would ask them to come back and give me a chance to get acquainted with them before I am ordered out of here to make room for some one who is sick.

The other night I had a visitation from five members of the Lambs Club. They were all in extremely high spirits and the house doctor refused them permission to see me. They pushed him aside and came in anyway. Among them was Gitz Rice whom you will remember as composer of "Dear Old Pal of Mine." Chairs were plentiful, but Gitz preferred sitting on the floor, from which he arose at too freguent intervals to come to my alleged bed of pain, kiss me on top of the head and say, "You old sweetheart!" They had all given their names down at the office, and when they had gone, my nurse, who had witnessed the proceedings, said, "I had no idea Grantland Rice would act like that." Of course I immediately corrected her error, but it was too late to deny the rumor which she had spread all over the place and I am afraid Grannie will go down in Doctors Hospital history as a man who sits on the floor and springs up every little while to kiss the patient on top of the head.

Aside from the Laniers' split-second call, I have been pleasantly surprised here just once. Vince Youmans came in and a house doctor took it on himself to conduct us to the housekeeper's rooms, where there was a piano. I made Vince play everything he had ever written, and it was grand. If I could afford to hire a composer-pianist like him to stay with me all the time, I could laugh at doctors and nurses.

John gets home next Sunday. Ellis is going to meet him and bring him right up here. I hope he still speaks English. Love to the family. (And to you).

R.

The following telegram is to Mildred Luthy:

NEWYORK NY            1931 MAY 11 AM 8 52
MRS KENNETH LUTHY=
133 TAYLOR HILLS AMERICUS GA=
AM NOT NEARLY AS DISCOURAGED NOW AS SINCE WE TALKED A FEW HOURS AGO STOP I MUST LIVE IN HIGH DRY CLIMATE THIS SUMMER FOR GOOD OF THE PUBLIC STOP IT OCCURED TO ME HOW LEAVENLY IF LIZ NEEDED THE SAME SORT OF CLIMATE STOP MISS FELDMAN WOULD WORK AS NURSE AND HOUSEKEEPER AND COOK FOR NOTHING STOP I TELEPHONED YOU WHETHER LIZ WOULD CONSIDER ANY SUCH ARRANGEMENT AROUND NEWYORK OR VERMONT OR CANADA AND I SWEAR I THOUGHT I HEARD NOT ONLY YOU BUT LIZ SAY YES AND I GOT QUITE A THRILL STOP WHEN I HUNG UP OPERATOR SAID ELLIS WANTED ME AND ELLIS ASKED WHOM I HAD BEEN AFTER SO LONG STOP THEN [WHEN?] I TOLD ELLIS I THOUGHT SHE SAID KATE HAD INVENTED THE SCHEME STOP EVERYBODY WAS IN HIGH SPIRITS OVER SCHEME STOP BUT IT SEEMS MISS FELDMAN CLAIMED AUTHORSHIP SO YOU CAN SEE THAT [WHAT?] I AM UP AGAINST STOP LIZ CAN GET WELL QUICK OR STILL STICK TO BARGAIN BUT POSTPONE

The following letter is addressed to Lardner's nephew (his sister Anna's son) Richard Lardner Tobin (later senior vice president of *Saturday Review*) in care of the University of Michigan *Daily*, of which he was editor in his senior year. Tobin had placed Lardner on the complimentary circulation list of the paper.

Doctors Hospital
East End Ave. at 87th St.
New York
October 2, 1931.

Dear Cousin:—
    A very swell elegant paper, Cousin. Keep up the good work. But don't let your sports editor think for one moment that he can fool this old codger by putting Bottomley's

name under Hoyt's picture and vice versa. Also, hasn't it occurred to you that you could relieve the unemployment situation by hiring a few night editors?

On and after next Wednesday, Mr. and Mrs. R.W. Lardner and son John will be living at 25 East End Avenue. It's a furnished apartment seven blocks down the street from here.

Cousin Ring

As the above letter indicates, the Lardners were about to move into a furnished apartment in New York, while their East Hampton house was being repaired. John had gone to work for the *Herald-Tribune*.

Saturday, October 31 [1931]

[To son James at Harvard]
Dear SIr,—

I can recall a Wigglesworth[1] who played on your team; otherwise I should have to keep asking Ronghild.

You may get up in the middle of Harvard Square and tell the Reds that I never wrote a picture for Chevalier and expect never to be asked to. If I were, I know I should swoon. At the present moment, I am awaiting a telephonic yes or no from Harold Lloyd as to whether I am to write the dialogue (not the scenario) for his new picture at an outrageous (not for Hollywood) price. If he says yes, I shall have to go out there in a couple of days and stay three or four weeks. If he says no, well and good. Again, if he says yes, I shall try to find some sappy Southern Californian who wants to bet against Notre Dame, so I can get even with my baseball sharpshooters. Otherwise, it will be necessary for me to back you vs. Yale.

Since starting this letter, I have had a telegram from Harold, who thinks my price is too high. I telegraphed back that I disagreed with him. He replied that he would give me a definite answer on Monday.[2] I know he is right, so if we get into a conversation on the telephone, I shall bargain with him until we come to terms. I need the money to pay the galumps who moved our house back to Sag Harbor. I shall try to ease in a stipulation to the effect that he pay an extra fare out there and back, so I can have a compartment and

---

[1] James Lardner resided in Wigglesworth Hall at Harvard.

[2] The arrangement with Harold Lloyd was never successfully negotiated.

work all the way going and coming. Your mother or older brother will let you know the result.

John is making good at the Herald Tribune and will probably be managing editor by the end of the year if the paper fails, as seems inevitable. He and Dicky Tobin went to the Princeton–Michigan game today. The game was for the championship of the slums and Michigan won, 21 to 0. If, as I presume, you depend on the Boston papers, you may not know this.

If King Howard wins the managership of the team and you are any kind of business man, you will strip him of enough tickets to pay your board, lodging and tuition.

The meals, nursing and beds here are much better than at the hospital. The day I left there, Dr. Erdmann, who works about five days a year, performed three operations, while fifteen doctors stood around and watched. His total fees were $25,000. One op was the removal, manicuring and replacement of the stomach of a seventy-year-old rake, who is now able to go out and get cock-eyed again.

Other East Hampton news is the death, by pneumonia, of Mr. Coppell. Why couldn't it have been she, is the question being asked in all the quail coveys.

Write to me here. If I'm gone, the letter will be forwarded by mail.

In a week or two, maybe this week, a series of mine[1] will begin in the Saturday Evening Post. Save the covers.

                    Mrs. Coppell.

*The following letter is to Mrs. Florence Hollis (who was about seventy-five at the time), the mother of Kate Rice, Mildred Luthy, and Lizabeth Vereen:*

25 East End Avenue,
New York City.
November twentieth, nineteen thirty-one.

Dear Mrs. Hollis:—

No matter what any or all of your daughters may have told you, I am not a chronic grumbler. But occasionally I do feel constrained to lodge what I consider a just complaint.

---

[1] The "series" consisted of six autobiographical articles: "Meet Mr. Howley" (in the November 14 *Post*), "Me, Boy Scout" (November 21), "Caught in the Draft" (January 9, 1932), "Heap Big Chief" (January 23), "Chicago's Beau Monde" (February 20), and "Alias James Clarkson" (April 16). Elder calls these pieces Lardner's "only real autobiography" (p. 337). They are reprinted in *Some Champions*.

Sensing the need of a Hollis in our home, I recently extended an invitation to Mrs. Luthy or Mrs. Vereen or both to come and visit us. They replied with a terse "No." The reply came by telegraph and was addressed not to me, but to my wife. Has the Master of the House no standing? If I were to ask you (as I do here and now) to pay us a visit, would you answer Ellis or me. I hope you would, and will, answer me and say "Yes."

Once in a while (I believe the last time was three years ago), we make up our minds to invite the Rices to a theater. When this happens, *I* telephone to *Grant* and he says "Yes" without consulting his wife or Floncey or Helga or Charles. He has *rights* which the Hollis girls seem to think I lack. This is a very serious matter with me and I would appreciate your decision.

Otherwise I hope you are in better health than most people I know. Sincerely,
Ring Lardner


[late November 1931]
Saturday, 3 A. M.

Dear James:—

As I have told your brother at Andover in a belle lettre I wrote him yesterday morning about this time, I have a new habit; I grow very, very sleepy every evening at dinner, stay up after dinner, nodding and blinking, until your mother scolds me into going to bed, fall asleep at eleven, awake at 1:30, all through with sleep, and spend the balance of the night working or writing mash notes such as this. The habit has persisted ever since I left the hospital, where a kindly night nurse gave me shots in the arm to insure me a night's sleep (thereby also insuring herself of one), but I have a hunch that during the coming week, I shall return to something near normalcy and then my correspondents (God help them!) will wonder why they aren't even receiving postcards from me any more.

Now don't imagine for one moment that I am suffering from a delusion that I owe you a letter—well do I remember replying to your last one and advising you to take advantage of King Howard's appointment to the post of football manager and make yourself and family independently wealthy by scalping. (I judge from recent events, however, that no tickets will be sold for Harvard games after this fall;

the public will be barred, as Husing was,[1] for the use of naughty words or for other misbehavior—In passing, my child, I might say that if you weren't a Harvard man, I'd write a little piece for The New Yorker regarding your school's haughty attitude toward the outside world. I know Bill Bingham and like him, but his refusal to have anything to do with the benefit games for the unemployed, his high hat stand in the Husing case, etc.—these and other items of the same sort have kind of cooled my love for your institution. Nevertheless, I have tried all week to bet on you and only last night succeeded in finding anyone with more than ten cents in Yale money. I had to give 8 to 5 (nonsensical odds) and the amount of the wager is $80.00 to $50.00. I lost my shirt and underwear on the world's series and not through bad judgment either, but incredibly bad luck. The defeat of Earnshaw in the last game was nothing short of murder—There was only one real hit (Watkins' home run) made off him.[2]

Anyway, I says to myself, "I'll get even on football." There was no chance to bet until November 7; then a bookmaker whom I know made this generous offer: Of all the games scheduled for that day, he would select fifteen; he would submit to me the list of fifteen and I could select six of them. If my six teams all won, he would pay me 6 to 1, but the betting limit was $10.00. (However, for friendship's sake, he would permit me to bet $20.00.) Well, just on the chance of having the laugh on him, I told him to send his list. John and I studied it carefully and picked the probable winners—nine instead of six so we would have three to argue about. I showed our selections to Mr. Rice, and he and two of his friends went in with us. I bet $20.00 and the others bet $10.00 each. Our six final choices all won. They were Colgate, Alabama, Lafayette, Temple, Nebraska, and Northwestern. (And our three alternatives—Michigan, Williams and Pittsburgh—were winners also) . I thought I was very bright, and so did my bookmaker.

---

[1] Ted Husing, the radio sets broadcaster with CBS, used the word "putrid" to describe the play of Harvard quarterback Barry Wood in a game against Dartmouth in 1931. William Bingham, Harvard athletic director, banned Husing from Harvard Stadium because of his language. Despite the disagreement, Husing placed Wood on his all-star team at the end of the year. Husing was permitted to return after two years banishment.

[2] In the 1931 World Series, the St. Louis Cardinals defeated the Philadelphia Athletics four games to three, with Burleigh Grimes winning over George Earnshaw, 4–2, in the deciding game.

On that same day, Georgia, which had already beaten Yale, licked New York University 7 to 6, a very lucky victory. But the Georgians and their followers were extremely cocky and thought they had a national championship team.

During the following week, Dan McGugin, who used to be a great guard at Michigan, is Yost's[1] brother-in-law, and coach at Vanderbilt, confided that Tulane was two touchdowns better than Georgia; his team had played them both. Mr. Rice was going south to cover the Georgia-Tulane game, so I gave him a check for all I had in the world and told him to bet it on Tulane, believing he would have a better chance to place it down there than I would up here. He wired back from Atlanta that he could find no takers, so all day Friday, the 13th., I hung on the telephone trying to unearth a bookmaker who had heard of Georgia money. I discovered it was impossible to lay a bet on Tulane at *any* *price.*

Beginning Monday morning of this week, I set out to bet on Harvard, succeeding, last night, as I have told you, in wagering $80.00 to $50.00. Once or twice I mentioned the Notre Dame–U.S.C. game; the bookies said Notre Dame was odds-on at 1 to 2 1/2. I wouldn't fall for any monkey business like that.

Sunday, 4 A.M.

I presume I ought to kneel down and thank the Almighty for getting by as fortunately as I did yesterday. I am thoroughly convinced that your hero, Barry Wood, got his Phi Beta Kappa key from a locksmith and that Notre Dame's coach, Hunk Anderson, will be driving mules in an Indiana coal mine next fall.

Forgetting (if we can) that first scrimmage, in which Harvard had a first down on Yale's seven-yard line, and the selection of plays that couldn't have scored a touchdown against Niles High School, let us leap into the fourth quarter where all the allegedly bright boys (Wood Casey at Harvard and Anderson, Jackswhich and Schwartz at Notre Dame) suddenly became the victims of brainstorms.

In war or in football, the first lesson is that the attack is more wearisome than the defense. In football it is a cardinal principle that the team just scored against shall kick off and not receive the kick-off. If the man who kicks off is any good, the receiving team will have eighty yards to go for a

---

[1] Fielding Yost was head football coach at the University of Michigan from 1901 through 1925.

touchdown. When it is finally forced to punt, your team will have the ball close to midfield. The blunder occurred only once at Harvard. At Notre Dame, it happened *three times*. And listen to this: When Notre Dame was leading 14 to 6, the broadcaster said, "Notre Dame *wisely* elected to receive the kick-off so it would be in possession of the ball," and on the first play after Notre Dame had received the kick-off, Schwartz threw a sixty yard pass from his own twenty-yard line, and the pass was knocked down. He proceeded to get himself into a hole and finally made a bad punt that gave U.S.C. its chance for a second touchdown. Even at that, Notre Dame could have kept its one-point advantage if it had slowed up its play. What is a five-yard delay penalty compared with defeat? Or three or four penalties?

Oh, well, let's not get mad. But I did get mad yesterday afternoon. Your mother, John and I were listening to both games over the radio (a new invention) and I am afraid your mother heard some "putrid" language.

In closing, I hated to see Harvard lose on your account and John's, and I hated to see those swell-headed Californians beat a superior team because it's Schwartz's last year.

There is one safe bet—that poor old Rock turned over in his grave at least three times yesterday P.M.

Remember me to the Howards and write.

A Second Guesser.

The letter below was written at two o'clock in the morning to Richard Lardner Tobin, who describes it as

> the work of a desperately ill man who has nonetheless an abiding interest in the sports world from which he came. The quote 'Mrs. Hoag' mentioned at the beginning was a small-town character in Niles, Michigan, whom I would have recognized as the silliest of all possible salutations to me. Also, I rather like the use of the postal telegraph press copy on which he is writing. As you will see, he is at this moment doing some pieces for the New Yorker, date line: 'No Visitors, New York,' which, of course, is Doctors Hospital. Since I was in Ann Arbor and Fielding Yost was still coaching out there, Uncle Ring is asking me to say hello to him personally, since they were once great pals.

Postal Telegraph—Cable Company
Press Telegram
Dec. 10, 1931, 2 A.M.

Mrs. Hoag (Mabel's mamma):— This isn't even a Western Union press telegram let alone a Postal press telegram, why should you let alone a Postal press telegram? Mackay may be a Catholic, but after all his daughter married a Heeb who plays everything in the key of F sharp. And can't play even in that key.

I guess I told you that I don't sleep o' nights any more, and my ankles are so swollen and itchy that all I can do is sit in a scratching position and turn out words, either for publication or for some one's private ear. This press telegram may be placed in the latter category and, as usual, what I write you is confidential. Mr. Rice's All-American team (to be in the December 26 issue of Collier's, which, appropriately enough, goes on sale the 18th.) is composed of the following rugby stars: Ends—Dalrymple, Tulane, and Catnip Smith, Georgia; tackles—Schweger (?), Washington, and an unspellable Pittsburgher, something like Quoutchi or Pouchi; guards—Hickman, Tennessee, and Munn, Minnesota; center—M-rr-s-n, Michigan; backs—Wood, Schwartz, Rentner and Shaver. No team represented by more than one man and may God have mercy on my soul and yours if you breathe a word even to your mother-in-law. There is nothing, however, to prevent you from digging up pictures for use at the proper time.

A few hours ago I did my annual radio broadcast. I called Morton Downey a soprano, which he is, but when he sees me and starts to sock me in the jaw, I'll tell him I have just been sick.

John has had five stories in the paper in the last three days and one of them each day carried a by-line. We are all swollen up like my ankles.

He (John) and I lost nothing on Notre Dame for the reason that no one would bet on the opposition.

The Princeton–Columbia–Penn–Cornell round robin yesterday was a terrific flop and the unemployed had to drive the visiting players home in their Hispano-Suizas. John Philip Suiza's band is on the Goodyear hour nearly every Tuesday and Saturday night. So are the Revellers, under a pseudonym. I read in the Michigan Daily that the Revs were in your town last week. Lah-de-dah.

In one of the next two or three New Yorkers will appear a comical parody on "Mourning Becomes Elektra"[1] It was

---

[1] "Quadroon," *The New Yorker*, 19 December 1931. Collected in *First and Last*.

a tough thing to write as two-thirds of it is menu cards which I copied from the program.
Love to Dean Yost.
A Cadaver.
I gather (you gather, he, she or it gathers) that B. Friedman is in kind of wrong at Yale owing to his lack of respect for Albie, and it is doubtful that he will be asked to return as assistant coach. Moreover, he has been more or less dissatisfied at New Haven, where the morons in charge have paid little heed, man, to the suggestions of B. Friedman. I realize that, until death do us part, a person named Fielding Yost will have a lot to say about the coaching at Michigan; nevertheless, I should like to see Benny get in (out) there. He could at least act as a formidable scrub team all by himself, just as Germany Schulz[1] used to do.
Ring*
*for icewater

Richard Tobin heeded the information his uncle had given him. The *Michigan Daily* of 18 December 1931 carried a story, with pictures, on Grantland Rice's All-American football selections. The *Collier's* story appeared the same day.

As a result of an October interview Lardner had given a *World-Telegram* reporter, the 9 November 1931 *Time* had quoted Lardner on Theodore Dreiser as saying: "The prince of all bad writers is Dreiser. He takes a big subject, but so far as handling it and writing it—why one of my children could do better." When Burton Rascoe defended Dreiser against Lardner's "attack" in his New York *Sun* column, Lardner wrote to him:

25 East End Avenue,
New York City.
December 16, 1931.

Dear Burton:—
I believe that a great many football fatalities might be averted by the adoption of the following rule:
"Before commenting on a statement attributed to an interviewee, the commentator must seek out the interviewee

---

[1] Adolph George "Germany" Schultz played football at Michigan. He was noted for his passing ability and for his defensive play as a "roving center." After fourteen years of coaching at such universities as Wisconsin, Michigan, and Tulane, he retired in 1922 from football.

and ascertain what the latter really did say. Penalty—Loss of two paragraphs."

Love and a merry Christmas to the Rascoe parents and progeny.

R.W.L.

Rascoe wrote back on Christmas Day from California explaining that he had quoted verbatim from the *Time* article and urging Lardner to "rebuke" the *Time* reporter and write a denial to the magazine.

In the meantime, Lardner sent a telegram of encouragement to Jim at Harvard just before a varsity wrestling match (in his senior year, just after his father's death, Jim would become New England intercollegiate wrestling champion in his 145-pound class):

```
                                    1931 DEC 17 PM 9
53
JAMES LARDNER=
    WIGGLESWORTH HALL HARVARD UNIVERSITY
CAMBRIDGE MASS
DON'T LET ANYBODY THROW YOU STOP AM
BACKING YOU HEAVILY STOP PLEASE SEND
NIGHTLETTER RESULT OF MATCH ALSO WHEN YOU
WILL BE HOME AND BRING YOUR DINNER CLOTHES
                DAD.

NEWYORK NY                          1931  DEC  24
PM 1 44
MRS FLORENCE HOLLIS=
    133 TAYLOR HILL AMERICUS GA
JUST TO WISH YOU A MERRY CHRISTMAS AND TO
ASK YOU TO TAKE CARE OF YOURSELF SO THAT I
MAY COME AND SEE YOU NEXT TIME AMERICUS
HAS A CENTENNIAL
                RING LARDNER.
```

On 2 January 1932, Lardner wrote to Dreiser:

25 East End Avenue,
New York City.
January 2, 1932.

Dear Mr. Dreiser:—

This is an effort to get the record straight.

Six or seven weeks ago a World-Telegram man, who wanted an "interview" and whom I had stalled until he convinced me that he was stall-proof, crashed my gate and discovered what I could have told him in advance—that I am a complete flop as copy. We drifted to the subject of what I was reading; it was a book about Jake Lingle, who was a friend of mine when I worked on the Chicago Tribune. (I left Chicago a year before Capone took charge). The idea I tried to convey to the W.–T. man was that I got more of a kick out of an actual transcript of testimony in a real murder case than from anything of that nature I had ever read in fiction, adding that one of the most fascinating documents I had seen was the stenographic report of Judd Gray's confession.[1] We discussed you and "An American Tragedy," and, to the best of my recollection, I said that no one, not even one of my children, could fail to make a human story like that uninteresting, and the more simply it was written, the better. In the "interview," as it appeared, I was quoted as calling you "the prince of bad writers" and saying other things about you which I certainly did *not* say. When I read it, I got all excited and was calmed down by my wife and my doctor who assured me that people who knew me would know I had been misquoted.

Well, it seems that "Time" lifted and reprinted one paragraph (the worst) and Burton Rascoe read it and jumped on me in his daily column. I wrote to him and suggested an amendment to the constitution, making it a punishable offense to quote from a quote from a quote, when it was such a simple matter to find out first hand what the victim of the interview really had said.

I assure you I am not in the habit of knocking writers (God help us all), and particularly novelists, whose patience and energy are far beyond any good traits I can claim. You don't know me and therefore will have to take my word, or the word of some of my friends, that I am incapable of the offense charged. On the other hand, Burton has known me twenty-five years and when he gets home, I'll "rebuke" him, as he suggests that I rebuke the interviewer.

As for "Time," in another recent issue it said I was slowly recovering from "pernicious anaemia." Aside from glanders, that is the only ailment I haven't had. But at least a dozen sufferers from it wrote to me asking what treatment I took, and I had to reply to all of them.

                    Sincerely,
                    Ring Lardner

---

[1] Judd Gray was the lover in "the Dumbbell Murder," a sensational case in March 1927. He and his mistress, Ruth Brown Snyder, were convicted and electrocuted for the murder of her husband.

I seem to have made quite a fuss over what you doubtless consider nothing, but I do want you to know that I'm not a knocker.

Dreiser responded:

Hotel Ansonia
New York City
Jan. 5, 1932

Courtesy and good will shine through your explanation of the *World-Telegram* and *Time* comments, and I thank you, though you need not have troubled. It is a long while since I have taken umbrage at any comment made either on myself or my work, since, good bad or indifferent, both are as they are, and, as for my work, the best I can do. Surely only critics are intolerant of those who do the best they can in so trying a world. None the less, the phrase "the prince of bad writers" cheers me. It is glistering irony that ought to be said if for no more than the saying. I am grateful to you for having called my attention to it.
Cordially and with assurances of my esteem,
Theodore Dreiser

Dreiser's ambiguity caused Lardner to reply:

Wednesday, January sixth. [1932]

Dear Mr. Dreiser: —
When I was in my teens, schoolmates and other acquaintances used to say of some one they particularly liked (some one who spent his money lavishly for drinks, ready-made cigarettes, etc.), "He's a prince," and for some reason the phrase nauseated me so that I have always avoided the word "prince" except when referring to the Prince of Wales, a thing I have seldom found occasion to do. So whether or not "The prince of bad writers" is glistering irony, it isn't my irony and I cannot accept the credit for somebody else's glistering.
It is only fair to warn you that when spring comes, your hotel will be a hotbed of Giant and Yankee ball players— unless they have decided to jump to the new Waldorf.
Sincerely,
Ring Lardner

Dreiser also replied more explicitly:

Hotel Ansonia
New York
Jan. 7, 1932

Dear Lardner:
 Plainly I did not make myself clear. But you must believe that I accept—and did—fully your assurance of innocence. More, *that I appreciated fully and gratefully* your troubling to write me and explain. Can I make this more definite? At the same time I rejoice in the phrase "The Prince of Bad Writers." The newspaper man who concocted it should have a medal of some kind—a real one. Let's call it "the phrase of the year" or "the year's best bit of irony."
 Anyhow you are a neighbor of mine. If you would trouble to walk so far we might drown this slight misunderstanding in hard likker. The mystic hour of five usually finds me turning from composition to speculation & drink.
                    Theodore Dreiser
As for the baseball wonders,—at worst they can only drown out the tuneful Latins herein resident at this hour.

 Lardner concluded the correspondence (and the "friendship," because the two writers never did meet) with this note:

25 East End Avenue,
New York City.
January 11, 1931.
[misdated; actually 1932]

Dear Mr. Dreiser:—
 On the contrary, you did make yourself plain and I am grateful to you for taking my word.
 I want to ask for a rain check on that hard likker invitation. It is my misfortune that when I get started, I seem to find it necessary to fight it out on those lines if it takes all winter, and having spent a whole year among the unemployed, I must now work until I am somewhere near even.
 We would be neighbors if I lived on *West* End Avenue, but as it is, the whole width of Manhattan divides us. I am

254

within wading distance of Welfare Island and hope to finish there.
     Sincerely
     Ring Lardner
     The Prince of Doltish Drinkers.

 Again, Lardner wrote to Richard Lardner Tobin at the University of Michigan. The play Lardner mentions was a one-act play by Tobin that had been included in a book of plays published by the University. Of the reference to shirking his work, Mr. Tobin writes:

> The mention of "Dowagiac" is a reference to a small town near Niles, Michigan. Stanley Walker, the famous City Editor of the New York Herald Tribune, had just hired me to start on the paper in June after graduation and, when this fact was made public, the Dowagiac paper ran a big editorial about the importance of working on college papers, using me as a prime example. It was, after all, the bottom of the depression and not many people were getting jobs that spring and summer. Apparently it impressed Mr. Lardner, too. The Bill Dickey whose name appears at the bottom was, of course, the famous New York Yankees' catcher, a drinking friend of Mr. Lardner, and well-known to me, naturally.

Thursday.
[ca. March 1932]

Dear Dickie:—
 The book of plays arrived from Ann Arbor yesterday. I read "Masquerade" last night and liked it, though it didn't "leave me laughing," as George Cohan says a play should do.
 If you are ever tempted to shirk your work, remember that Dowagiac has its eye on you.
 And if you know of another record I would like you might, when you have time, ask the Schirmer boys to send it along.
 It was tough luck for you to have that postponement Monday, but not so tough for me and my unspeakable Giants.
     Bill Dickey.

 The following letter is to Adelaide W. Neall, an editor with George Horace Lorimer's *Saturday Evening Post*:

March 16, 1932.

Dear Miss Neall:—

You are almost forgiven and will be entirely so if you will see that the one-line insert (appropriately marked Insert A) in the sixth galley of the proof is attended to, and if you will rush me the proofs of the second installment.[1] The insert will show the readers if any that we are more or less up to date, and the second installment will require some revision because Babe Herman[2] was included in the Cincinnati trade, something I had not been warned against. "Insert A" is near the bottom of this sheet.

My mark of elision in proofreading is a ⟿ as you have probably guessed. I shall try to master the Post's.

Whether or not you are interested, I went visiting the Philadelphia sick after leaving your office Wednesday, and wound up sicker than any of them, without breaking a resolution or a law and on the train coming home an utter stranger told me a joke about the Lindbergh baby, which I laughed at so heartily that he left the washroom offended.

Sincerely,
Ring Lardner

Insert A— 6th galley of proof:
because they trade it Herman to Cincinnati.

New York, New York
May 13, 1932.

Dear Mr. Meconnahey:—

Please pardon my tardiness in replying to your letter. I have not been able to write or even dictate.

---

[1] Lardner's reference is to "When the Moon Comes Over the Mountain," the second in a series of six new "busher" stories published by the Post in 1932 and as a book titled *Lose with a Smile* by Scribners in 1933. The stories are imitative of the Jack Keefe series, consisting of letters between rookie Brooklyn outfielder Danny Warner and his girl Jesse. Though the stories are a pale version of *You Know Me Al*, and not at all the novel that Perkins had hoped Lardner might produce, they do exhibit all Lardner's earlier mastery of the "busher" dialect and the epistolary form, and they are a remarkable effort by an extremely sick man who was unable now to write for any sustained length of time.

[2] Floyd "Babe" Herman was a star outfielder for the Brooklyn Dodgers, who was traded to Cincinnati before the 1932 season. He had a batting average of .393 in 1930, and a cumulative average for thirteen years in the major leagues of .320.

Sid Skolsky's stuff was more nearly accurate than those things usually are.

I believe that I like "Golden Honeymoon" best of my immortal works, but I don't know why.

Sincerely,<br>Ring Lardner

The letter below was written to John McGraw, baseball manager of the New York Giants and an old friend of Lardner's, who had just been forced by ill health to retire.

Doctors Hospital
New York City
June 4, 1932

Dear John:

This is iust to say that I'm terribly sorry to hear of your resignation as manager and of the serious nature of the illness that caused it. Baseball hasn't meant much to me since the introduction of the TNT ball that robbed the game of the features I used to like best—features that gave you and Bill Carrigan and Fielder Jones and other really intelligent managers a deserved advantage, and smart ball players like Cobb and Jim Sheckard a chance to *do* things.

You and Bill Gleason and Eddie Collins were among the few men left who personified what I enjoyed in "the national pastime." Moreover your retirement has ruined my hope of a resumption of amusing (to me) relations with Frank Belcher when, and if, I am ever physically and financially able to go into the Lambs club-house again. Two or three years ago, when the Giants lost a game or a series, I used to torture him by saying that it was due to bad management. When I had him on the verge of tears, I would "break down and confess" that I was kidding and that I really considered you the greatest of managers, and it was honestly pathetic to see him brighten up at my sudden change of front. If you ever had a loyal supporter, he was and is it.

Often I have wondered whether you ever enjoyed the feeling of security and comfort that must be a manager's when the reporters assigned to his club are "safe" and not pestiferous—a gang such as Chance and Jones and Jim Callahan were surrounded with for a few years in Chicago, and I don't say that just because I happen to be one of the gang. We had a rule, and lived up to it, that none of us would ever act as assistant managers, would be worthy of whatever confidence was reposed and would never ask, "Who's going to pitch tomorrow?" The result was mutually beneficial. We were kept posted on whatever changes, deals and trades were "in the air" and therefore knew what we were talking about when the trade or deal was put through or called off. The managers referred to didn't wince when they saw one of us approaching. They were our friends and we were theirs. So far as I was concerned, Frank Chance knew that I was very close to Schulte and lots of times when Schulte was not "behaving," Chance would drop a hint to me, knowing that I would warn Schulte, and I am positive I was thus enabled to save Schulte money and Chance the unpleasant task of fining and suspending him . . . .

I do hope you get better soon and that eventually you get "back." I am lucky in that I have no physical pain. My chief trouble is an increasing hatred of work, and it happens that work is necessary. Please remember me to Mrs. McGraw, or, as the internes would call her, Mrs. "McGror."
Sincerely,
Ring Lardner[1]

Lardner's nostalgic reference in the letter above to a "safe gang" of baseball reporters is at odds with today's philosophy of journalism that it is the reporter's responsibility to expose the "truth," regardless of consequences. For Lardner, a part of his responsibility was to respect the confidences of baseball managers such as McGraw and Chance.

The letter below is to Ellis's sister, Ruby Abbott Hendry:

July seventh. [1932]

Dear Rube:—

Thank God for John, if only because he made you write. I thought I was the Hendrys' Forgotten Man; Ellis evidently thought so, too, for when she saw your writing, she opened the letter—and read it.

Arthur Jacks used to have an exasperating (till you knew him) trick of always "topping" people. If I complained of a headache, he had a worse one. If Rex mentioned a sore throat, Arthur had all the symptoms of diphtheria. So I will proceed to annoy you by pointing out that Robin's present unemployment is not nearly as "bad" as my plight throughout 1931 and several weeks of this blessed year. There was work to be done, but the mere sight of a typewriter gave me the heebie-jeebies. When I was able to subdue them and attempt to work, I was immediately overcome by sleeping sickness, though nothing short of chloroform would put me to sleep in bed. I would lie awake

---

[1] This letter quoted from Elder, pp.361–62. Unlocated elsewhere.

and think of debts and expenses; jump up determined to work; begin to work and either get the shakes or doze off, and then go back to bed and start the whole performance over again. I maintain that when a person is idle through no fault of his own, it is less irritating than when he realizes that "loose living" is "the cause of it all."

Dickie Tobin, having got through Michigan, is rooming in town with John. They are both, as you probably know, reporters on the Herald Tribune. They have the same off-day and will probably come out here about once every two weeks during the summer. David will be our contribution to Andover this fall; Jim will go back to Harvard and Bill will enter Princeton, *if* the magazines don't "ask" the old man to take another cut. Magazines and newspapers are, of course, face to face with the Grim Reaper, their only consolation being that radio, which beat them out of a lot of advertising, is now as badly off as they.

The New Yorker, being a "class" publication, doesn't pay much, but it's kind of fun to be a radio critic. If I don't get fired, I will crusade against the vulgarity and stupidity of some of the comedians and the immorality and illiteracy of most of the songs. It won't do any good, excepting to my disposition, which is soured by listening to the atrocities perpetrated by jokers, lyric writers and alleged singers.

I sympathize wholeheartedly with Boots on the subject of July Fourth, and I was mean enough to be glad that it rained all day hereabouts. The most fun I have all year is tossing into the waste basket the annual request for a contribution to the Village Fireworks Fund.

You ought to make a proposition to your friend, Mr. Marr. During dull times—and it must be dull times for good architects—have him draw new plans and remodel the cottage with the understanding that he will receive ten percent of any amount over $100,000 that it sells for when good times return. I have always thought it was extremely attractive—both the cottage itself and the site.

The bus cure for insomnia would work on me with a vengeance. Once I rode in one from Miami to Palm Beach, a trip taking only a couple of hours. An hour more and I would have shot all the other passengers and gone to sleep permanently in the electric chair. Buses and berths were not designed for people over five feet eleven. When I go to bed in sleeping cars now (which I don't), I wonder how in the world I stood it an average of two or three times a week all those years. Probably I was encouraged by the knowledge that there were always four or five pitchers who couldn't get through a car door without crawling on their hands and knees.

Please give my love to Mrs. Hendry aud the kids and Robin, and keep a lot for yourself. And please don't ask Florence—I wrote her a five hundred-word letter once and she hasn't sent me a postcard in reply.

I am addressing this to Detroit on advice of Ellis, though my own very good judgment tells me you are still at the lake. Well, you will live just as long if it never reaches you.

Come and see us and I will cook you a meal such as only I can cook—lamb chops, potato salad, pie—just as I cooked for you in Brookline twenty-one (Good heavens!) years ago.

RWL

East Hampton
Bastille Day
[1932]

[To Mildred Luthy]
Dear Millie:—

Two or three years ago I scolded you for using a comma where a semicolon belonged (or something) and you were furious, so I'm afraid to tell you how your last letter impressed me, or rather, depressed me. Honestly it sounded as if you considered me a perfect or imperfect stranger and when I had finished it, I was amazed that the salutation hadn't been "Dear Mr. Lardner" or "Dear Sir." I won't answer such questions as how do I like my house in its new position or is my interest in radio something new. Listen, Miss, I ain't Dr. Erdmann,[1] with whom you are trying to make dinner conversation. I remember you quite well and can talk to you on much more familiar topics—Ovaltine, for example. Aren't you the lady who once recommended it as a cure for my Intractable Imsomnia? Well, the other night (July fourth) I was listening in on Little Orphan Annie and the man said, "If you are going to stay up and see the fireworks tonight, take a glass of Ovaltine *before* supper and another glass *an hour* later, and it will keep you *wide awake* and *fresh* for the evening's entertainment. Now Millie, this man is employed by the Ovaltine company and he ought to know what the lovely stuff is good for. Yet I can scarcely believe you would try to coax me into consuming a beverage that not only must drive a person to beverages more pleasant, expensive, habit-forming and devastating, but also keep him wide awake and, above, all things, *fresh*. I simply am too fond of myself to entertain

---

[1] Dr. Erdmann was a surgeon at Doctors Hospital (see letter of 31 October 1931 to James Lardner).

the thought that you don't remember me a little, and if you do, you surely are aware that I seldom have an ambition to keep wide awake, unless there is a game of setback in prospect, and never fresh. I do think an explanation is in order.

Moreover, I have this against you: One of the reasons I left the hospital before my time was to be in a position to serve as a member of the reception and entertainment committee when you and Jane came to East Hampton. I don't believe the Rices are ever coming but Helga is here and so hard up for work that she insists on inviting our two Danes to have a meal with her once or twice a week. Ellis seldom goes out in the evening and I am afraid she gets quite lonely without Kate. Even when she goes out, I would insist on your staying home and entertaining Jim, Bill and me; I am not suggesting that you wouldn't be invited other places, but merely hoping that your attitude toward parties is the same as it used to be. Dave misses Jane, as also do Liz Wheeler and the other Lardner boys. If you ever did want to go out, I would love to serve as Jane's nurse because it would give me a comfortable sensation of having to do something that isn't work. Please think it over, Millie, and consider carefully that the summer will be over before we know it . . . .

I know a person doesn't always, or often feel like writing. But please try it again, Millie, and don't treat me as if I were a silent policeman.

R.[1]

In the midst of the Depression, the 1932 political campaigns were intense. When Heywood Broun ran for mayor of Hartford on the Socialist ticket, Lardner, though nominally a Republican, supported him out of friendship, and that support led to a misunderstanding. In its 9 July 1932 issue, the *New Leader* listed Lardner as one of several contributors who had agreed to write articles supportive of the Norman Thomas–James Maurer Socialist ticket. The articles were to appear during the sixteen weeks of the campaign in a weekly tabloid edited by Edward Levinson, then an assistant editor of the *New Leader*. Lardner objected in the following note:

---

[1] No original discovered of this letter. Quoted by Elder, pp. 364–65.

East Hampton, Long Island
July 29, 1932.

Dear Mr. Levinson:—
  I agreed to contribute to the Thomas and Maurer campaign publication, but did not say I would write on my reasons for supporting Norman Thomas. If there is any misunderstanding, please let me know.
  Sincerely,

At Broun's request, Lardner did eventually write a rather facetious letter, which the *New Leader* published on 5 November 1932 as a statement of political support for the Socialist party:

RING LARDNER EXPLAINING WHY HE WILL
VOTE SOCIALIST

  On November the 8th my vote, as such, is liable to be cast for the Socialist candidates for president. I have the impressive figure of Heywood Broun in mind when I say this. The big fellow, I am told, is very thick with your candidate for national honors, Norman Thomas, and it seems probable that if the latter is elected he will take Broun, the rail-splitter, to Washington with him to occupy some comfortable berth in the cabinet. As a citizen of New York I feel that Broun's place is in Washington, and I would be willing to cast three or four votes and any number of aspersions to get him there.
  My friends reel back in amazement when I tell them, after a certain amount of preliminary fencing, that I am going to vote the Socialist ticket. Their comments are not printable, but the gist is as follows:
  "You are just wasting your vote, kid. Who do you like in the fifth at Empire City?"
  Throwing out the last sentence for reasons of policy, I am moved to ask in turn:
  "What am I doing when I vote for Hoover or Roosevelt?"
  This, you understand, is strictly between myself and the Socialist National Campaign committee. Under no circumstances would I care to have such old

golfing buddies as John McCooey and Everett Sanders know that I am planning to knife them at the polls.

The other day my doctor, while strapping me to a bed, pointed out that if Mr. Thomas is elected Mr. Hoover and Mr. Roosevelt will be out of a job.

"Don't worry, doctor," I replied, recognizing him without difficulty. "There is a big demand for comedians, and both those boys will be able to land swell jobs on the radio."

He parried this thrust with a gag from one of the Old Music Box Revues, and left me composing this campaign plea, which should stir up no little discussion around White's drug store in East Hampton. Until you are ready to hand me my piece of America, I remain,

Without rancor,<br>Ring Lardner.

After a lapse of nearly a year in his correspondence with Perkins, Lardner wrote the following letter, which hints strongly of self-doubt and depression:

Tuesday, August 16

Dear Max:—

Early in the summer, one of the Post's associate editors wrote me such a tactless letter, suggesting that the new series of baseball letters be brought to a conclusion in two more installments that I, then in a low mental condition, thought the whole series must be pretty bad though I had felt quite proud of part of it when I had sent it in. His words were chosen with a view, I guess, to lessening the shock of the premature conclusion, whereas if he had written frankly, saying that the Post could no longer afford to pay the very liberal price it had set on the series, I would have understood perfectly and thought little of it. For a time I banished the idea of offering the series to you for a book, but later on I reread some of the acceptance letters from Lorimer and other Post editors, as well as a bunch of nice "fan mail," and got steamed up about it again. I honestly don't know how the present interest in baseball compares with the past, but I presume that Brooklyn's recent spurt (the "hero" is a Brooklyn player) ought to be a help. Please read the whole thing when you feel strong and healthy and tell me what you think. I enclose the final installment, which should be published in a week or so. If Brooklyn wins the pennant, a book appearing simultaneously with the world's series might go.

R. L.

Perkins received Lardner's letter the next day and immediately wrote to say that Lardner's royalties were due in December, but he would send them sooner if Lardner wished. He also commented:

> I had always supposed that we would publish your Saturday Evening Post baseball articles in early 1933, but because of all the things I have had to do lately, I only read one, the early one. I am getting all there are, and probably now the last one has been published. I thought your radio pieces in the New Yorker were extremely good, and read all of them in the idea that they might make a book, but I hardly think so because they deal with such transitory matters.

The "radio pieces" were the often-attacked series of articles Lardner wrote in 1932 and 1933 for the *New Yorker* on standards of radio entertainment. They constitute a curious crusade by a dying man against faulty grammar, tastelessness, and sexual allusions in popular songs to which Lardner listened on the radio from his hospital bed. Among the more memorable passages in these articles are the parodies of Cole Porter's "Night and Day": "Night and day under the fleece of me/There's an Oh, such a flaming furneth burneth the grease of me . . . . Night and day under my dermis, dear,/There's a spot just as hot as coffee kept in a thermos, dear . . . ."

Thursday, August 18.

Dear Max:—
    A check for that $222.73 early next week would be a life-saver; or rather, a life insurance saver. However, if it isn't convenient I can manage to get over the hurdle in some other way.
    I mailed you the proof of the final Post installment yesterday or the day before. It hasn't been published yet, but certainly ought to be within three weeks. You are right about the New Yorker stuff—It is much too topical and local for publication in a book.

I am very much steamed up over the news of Zelda's novel[1] and hope you will keep me posted on the date of publication, etc.
Sincerely,
R.L.

Included with the royalty check that Perkins sent five days later was a report from Scribner's indicating a total sale at this point of 20,366 copies of *How to Write Short Stories*, 8,633 copies of *What of It?*, 12,904 copies of *The Love Nest*, 6,764 copies of *The Story of a Wonder Man*, and 15,261 copies of *Round Up* (in addition to the 70,000 copies sold through the Literary Guild).

Doctors Hospital
East End Avenue at 87th Street, New York
November 5, 1932.

H.L. Mencken,
704 Cathedral Street,
Baltimore, Md.

Dear Henry:
Your suggestion that we meet far too seldom has been in my head for ten years. If I ever escape from here I will see what can be done about it. Meanwhile, kindly publish another book.
Sincerely,
Ring Lardner
RL:HR
I think we ought to make it a trio and include that ole devil H.R.M. Landis of Philly.[2]

In the following letter to his son James at Harvard, Lardner demonstrates the high standards that he applied to the writing of popular music:

---

[1] Zelda Fitzgerald's novel was *Save Me the Waltz*, which was about to be published by Scribners. It is a strikingly autobiographical account written in about six weeks during her confinement in a Baltimore hospital after her second breakdown.

[2] Comment in ink at end of letter. Possibly a reference to the autocratic baseball comissioner—"His Royal Majesty" Kenesaw Mountain Landis.

Doctors Hospital
New York
Sunday.
[6 November 1932]

Dear Jim:—
    I enclose an amended version of your song. As I said in my telegram, I *think* your refrain begins on the wrong word and on the wrong beat—Anyway, it's unsingable as you have it, as you will find out if you try. Your music demands a two-syllable rhyme scheme (except in the middle eight bars, where you have written "ritardo"—incidently, you don't want any retard; it ruins the number as a dance tune). If I were you, I'd rewrite the music to those middle eight bars, simplifying it: you can almost do it with a couple of monotones, allowing the harmony to embellish it, or you can go into an entirely different key—A flat for instance.
    As the song stands, no one but a man can sing it. To rectify this fault, write a verse (holding it to eight bars if possible, but making it sixteen if necessary) in the third person, along these lines: "Joe Serviss was a handsome brute," then words to the effect that he had a girl, but he didn't like to work, etc., winding up with something like, "And so when he proposed to her, why this is what he said:" (I guess you'll need sixteen bars to tell the story) . The last word of the verse must come on the first beat of the eighth or sixteenth bar, and the "Oh," preceding the refrain, is the last beat in that same bar. The last note in the verse can be either a quarter, a half or a dotted half. If not a dotted half, you must put a half rest or a quarter rest between it and the word "Oh."
    In the third bar of the refrain, you will notice that I have changed the tune to get away from the resemblance to "River Shannon" and innumerable other songs. If you don't like my alteration, you can make it four straight Cs, with the harmony to help it, or C,B,C,B or C,A,C,A or C,F,A,C. (While on the subject, never mind about the harmony unless you have some special idea regarding one or two spots. If and when the song gets to an arranger, he'll do just what he pleases.)
    As I told you, your afterthought seventh and eighth bars was an improvement, and it should also be kept that way in the final bars of the song.
    I think your broken time is a mistake and I have rewritten it in straight time. As a matter of fact, I wouldn't be surprised if the tempo oughtn't to be changed to two-four—I am considering it from the dancing angle. This can be determined, and easily fixed, later on.

In my version, the title appears in the first and last lines of the refrain, which always helps a song commercially. However, you mustn't think this song is commercial in a "big way"—Very few are these days. But it's too good not to work on, and I may find one or two people who will introduce it on the radio.

I have taken a few liberties with your words, necessitated by the swing of the melody and the two-syllable rhymes; I have also taken a slight liberty with the pronunciation of "robust," but I think it makes a good finish the way I have it.

One explanatory verse will be enough, but you might be pondering a second refrain.

On whistling over the refrain, I am "struck" with the thought that if you use the C,A,F and A third bar, you ought to duplicate those four notes in the fifth bar (and of course, all the corresponding bars). But suit yourself.

I think you have a good start and I'm glad to see you working at something like this. Make the verse simple musically and *comical* lyrically. Don't rush.

It's good news that you have even a chance to get on that old davil dean's list, but if you miss this time, don't let it worry you.

Who were those ringers that posed as Harvard's team yesterday? There is one consolation—I won't have to give 3 to 1 on Notre Dame against the Army.

Write when you have time. Your mother is moving into town day after tomorrow. If you intend to write to her, you'd better address her here, in care of me. Don't forget to wire me how you come out with the dean, and when you have fixed this song, send it back and I'll see what can be done with it.

Pa.

Keep me posted on your football. Are you inclined to try baseball? Fred Mitchell[1] is an old (and queer) friend of mine and I might get him to pay you a little attention.

Later: It occurs to me that your idea is to make it a mock ballad. If so, of course we'll keep it in 4/4 time and mark it slow.

On 9 November, Mencken wrote saying he would visit shortly and promising "some dreadful scandal to tell you, some of it relating to persons hitherto regarded as impeccable Christians." Lardner replied:

---

[1] Fred Mitchell was a former major league pitcher–catcher who was then coaching at Harvard.

Doctors Hospital
East End Ave. at 87th St.
New York
November 13

Dear Henry:—
 I think the chiropractors will let up on me in about two weeks. If you will tell me what days you are in New York, I will telephone and insist that you keep your promise. Meanwhile, please don't forget the scandal.
                    Sincerely,
                    RL.

Lardner was overly optimistic. At the end of January, he was still hospitalized, and his doctors were advising that he seek a better climate in California.
The letter below is to Seymour Glaenzer, editor of the Laugh Club publications, a series of paperbound anthologies of humor:

New York, New York
December 22, 1932.

Dear Mr. Glaenzer:—
 If you don't mind, I would rather not give permission for the use of any of my work in Laugh Club publications. I have always been opposed to any story or volume of stories that guaranteed the reader laughs, a practice which puts him on the defensive and is likely to end in alienating whatever affection he may have had for one's writing. If I had known that "Comic Relief" was to be peddled on such a basis, I never would have consented to the inclusion in it of any work of mine.
                    Sincerely,
                    Ring Lardner

NEWYORK NY JAN 30         1933   JAN   31
AM 9 20
HL MENCKEN=
 704 CATHEDRAL STREET 3RD FLOOR (RD]=
HAVE SEVENTY FIVE HUNDRED WORD FICTION STORY SO GOOD THAT POST COSMOPOLITAN AND COLLIERS DONT WANT IT STOP WOULD YOU LIKE A CHANCE AT FOURTH REFUSAL STOP IF SO WHERE SHALL I SEND IT STOP PLEASE WIRE ME CARE DOCTORS HOSPITAL STOP AM LEAVING FOR DESERT RETREAT NEXT SATURDAY
                    RING LARDNER.

The next day, Lardner mailed the story, "Poodle," to Mencken, with the enclosed letter:

Doctors Hospital
East End Avenue at 87th Street, New York
January 31, 1933.

Dear H:—
Here's the one-part serial. The Post just didn't seem to care for it, Bill Lengel[1] said it was swell, but he ain't the boss, and Collier's objected to its length and tenuousness. What can *you* think of? I really advise you not to return it because I am leaving (by boat) Saturday for the Mojave Desert and it doesn't look to me as if it would stand a trip that long, or even one as far as the waste-basket. My address will be La Quinta, California, and I expect to be there till the first of May.

Please don't imagine that I didn't appreciate your offer to come and see me here. To begin with, I was no treat; besides, the doc wouldn't permit visitors for quite a while, though God knows you would have done me good, whereas some of the boys and girls who crashed the gate set me back weeks in half an hour, finally forcing me to take advice and arrange the impending hegira. When I return I will remind you of your promise or pay you a visit I don't owe.
                        Yours,
                        R.L.
After February 4—La Quinta, Calif.

Elder quotes from a letter sent the same day to Lardner's sister Lena in Niles, Michigan:

[31 January 1933]

The doctors think it is necessary for me to get out of this climate and into the desert. So Ellis and I are leaving next Saturday by boat, via the Panama canal, for California (on borrowed money) and will stay for three months . . . in a dry quiet place, hoping my condition will improve enough to permit me to work again. It is hard to leave John and not to see the other boys occasionally, but I think it will be best in the long run.

The next letter, the last Lardner ever wrote to Max Perkins, is particularly significant for its varying tone.

---

[1] William Lengel was associate editor of *Cosmopolitan* at that time.

Lardner's depressed state of mind over his bad health and declining creative power is evident, but so is his ability to retain his sense of humor.

Doctors Hospital
East End Ave. At 87th St.
New York
February 3, 1933.

Dear Max:—

    Some day I will probably realize that there is a depression. I wouldn't have asked you for any advance if I hadn't got into a sudden jam. The doctor and I decided that my place was the desert for a while, and not having done any real work since June, I was obliged to borrow money. I borrowed less than I needed, figuring I would sell a story to the Post. Once I wrote a complete story, "Alibi Ike," between 2 P.M. and midnight, with an hour off for dinner. This last one was begun in July and finished ten days ago, and the Post turned it down just as promptly as it had accepted "Ike." Since then, Bill Lengel has said it was great (but he ain't the boss), Collier's has rejected it as too long and tenuous (It runs 7,500 words) and Mencken has told me it was too much of a domestica symphonica or something for the Mercury. Mr. Graeve[1] (Delineator), suggested, perhaps sarcastically, by Mencken, now has it as a week-end guest and I have asked him to return it to my brother on the Times, who will give it to some poor author's agent to peddle. I have always scoffed at agents, but I am leaving tomorrow morning for La Quinta, California, to be gone till the money has disappeared. I have promised the doctor that I won't work on anything but a play which George Kaufman has been waiting for me to start for three years; of course, I will have to cheat a little, but I can't cheat much.

    What I started to say is that the fiction story (really not bad, and just as really not a Pulitzer prize winner) has a great many local stops to make, and if I were to stay here and wait till the last possible purchaser had said no, I would die of jitters. Your loan has made it possible for me to get out of here before I am committed to Bellevue, and I am truly grateful. I won't need the "other" two hundred, and if the sale of "Lose With a Smile" never totals the amount you have advanced me, I will see to it that you don't lose. The agent can make the rounds much quicker than I could from 3,500 miles away.

---

[1] Oscar Graeve was editor-in-chief of *Delineator*.

This letter doesn't seem to be properly constructed or quite clear. That is a symptom of my state of mind, but the fact that I can laugh at the succession of turn-downs of a story which everybody but the Post has had a kind word for but no inclination to buy, makes me hopeful for the future. Maybe someday I can write a piece about the story's Cook's Tour—it is the first one I ever wrote that wasn't accepted by the first or second publication to which it was offered, and that either means go west old man or quit writing fiction or both.

Thanks again, and honestly I want you to forget the "balance" because I can easily get along without it.

Will you send me a couple of copies of "Lose With a Smile" when it is published?

Yours,
RL

The widely-traveled "Poodle" finally appeared in the January 1934 *Delineator*. Perkins wrote immediately to Lardner's brother Rex offering to publish it in *Scribner's Magazine*, but it had already been accepted by *Delineator*.

Lardner's doctors had advised strongly that he try the desert climate of La Quinta, California, a resort near Palm Springs. After arriving there, Lardner wrote a letter to Mencken deploring *Herald-Tribune* columnist Lewis Gannett's enthusiastic review of Sinclair Lewis's *Ann Vickers*, published a month earlier. Lardner recognized the inferiority of this novel to Lewis's best work.

La Quinta
February 28, 1933.

Dear H.—

You ought to be a literary agent and I a designer of gowns. I followed your advice about Mr. Graeve of Delineator—in sheer desperation, I must admit, and not with any idea that you were right—and he accepted the story with the comment that it was so unsuitable to his publication that he just couldn't resist it. Thanks.

Inasmuch as I always write on subjects familiar to me and am not at all with either fornication or treachery, I don't see how I can crash the Mercury. But when the Post rejects the next one, I'll at least ask you where to find a sucker.

Listen, Mr. Gannett: In five or ten years, when your judgment is more mature, please re-read "Elmer Gantry" and "Babbitt," not from the standpoint of a debunker, but from that of a critic of literature and with an eye and ear to faithfulness in characterization, fidelity in dialogue and truth

in this, that and the other, and then review both books in a special $1.00 issue, and I'll subscribe for at least six copies.
Yours,
RL.

Mencken agreed: "I begin to have an uneasy feeling that you may be right about the Lewis books. Lewis has made a big success with his last, but it seems to me to be dreadful stuff."

Then Lardner wrote to his sons and nephew, Richard Lardner Tobin (who was then sharing an apartment with John in New York), describing the boat trip from New York to Los Angeles:

February 28, 1933.

Bill, John (and Dickie), David, James: —
This is a circular canary. A what, Baron?[1] An orbicular crow, a spherical sparrow. Baron, are you sure you don't mean a round robin? Why, yes, of course, Charlie! What did you think I meant?

I adopt this method of writing to you little ones because I won't have time to write you separately; besides, I should hate to say something comical to one of you and forget to say it to the others. The order indicated in the salutation is probably the best from a standpoint of speed in transmission. When Bill has read and, perhaps, memorized these words, he is supposed to send them on to John, who, after mumbling them to Dickie, will forward them to David, and the last-named (in every way) will mail them to Jim or, as some call him, the dead letter office. If this proceedure is agreeable to you, I will write once a month, possibly oftener. If it isn't, you can take the consequences. I trust that Bill, John and David will vindicate my judgment in routing by being prompt to re-address and re-mail.

Well, let me tell you that boat-ride was okeh after a storm had laid Mrs. Lardner low the second day out, and would have been more okeh if my feet, unshod since last April, had not swole to elephantine proportions. All the girls on the ship dubbed them the Giant Redwood Trees of California. Yes, the boat-ride was okeh, but don't ever take it just to have a look at the Canal. It is little more than a glorified Sault Ste. Marie, and when you have seen one lock, you have seen two locks, or my hair.

---

[1] The Baron/Charlie dialogues in this letter are a take-off on the Baron Munchausen character that Jack Pearl was then doing on the radio.

One afternoon I sat on the prowl pack—Pardon me, Baron; the what? The sauntering fifty-two cards. Why, Baron, I believe you are trying to say the promenade deck. That's it, Charlie! The promenade deck—and I was reading Van Loon's geography and the deck steward remarked that it was a great book. Being a democratic fellow, I replied to him and observed that one of my sons had given it to me at Christmas. "Isn't that queer, Mr. Lardner?" he said. "Because I was planning to give it to one of my sons for his birthday. That's a paradox." So now you know what a paradox is. Personally, I had always thought it meant two physicians in consultation, or just two physicians.

Warner Baxter[1] was a shipmate and walked twelve or fourteen laps around the deck each evening before dinner. This is called the Baxter Mile. Mrs. L. pretended she didn't know who he was, but she followed him with her eyes every time we turned our Baxter. Another mate was Mr. Collins, treasurer of the Curtis Publishing Company. He introduced himself to me and I tactfully said, "Oh, have they still got a treasurer?" This may result in the S. E. Post's rejecting a new story I mailed last Thursday. I recall telling some of you chaps that the story before this one was rejected by the Post, Cosmopolitan, Collier's and the Mercury, the two middle ones saying it was too long, as it certainly was, and Mencken saying it was not his style. But he suggested that I try Delineator, adding that women's magazines were the only ones making money. I didn't know whether Delineator was a weekly or a college year book, but I followed Mencken's advice and tried it, and it accepted the story, the editor remarking that it was so unsuitable for his magazine that he couldn't bear to turn it down. He paid, or is going to pay, one-fourth of the Post's price and, according to him, four or three times as much as Mencken would have paid. So, fellows, we have crashed Delineator and there are no more worlds to conquer.

The boat landed at San Diego at noon of Friday the 17th and stayed there long enough to permit the madam and myself to go to the races at Aqua Caliente. At that dismal joint the finishing touches were put to my feet by a half-mile walk almost straight up hill. We would have quit even on the day but for the presence in the seventh race of a horse named June Moon. Golden Prize or something was favorite and I would have played him but for the June Moon hunch, as favorites were doing pretty well. Little Ellis, always timid, wanted me to play June Moon for show, she urging that June Moon had been a show. I urged right back that it

---

[1] The movie star.

had also been a straight play. For one instant I had a flash to bet on Golden Prize to win and June Moon to show, and that is exactly what they did, but I neglected Golden Prize and played June Moon across the board, and the show money barely paid for itself.

If I could afford the trip, I would go in to Los Angeles, now that Vidmer's[1] here, and shoot him. They would never suspect me, because I would have to go barefooted and they would think I was a Hollywood boy. Don't get chesty, John, for winning arguments from your sports department, unless you win one from George Daley,[2] who Sees Everything, Knows Everything, Is Everything. I done tol' your ol' mammy that you had written most of Bill Macbeth's Corbett stuff. Jim was really a good old soul who made good in vaudeville because he had sense enough to act as straight man instead of trying to be the comic; the team of him and Billy Van was actually worth seeing. His eating habits, such as two helpings of coffee, doughnuts and wheatcakes in the Lambs at one or two in the morning, were not conducive to longevity.

I am sorry (still addressing John) that Gannett appeared to like your book.[3] I was hoping he would pannett. But you can bet that F. Adams wouldn't have said it was funny if he hadn't thought so, and he is anything but a bad judge. However, I will do my own judging when, if ever, I see the book. I presume, and hope, I'll get most of the reviews in my clippings. Remember my advice and don't give first refusal rights to any of those publishers, unless they pay you for them, and even then, don't tie up for more than one or two books with a decent firm, such as Farrar and Rinehart or Simon and Schuster.

I had a letter yesterday from your ma, Dickie, who said, among other important things, "D.S. Schoffern is dear and Oh, the difference to me!" Having known her for forty-seven years, man and boy scout, I am aware that when she writes "dear" she means "dead." We are all a-flitter to see the "Peter Stuyvesant Review," or whatever the name of it is.

---

[1] Richards Vidmer was a sportswriter and columnist on the *Herald–Tribune*. Whatever dispute Ring or John Lardner may have had with him is unknown.

[2] George Daley had become sports editor of the *Herald–Tribune* in 1931. He introduced the all-star football game to New York.

[3] John's book was *The Crowning of Technocracy*, by John Lardner and Thomas Sugrue.

Bill, how about finishing in Group 1 or Group 2 this semester? They tell me it's almost impossible not to at Princeton.

Dave, for my sake and dear old Andover (sometimes they call her Nancy) get a new picture taken so I can destroy the one of the noseless Jap which now makes our parlor table a living Bedlam on horseback.

Jim, we received one, not two, cables from you and what we'd like to receive is a letter stating what marks you got in each and every subject. Soon I shall write to Tom Shaw or Jack Doyle[1] and ascertain the preseason odds on the clubs in each league (some of them, I mean) and possible parlays such as the Yankees–Pittsburgh, the Yankees–Cubs. I wish some one would tell me whom Brooklyn got in exchange for Vance.[2] Brooklyn, my lads, is not out of the race yet. It came pretty close last year without much help from the Doozzler.

We are expecting a visit soon from Claudette and Norman,[3] and possibly one from Jean Dixon.

Meanwhile, the play's[4] the thing
Which is worrying the life out of your
                Shoeless Uncle Ring.

The National League race, I say, is between Pittsburgh and Brooklyn, which the acquisition of Joe Judge will strengthen. In the other league, watch the Red Sox so Cocky Collins won't have to do it alone.

The following letter is to Jean Dixon, a prominent Broadway and now Hollywood actress who had been a member of the original *June Moon* cast. Lardner had maintained a correspondence with her since the production of *June Moon*:

---

[1] Shaw and Doyle were sports promoters. Doyle was founder of the famous Vernon Arena frequented by motion picture stars, sports figures, and celebrities for many years.

[2] After winning twelve and losing eleven games for Brooklyn in 1932, the poular Clarence "Dazzy" Vance had been traded to the St. Louis Cardinals.

[3] Claudette Colbert and Norman Foster had been close friends with Lardner since Foster had played the lead in June Moon. Colbert was on the eve of a distinguished film career.

[4] Lardner was now working on the new play with Kaufman.

La Quinta
March seventh.

Dear Jean:—
   The vague address on this envelope was given me by a Mr. Kaufman of the Pulitzer Prize Kaufmans. I have no doubt it is wrong because his mind, at the time, was occupied with what he thinks of as the London Horror, which consists in the fact that it takes *six minutes* longer to play a performance of "Dinner at Eight" over there than in New York. I tried to comfort him with the suggestion that it was owing to the difference in longitude, but he continued to mope.
   My earnest wish is that when a few of my ailments show signs of improvement under the desert sun, as promised, you will be nice enough to pay me and Madame X a visit. We have no inducements excepting decent food and absolute quiet, so much of the latter, in fact, that I am afraid the joint won't stay open as long as I want it to. No doubt you have been at Palm Springs; we are eighteen miles east of it. Some people drive here from Los Angeles in five hours. For myself, I prefer the ease and luxury of railroad travel, and the Southern Pacific has a convenient train (quaintly termed "The Apache") which leaves Los Angeles at 12:15 and arrives at Indio (our nearest railway station) at 4:29. Are you still good-hearted enough to make such a trip when I am in better condition to act as genial host?
   I pass my sitting-up hours at the typewriter, working on the first act of a future Pulitzer winner. George has promised that if I can complete an act and a half that are worth tearing to bits, he will come out here to do the tearing. I have a secret hunch that he wants to come anyway, so perhaps the act and 1/2 need not be as good as normally.
                                        Ring

The play on which Lardner was working was, significantly, about a reformed alcoholic wbo falls off the wagon as an act of revolt against a lack of human sympathy and understanding on the part of his fiancee's family. Lardner had written one act of this play and a fragment of a second act before he died.

March 29, 1933

Bill, John, Dickie, David and James:—
   Would you like to know what I have been doing lately? (Oh, goodness, what has father dad unk popsie wopsie been doing lately?) Well, occasionally working on the first draft

of the first act of a play, and now I am on the 23rd page of rewriting, which is just about one-third of the way through. For this first act, my burdens, is nearly an hour and a half long in its present plight, which will give Mr. Kaufman the opportunity he lacked in "June Moon" of masticating and spitting out five and six pages at a time. I would have been in the midst of Act 2, the comical act, if hell hadn't popped loose a fortnight ago. Possibly as an aftermath of the temblors (if you think you're pronouncing that word right, look it up) things began happening in La Quinta and as they are things that might happen to anybody named Mr. and Mrs. Ring Lardner who came to the place called La Quinta in search of absolute La Quieta, I will outline them by way of warning (via Warneke):

Vincent Lawrence, former playwright, now Hollywood scenarist, and Dorothy Speare, novelist, entered our hut uninvited and wanted to know whether I had an idea for Harold Lloyd. Mr. Lawrence wrote his last picture, "Movie Crazy" or something; it was a flop, so Harold came back to him for more. I said I had no idea, but would try to think of one. I did think of one and it was a good one; so I thought and so Mr. Lawrence thought. However, it is well-known (to me, at least) that I can't tell things in synopsis form, or any other form—I have to write them out at length.

Well, a week ago Sunday came. The Rices were visiting us, I think. So was Phillips Holmes. So, suddenly, were Mr. Lawrence, Miss Speare, Harold Lloyd, Sam Harris,[1] some anonymous girl, and Louella O. Parsons and her latest husband, one Dr. Martin, who says he knew me in Chicago, which he did not if I am any judge. Louella also said that when she was working on the Chicago Tribune, she and I used to go on lots of parties together, which we did not if I am any judge.

Harold was all steamed up over my having an idea, and I was all steamed up over the same miracle, but when he and I managed to get a moment alone, it developed that all he wanted was the bare idea, told in two paragraphs (as he phrased it) and his scenarists and gag men would attend to the rest. Well, to be modest, this was like sending Babe Ruth to bat and letting him stand there till the umpire had called one ball, then taking him out and substituting a good hitter. Harold and I both steamed down as quickly as he had up— and I had wasted two or three days of thinking and writing. Unless, as Mr. Lawrence suggests, Buster Keaton can be

---

[1] Sam Harris was a Broadway producer who won three Pulitzer Prizes for *Icebound* (1923), *Of Thee I Sing* (1932), and *You Can't Take It with You* (1937).

caught sober and interested in the same idea, which remains, yours sincerely, a good idea, reeking with gags that Harold and his gag men wouldn't think of in a month of Sundays, and if there were a month of Sundays, you could all call yourselves Little Orphan Annie.

Now Louella's interview with G.B. Shaw at the Hearst ranch may have been printed in papers to which you have access. If not, you are much obliged to me for the following excerpt from it, to appreciate which you must know that if Louella is fifty-five years old, she's fifty-six: "'Mr. Shaw,' I said, 'is it true that Gene Tunney was the original of Cashel Byron?'[1] 'Young woman,' he replied, 'Cashel Byron was superannuated before you and Tunney were born.'"

Bill — Does this projected publication promise you or anyone else a living wage? Would you room and board at the Swopes'?

John — What's this I hear about you and one Sorghum having written a tune or a book called "The Crooning of Telegraphy"? If there is such a product, who is hoarding it?

Dickie — I imagine that Mr. Daley did Mr. Vidmer an injustice. The latter probably wrote a story about a ball game and it sounded like a story about an earthquake. All your baseball writers are tricky.

David — Please rush me a photograph of yourself. Ellis is mad and I am glad because I tore up a caricature of a noseless Jap which she was telling the waiters was sa jungest kind.

James — If you qet a bronze medal for defaulting to a Swiss in a consolation bout, why not stay away from the meets and win a Cecil Pulitzer scholarship?

Anxious

"Myrt," to whom the following letter is addressed, was Lizabeth Vereen, the sister of Kate Rice.

La Quinta, Calif.
Saturday, April first. [1933]

Dear Myrt: —

The enclosed is not just a cash prize for you, but the Lardners will be much obliged if you will turn it over to your sister Kate. It is a debt we owe her and please tell her

---

[1] Cashel Byron was the protagonist in George Bernard Shaw's novel of the same name.

not to send it back again—That would simply mean returning it to her, and so on ad infinitum.

Today the thermometer registered 100 in the shade (I don't know where they found the shade) and everybody was saying how wonderful! a temperature like that and you don't feel it: Well, Mrs. Vereen, this one felt it and longed for the refreshing breezes of an August afternoon in Macon. I must admit, though, that when the sun has disappeared behind our mountain, the weather is invariably perfect, as advertised.

With the slump in picture production, most of Hollywood can be found in La Quinta. Our next door neighbors all week have been Lilya Tashman and Edmund Lowe,[1] who, I presume, are married. Mr. Lowe had grown fat—a terrible blow, Ellis says, to the waitresses at the hotel. Miss Tashman, when she whispers, can be heard in Seattle and today she lost her diamond and emerald broach, which was no whispering matter. I am told she is supposed to be the best-dressed of all the picture people. She would look better to me in a soiled old Mother Hubbard than the beautifully pressed trousers she always wears.

We were expecting Floncey this week-end, but haven't heard from her. Norman and Claudette (Colbert or Foster) are coming tomorrow to spend the day with us. It will be an excuse for me not to work. Poor Norman had an automobile accident two weeks ago and knocked out a couple of front teeth. He is to start work Monday on a new picture and had put in a pleasant week at the dentist's—a secret from his producers.

The other enclosure[2] (the one without Lincoln's picture) will tell you the latest news of me—and *to* me. The writer is

---

[1] Lilyan Tashman came out of the Follies in 1917 to appear in several Broadway musicals before she went to Hollywood, where she met and married Edmund Lowe while they were both making *Ports of Call*. He was already established as a leading man in films. She died in 1934.

[2] Enclosed with the above letter was the following newspaper clipping:

**Hate Is Back of Ring Lardner's Fun; He Hates His Characters, Says Writer**

Ring Lardner, who is said to do his writing from a sick-bed somewhere in the west, is popularly regarded as a funny man. But hear Clifton Fadiman's opinion in this week's The Nation. Fadiman says:—

The special force of Ring Lardner's work springs from a single fact; he just doesn't like people. Except Swift, no writer had gone farther on hatred alone. I believe he hates himself; more certainly he hates his characters; and most clearly of all,

evidently a fellow from whom you simply can't keep a secret. But I do resent being called police dog, or dog of any kind.

I hope all the Hollises are well and that Mr. Crisp is much better. Love to everybody, including Mrs. Vereen.

A Born Hater.

La Quinta, California.
Sunday, April 9.

Dear James:—

I think I promised to tell you the official odds on the pennant races as soon as they were told to me. Here, then, they are:

Yankees, 1 to 3; Washington, $3\pm$ to 1; Athletics, 4 to 1.

Pittsburgh, 2 to 1; Cubs the same; St. Louis, 3 to 1; Brooklyn, 6 to 1; Giants, 4 to 1.

Parlays: Yankees with Pittsburgh or Chicago, 3 to 1; Yankees with St. Louis, $4\pm$ to 1; Yankees with Brooklyn, 8 to 1.

The price on the Yankees makes things tough. Yet, counting them as safe, I could make bets that would insure me an even break (if the Cubs or Pittsburgh won) or a profit (if St. Louis or Brooklyn won). There's no fun to that, however, so I'm playing the Yankees straight and parlaying them besides with Pittsburgh and Brooklyn. If the Yankees lose, you will find my body in a sour apple tree. If they win and my National League selections lose, I'll be ahead a

---

his characters hate each other. There is no mitigating soft streak in him as there is in the half-affectionate portraitures of Sinclair Lewis; and none of the amused complacency of H.L. Mencken.

He has found nothing whatsoever in American life to which to cling. Other writers who reveal this masochist pattern in a less pure form are George S. Kaufman and F. Scott Fitzgerald. But neither of these is cursed with Lardner's intuitive knowledge of the great American swine . . .

Read beneath the lines and you will see that everything he meets or touches drives him into a cold frenzy, leaving him without faith, hope or charity.

What Lardner, even in his simplest magazine stories, is interested in getting at is the core of egotism from which even our apparently most impeccable virtues spring.

Somewhere Lardner had a remark about "this special police dog" which "was like the most of them and hated everybody." Lardner himself is the police dog of American fiction, except that his hatred is not the product of mere crabbedness but of an eye that sees too deep for comfort.

trifle. If they win and Pittsburgh wins, it will be quite nice. And if they win and Brooklyn wins, it will be lovely.[1]

We are starting for home the end of this week and after making brief stop-overs in Niles and Detroit, will reach New York on or about the 24th. I will probably hang around the metropolis a week, to see Dr. Gerber, Dr. Tyson and Dr. Kaufman, but your mother will go to East Hampton and that is where you had better address future letters, of which I hope there will be a great many.

I'd like to know how you are getting along with your strenuous course.

Popsy.

When the Lardners returned to New York, Lardner did indeed see his dentist ("Dr. Gerber"), his physician ("Dr. Tyson"), and George Kaufman (about the new play on which they were working). A letter[2] "to a friend," probably written at this time, exhibits Lardner's desire professionally and personally to "keep on going":

Ellis is in East Hampton and I am staying in town for two reasons—one is a long-delayed session with the dentist, which will last at least two weeks, and the other to play with George the first two acts of our next collaboration. I am fortunate, I guess, to be one of the chosen to work with him. There are flocks of more experienced playwrights seeking his partnership and the only thing that wins consideration for me is the fact that he keeps promises and as soon as we had finished "June Moon," we agreed to do another one on a subject I had in mind—as soon as I got around to it, which has been a long, long time. I only hope I can stay well enough to work. If I can, I promise you and the rest of the world one thing: that never again will I take a vacation when I am through with a job. I think it is the biggest mistake a person can make—not to keep on going. I never felt better in my life than when I was working twenty hours a day, trying to get "June Moon" into shape, and never felt worse than afterwards, when it was in shape and I treated myself to a "layoff," which was mostly spent in the lovely atmosphere of hospitals.

---

[1] Unfortunately, the Washington Senators beat out the second place Yankees by seven games in the American League, and the New York Giants finished five games ahead of Pittsburgh in the National League. Brooklyn finished sixth, twenty-six and a half games back. The Giants won the Series, four games to one.

[2] Quoted by Elder, pp. 282-83. Unlocated elsewhere.

In June, Lardner returned to East Hampton, where, because it was the beginning of summer vacation, the boys had gathered, too, except for John, who was in nearby New York. Lardner was quite weak and was confined mostly to his workroom and sleeping porch, overlooking the ocean.

Of the following letter Richard Lardner Tobin writes:

This letter . . . was written from East Hampton in either the late spring or early summer of 1933, just before Mr. Lardner died. As he indicated in the letter, he has just left Doctors Hospital for East Hampton, where he died September 25, 1933. I find it fascinating, (and I remember it to be true), that Ring Lardner was writing lyrics for Jerome Kern, but I don't for a moment doubt it because he was, obviously, intensely musical. The 'Jim' mentioned in the first paragraph is Ring's second son, James, who was later killed in the International Brigade in Spain and, about this time, an unhappy student at Harvard—unhappy because he knew more about literature than the people who were teaching him.

East Hampton
Late spring or early summer of 1933]
Solomon Gr—dy.

Dear Dickie:—

Attached are two or three documents[1] of value to you and me. The envelope is sent in the hope you will see it to its way via the New York PO. I don't dare send it from here or Jerome Kern would have to put the lyrics enclosed into his farewell opus and while Jim is home for the week-end giving it to him is like sending it to the dead letter office. Sherwood Anders-n and Rabbit Maranville paid calls before I left No Visitors, N. Y., for this bed o' pain. Anders-n and I got to talking why we'd ever left our small towns. Maranville says the Yankees are a cinch so he isn't putting up anything on them. I've got what the boys call a yard and a half unless Doyle wiggles out, and he's trying.

Claudette Colbert was in town before I left and came up to say hello. I never knew they was so many interns in Doctors' Hospital. Every five seconds a new one would come in and say, "Can't I get you some icewater, Mr. Lardner?" or "I'm going out, would you like anything

---

[1] The "documents" were some lyrics Jerome Kern apparently did not use and a check for Richard Lardner Tobin.

from the drug store?" Her hair is now pink but she's cute, anyway.

Your aberrated mother hasn't send me any of your clippings but I caught one Sunday under a by-line. Good stuff, congratulations. When you see my son John tell him we now have mail delivery in East Hampton.
                                                    Ring.

Ring Lardner
East Hampton, Long Island
Thursday, July twentieth.
[1933]

[To Mildred Luthy]
Dear Millie: —

The young man who said "Hello, sweetheart" to you on the telephone doubtless knew whom he was addressing and wanted a little encouragement. When you replied to him so cruelly, he had to think of an explanation that would salve his wounded pride.

Your child is really beautiful and has the Hollis charm, which means that hundreds of members of my poor sex will suffer. If I didn't know how bored and uncomfortable it would make her, I would insist on her visiting me at least once a day, just so I could hear her talk and see her close up. I have refrained from demanding her presence (except once) because I don't want her to think of me as an old pest, but lots of times I watch and admire her from my cell without interfering with her normal activities. I offered to answer all the letters she got from Americus if she would let me read them all. She accepted the offer but evidently changed her mind.

This is a gala night in East Hampton, with Floncey opening in the local stock company's play. Enough people to fill the theater are going from the Rice and Lardner houses. As usual, the undersigned will have to be satisfied with hearing about it. Floncey has a much bigger part than in "June Moon" and I presume Kate is quite nervous, probably more so than the artiste herself.

John's vacation begins next Monday and on Thursday, Albert[1] and all the Lardners excepting the old man are leaving by automobile for Chicago and the Fair. They intend to see how cheaply they can make the trip, for two reasons—the "fun" of the experiment and the fact that they won't have anything to spend. Two Scandinavians and I will

---

[1] Albert Mayer was the Lardners' chauffeur for more than twenty years.

have the house to ourselves for a couple of weeks, and I'll bet you guess my plans for the first two or three days and nights. After that I may accept the hospitality of the Rices for one meal (they haven't invited me yet) but I am terrified while I am there because, as you know, they are never safe from invasion by people I used to like, but who, in my old age, make me jittery. There is simply no sense in a person's reaching the anti-social state I seem to have attained and if I had any will power, I would snap out of it.

Which subject naturally leads to the Boswell Sisters.[1] Did you know they were in London, singing in a night club? That is, they were till Connie got the mumps. I imagine it improved her looks, but interfered with her singing and, worst of all, with her interesting conversations on the Life and Loves of Connie Boswell.

Lizabeth,[2] who does *not* make me jittery, has been kind enough to obey my positive orders to call. I think she looks very well, infinitely better than last time she was here. The other night, Ellis went to Kate's to play backgammon, and I made Liz come here and play contract with Bill, Jim and me. Before the game she protested that she knew nothing about it, and then proceded to show up the Lardners. She and I gave my little ones a good beating, and I assure you it was her doings, not mine.

Please give my love to your mother and tell her I think of her often and particularly when there is a beautiful moon, such as we had earlier in the month. One of you told me she was a moon lover and it makes me proud to know we have that taste in conmon—as well as a few others.

Try to get well and strong for your trip up here, and arrange to stay a long, long time.

R.

The next letter responds to a letter from Dorothy Dudley Harvey, whose book *Dreiser and the Land of the Free*, published in 1932, contained this statement: "Ring Lardner, asked by a producer to serve with Dreiser and Robert Frost as one of three founders of an American theatre for only

---

[1] Connee, Vet (Helvetia), and Martha Boswell, an internationally-known singing trio, were among the first to introduce swing. Connee, the trio's soloist and arranger, overcame a childhood paralysis to be the motivating force in the trio.

[2] Elizabeth Vereen, Kate Rice's sister.

American plays, refused on the ground that Dreiser was both ridiculous and immoral."[1]

East Hampton, Long Island
July 21, 1933.

Dear Mrs. Harvey:—
Honestly I have a dozen real alibis for not having answered your letter before, but I won't bore you with them. I do hope, though, that you haven't taken my silence as consent to the report in your book of my attitude toward Mr. Dreiser. I am telling you the truth when I say that I can't recall ever having heard of the Art Theater you mention, and the true explanation of your sister's story must be either that some one was impersonating me or I was under an anaesthetic. Never consciously did I speak of Mr. Dreiser's work as repellent to me in any way. I have never met him, but have had some very pleasant (to me) correspondence with him. I have undoubtedly expressed the opinion, in private conversations, that I thought his style awkward. Otherwise I admire him intensely for the drama of his writing and its wealth of detail. I am sorry to add that your book never reached me and probably was held up somewhere along the route taken by your letter.
Sincerely,
Ring Lardner

A few days later, Lardner sent a telegram to Mrs. Hollis:

EASTHAMPTON NY          1933 JUL 31 PM 4 20
MRS FLORENCE D HOLLIS=
AMERICUS GA
AN ASTRONOMER IS GOING TO TELL US ALL ABOUT THE MOON THURSDAY NIGHT OVER NEWYORK STATION WJZ NINE FIFTEEN YOUR TIME STOP THE MOON WILL BE NEARLY FULL THAT NIGHT STOP IF HE SAYS ANYTHING YOU DONT LIKE LET ME KNOW AND I WILL ECLIPSE HIM STOP LOVE=
RING.

In the June 1933 *American Mercury*, Mencken had praised Lardner's *Lose with a Smile*, arguing that Lardner would eventually be acknowledged by literary scholars as a

---

[1] Dorothy Dudley, *Dreiser and the Land of the Free* (New York: Smith and Haas, 1932), p. 470.

major American writer. One month and a day before Lardner died, he wrote to thank Mencken:

East Hampton, Long Island
August 24, 1933

Dear H.—
It is almost time I thanked you for that piece about the baseball book, which you know perfectly well did not deserve any of the space you gave it. Believe it or not, I appreciated it more than the checks it brought from Brother Lorimer.
Yours,<br>R. L.

The same day, Lardner wrote what may have been his last letter. It is addressed to a Miss Wilma Seavey, who later married Paul Ogden. She had written to Lardner after a friendly argument with her future husband over Lardner's attitude toward his characters. His response is of particular importance because it is his only direct comment on Clifton Fadiman's interpretation of Lardner's work.

East Hampton, Long Island
August 24, 1933

Dear Miss Seavey:—
 I must apologize for delaying so long in answering your letter, but my health has prevented me from attending to my correspondence for the last few months.
 I don't suppose any author either hates or loves all his characters. I try to write about people as real as possible, and some of them are naturally more likeable than others. In regard to your argument, I think the decision should be awarded to you, because I cannot remember ever having felt any bitterness or hatred toward the characters I have written about. I am grateful to you for your defense of me.

Yours Sincerely,<br>Ring Lardner

Though Lardner had seemed better after the stay in La Quinta, he soon began to decline rapidly. Miss Feldmann, who was a trained nurse, returned late in the summer to care for him. His last written communication was probably the following telegram congratulating John for a front-page story John had written for the *Herald-Tribune*:

EASTHAMPTON NY    1933 AUG 31 PM 5 18
JOHN LARDNER:
HERALD TRIBUNE NYK
  VERY PROUD OF MY SONS ECLIPSE OF SUNS ECLIPSE ON PAGE ONE
      STOOPNAGLE.

On the evening of 24 September, after Jim and David had departed for their fall terms at Harvard and Andover, Lardner played some bridge with Ellis, Ring Jr., and Kate Rice. The next morning, he suffered a heart attack and, later that day, he died. He was only forty-eight.

As he had requested, his body was cremated without ceremony. While a great many in the worlds of sport, journalism, popular music, drama, cinema, and literature grieved and testified to their sense of loss, Lardner characteristically avoided the ultimate public appearance.

# Index

*LT: Letters To*
*LF: Letters From*

Abbott, Dorothy (Ellis's sister). See Kitchell, Dorothy Abbott.
Abbott, Ellis. See Lardner, Ellis Abbott.
Abbott, Florence (Ellis's sister). See Torrence, Florence Abbott.
Abbott, Frank Parker (Ellis's father), 1, 41, 45, 53, 58–61, 64–65, 67, 70, 74, 76–79, 83, 93, 95–97, 99, 102. LT: 53, 78–79
Abbott, Jeannette Hascall (Ellis's mother), 24, 54, 58–60, 65–66, 70, 93, 95–99, 102–04, 106–07, 123–25, 129, 204, 206. LT: 58, 61, 95–99, 103–04, 106–07, 124–25, 129
Abbott, Frank (Ellis's brother), 92, 96, 104, 123–25, 132–34, 196. LT: 124–25, 132–34
Abbott, Jane ("Jeannette") (Ellis's sister). See Kitchell, Jane Abbott.
Abbott, John (Ellis's brother), 96, 123–25, 132–34. LT: 124–25, 132–34
Abbott, Ruby (Ellis's sister). See Hendry, Ruby Abbott.
Abbott, William C. (Ellis's brother), 123–25, 128, 132–34. LT: 124–25, 128, 132–34
"Absolution," 156–57

Adams, Franklin P. ("F.P.A."), 105–06, 114, 182, 274. LT: 105–06, 127
Ade, George, 133–34, 146–47. LT: 146–47
Albee, Edward, 169
"Alibi Ike," 152, 157, 194, 270
*All the Sad Young Men*, 182, 199
*American Golfer, The*, 177
*American Language, The*, 139
*American Magazine*, 132, 157, 209
*American Mercury*, 156–57, 176, 195, 211, 270–71, 273, 285–86
*American Tragedy, An*, 252
*Amos and Andy*, 238
Anderson, Ellen Graham, 178
Anderson, Hunk, 247
Anderson, Maxwell, 170n
Anderson, Sherwood, 196–98, 282
Andrew, Jess C., 146
*Ann Vickers*, 271–72
Arlen, Michael, 176, 187, 208
*Arrowsmith*, 200
Ashford, Daisy, 126, 173
Astaire, Adele, 228, 235
Astaire, Fred, 228–31, 235
Aubert, Jeanne, 234
Austen, Jane, 80n
*Babbitt*, 271
*Baltimore Sun*, 140n
Balzac, Honoré de, 67
Banta, John, 84, 88
Barrie, Sir James, 126
Barthelmess, Richard, 171n, 177, 182
Baseball war, 39
Baston, Albert Preston, 111

"Battle of the Century, The,"
 134–37, 142
Baxter, Warner, 273
Bayes, Nora, 57
Beckett, Samuel, 169
Beach, Harrison L., 162–63
Beeson, Billy, 1, 3
Belcher, Frank, 257
Bell Syndicate, 1n, 119,
 122–23, 138, 156, 168,
 194, 204–05, 210, 232–33
Berlin, Irving, 191
*Big Town, The*, 113, 119n,
 129–31, 144, 166, 194
Bingham, William, 246
Bobbs–Merrill Publishing Co.,
 109, 112, 118–21, 123,
 129, 131, 138, 142–43,
 147, 163, 165–67.
 LT: 112, 118, 125–26,
 138, 167
*Bookman*, 178n, 199, 210
Boston *American*, 1n, 15,
 79–81, 83, 86, 94, 95–98
Boston *Globe*, 235
Boswell sisters, 284
Bottomley, Jim, 242
Boyd, Ernest, 171
Boyd, Madeline (Peggy), 171,
 201
Boyd, Thomas A., 159, 201
Brady, William A., 135–36
Briggs, Claire, 53, 60, 105–06
Bruccoli, Matthew J., 1n
Broun, Heywood Campbell,
 82n, 141, 171, 187,
 205–06, 261–62.
 LT: 141–42
Broun, Ruth Hale, 187–88
Brown, Joe E., 194
Bruhn, Lottie, 220
Buchanan, Jack, 187
Buck, Gene, 148–49, 159–60,
 163, 172, 177, 181–83,
 188–91, 200–01, 205,
 207–08, 215
Buck, Helen Faulkner, 148,
 172, 181n, 200
Burleson, Albert S., 128

Busher stories, 39, 49, 104,
 109, 117–21, 131,
 193–94, 204, 207, 256,
 263–64
"Caddy's Diary, A," 143
Callahan, Jimmie, 94, 257
Capone, Al, 252
Cantor, Eddie, 148n
Carey, Max, 234
Carpentier, Georges, 134–36
Carrigan, Bill, 257
Century Company, The, 115
Century Film Corporation, 193
Chamberlain, John, 222
Chambers, D. Laurence,
 138–40, 165. LT: 138–39
"Champion," 147, 151, 152,
 194
Chance, Frank, 47, 50n,
 51–52, 62, 257–58
Chaplin, Charles, 183, 200,
 207–08
Chicago *American*, 1n, 10–11,
 98, 102
Chicago City Hall, 184–86
Chicago *Examiner*, 1n, 4, 11,
 13, 20, 99
Chicago *InterOcean*, 1n, 4, 6,
 20, 79
Chicago *Tribune*, 1n, 20–21,
 22n, 23–24, 33, 37, 39,
 49, 57, 66–68, 72, 78–79,
 86, 93–94, 103, 105, 107,
 113–14, 116, 119,
 121–22, 186, 192n, 198,
 232–33, 252, 277
*Citizen Kane*, 181n
Claire, Ina, 176
Clarkson, James, 11
"Clemo Uti—'The Water
 Lilies,'" 169
Cobb, Irvin S., 127–28, 143,
 146, 176
Cobb, Ty, 257
Cochran, Charles B., 135–36
Cohan, George M., 212–13,
 215, 217, 226, 255
Colbert, Claudette, 275, 279,
 282–83

*Collier's*, 115–16, 148, 249–50, 268–70, 273
Collins, Eddie, 257
Connolly, Marc, 199–200, 206
"Contract," 217
Conway, Karl, 210
Conway, Sylvie, 210
Coolidge, Calvin, 161
Coppess, Irvin, 92
Corbett, James J., 135n, 201
Cornell, Duffy, 29
Cornell, Katharine, 188
*Cosmopolitan*, 120, 144, 172n, 174–75, 177, 179, 192–93, 209, 213, 268–70, 273
Costain, Thomas B., 144, 160. LT: 144, 160
Courtney, Inez, 234
Coward, Noel, 187
Coy, Edward H. ("Ted"), 220. LT: 220
Crandall, Mrs., 60, 63, 66
Craven, Frank, 189
Crews, Laura Hope, 188
Crews, Ralph, 133
*Crowning of Technocracy, The*, 274, 278
Crowninshield, Frank, 170, 172, 177. LT: 170
Crusinberry, James, 120
Culver Military Academy, 59–60, 62–63, 65, 67–68, 71, 76, 80, 84, 87
Curtis Publishing Co., 194, 273
Daley, George, 274, 278
Dane, Karl, 206
Davies, Marion, 207–08
Davis, Bob, 2, 201. LT: 201
Davis, George, 14
Davis, John W., 161
Davis, Owen, 198, 200
"Day with Conrad Green, A," 183
*Delineator*, 270–71, 273
Delong, John, 53
Dempsey, Jack, 134–36, 153, 203–06, 236

Depression (1930s), 224, 232, 255, 259, 261, 270
Deuel, Harvey, 192
Dever, Mayor (of Chicago), 185–86. LT: 185. LF: 185–86
Dickens, Charles, 80n
Dickey, Bill, 255
"Dinner Bridge," 211
Dixon, Harland, 229–30
Dixon, Jean, 275–76. LT: 276
Dole, Julia, 93
Donohue, Jack, 191–92
Donohue, Jagger, 14–15
Doran, George, Publishing Co., 109, 131, 143n, 144, 165–66, 176
Dorgan, Dick, 162n, 172
Dorgan, Ike, 136–37. LT: 137. LF: 137
Dorgan, Tad, 162n, 172
Douglas, Kirk, 194
Downey, Morton, 249
Doyle, Jack, 275, 282
Dreiser, Theodore, 250–55, 284–85. LT: 251–55. LF: 253–54
*Dreiser and the Land of the Free*, 284–85
Dreyfuss, Barney, 234
*Drifting Cowboy, The*, 192
Dryden, Charles, 18–20, 53
Dunne, Finley Peter, 20, 134n
Durand, Rene, 151–52, 181
Dyckman, Clyde, 184–86
Earnshaw, George, 246
Eckersall, Walter, 20, 60, 67
*Egoist, The*, 80
Elder, Donald, 66n, 175n, 216n, 227n, 238n, 244n, 258n, 261n, 269, 281n
*Elmer Gantry*, 271
*Elmer the Great*, 194, 212–13, 215–16
Errol, Leon, 146, 183
*Esquire*, 162
Evers, John, 50, 62
"Ex Parte," 217
"Facts, The," 152

Fadiman, Clifton, 279n, 286
Fallon, William, 208
Farrar, John, 199
Feldman, Gusti, 195–96, 216, 228, 242, 286
Ferber, Edna, 139, 208
Fields, W.C., 134, 171n, 190, 234
Fish, Sidney, 205
Fitzgerald, F. Scott, 127, 145, 148–54, 157–60, 163–65, 167, 170–73, 175–84, 186–92, 197–201, 205–08, 211–15, 223–26, 280n. LT: 152, 158–61, 163–65, 170–73, 175–78, 181–83, 186–92, 197–201, 205–08, 211–12, 214–15, 225–26. LF: 149, 214
Fitzgerald, Frances Scott ("Scottie"), 154, 197, 226
Fitzgerald, Zelda Sayre, 127, 145–46, 148–49, 153, 157–60, 164–65, 167, 170–73, 175–77, 181, 183, 186–92, 197–201, 205–08, 211–12, 214–15, 225–26, 265. LT: 145–46, 154, 157–60, 164–65, 170–73, 175–77, 186–92, 197–201, 205–08, 211–12, 214–15
Fitzsimmons, Robert, 201
Flatley, Nick, 160
Fleischer, Nat, 135n
Fletcher, Louis J., 38–39
Fonda, Harold, 92
Forrest, Sam, 226
Foster, Norman, 275, 279
Foy, Eddie, 231
Frazee, Harry, 182, 190
French, Samuel, 239
Friedman, Benny, 250
Frost, Robert, 284
Fullerton, Hugh, 4, 11, 66, 79, 103–04, 132, 156, 204
Gallagher, Ed, 191
Gannett, Lewis, 271–72, 274

"Gee! It's a Wonderful Game," 57, 89–90
Gerard, James Watson, 117
Gibbons, Jack, 206
Gibson, Helen, 81, 85, 87, 91, 93, 95, 98, 108
Gibson, Stewart, 92
Giffin, R. L., 109. LT: 109
Gilbert, Kenneth, 146. LT: 146
Gillen, Harold W., 109–12. LT: 110–112
Gilmore, Margalo, 188
Gish, Dorothy, 197n
Gish, Lillian, 177, 182
Glaenzer, Seymour, 268. LT: 268
Gleason, Bill, 257
*Gold Rush, The*, 183
Goldberg, Irma, 172
Goldberg, Rube, 172
Golden, John, 159, 239. LT: 239
"Golden Honeymoon, The," 144, 150–52, 157, 159, 174, 257
Graeve, Oscar, 270–71
Grange, Harold ("Red"), 187
Gray, Judd, 252
Grayson, Billy, 75–76, 78–79
*Great Gatsby, The*, 165, 167, 170, 175, 178–80, 182, 186, 200
*Great Gatsby, The* (play), 197–200
Guest, Edgar A., 219
*Gullible's Travels, Etc.*, 112–14, 119, 123n, 127, 147–48, 163, 166
Hahn, Edgar, 14
"Haircut," 174–75, 179, 219
Hamill, Pauline Micks, 33–34
Hammond, Percy, 155, 186, 200, 217
Hanley, Jimmy, 201
Hansen, Harry, 201
"Harmony" 49
Harris, Sam, 277
Hart, Moss, 234
Harter, Evan, 9

Hartman, Siegfried, 194
Harvey, Dorothy Dudley, 284–85. LT: 285
Hawks, Edwin, 84, 88
Hawks, Helen, 4, 8, 23, 33, 133
Hay, Mary, 171, 177, 182, 191
Hayes, Helen, 192
Hazzard, Jack, 197, 208
Hearst, William Randolph, 97, 177, 207–08
Hearst Castle, 208, 278
*Hearst's International*, 175
Hemingway, Ernest, 150, 162, 214
Hendry, James Abbott, 108
Hendry, J. Robin, 124–25, 132–34, 203, 258, 260. LT: 124–25, 132–34
Hendry, Ruby Abbott, 4, 8, 20, 54–55, 60, 63, 65, 71, 83, 93–94, 96–100, 102–03, 107–08, 123–25, 132–34, 148, 203, 258–60. LT: 55, 102–03, 107–08, 124–25, 132–34, 203, 258–60
Herbert, Victor, 159–60, 161n
Herman, Floyd (Babe), 256
Heston, William M. ("Willie"), 187
Hoffman, Danny, 15
Hofman, Artie, 48, 51, 113, 120n
Hollis, Florence, 238, 244, 251, 284–85. LT: 244–45, 251, 285
Holmes, Howard E. ("Ducky"), 51
Holmes, Phillips, 277
Hoover, Loring, 13, 15, 92
Hopper, DeWolf, 38
Houdini, Harry, 183
*How To Write Short Stories*, 151–53, 156–57, 159, 163, 165–66, 176, 179–80, 217, 265
Howard, King, 227, 244–45
Howard, Leslie, 188
Howard, Sidney Coe, 168n

Howland, Hewitt H., 112–23, 125–31, 137–41, 143–44, 165–66. LT: 113–23, 125–31, 138, 141, 143–44. LF: 165–66
Hoyt, Waite, 243
*Huckleberry Finn*, 20n
"Hurry Kane," 212n, 215
Hurtz, Fred, 92
Husing, Ted, 246
Huston, Walter, 212n, 215–16
Hutchinson, Duke, 4
Hyde, Henry, 140
"I Can't Breathe," 217
"I. Gaspiri," 169, 226
*In American*, 178n
"In the Wake of the News," 20, 39, 103
*Innocents Abroad, The*, 165
Irwin, Helen, 63, 102–03
*Jack Dempsey*, 135n
Jacks, Arthur, 4, 83, 88, 90, 93, 127, 177, 258
James, Will, 192–93
Janis, Elsie, 183
Jeffries, James J., 135n
Johns, Mabel, 225
Johnson, Ban, 39n, 75, 94
Johnson, Jack, 100
Johnson, J. Rosamond, 187
Johnson, Wilma Abby ("Ginnie"), 1, 3–12, 14–17, 24–27, 32–33, 38–39, 51–52, 93. LT: 5–6, 11–15, 18–19, 25–26, 32–33, 38–39
Johnston, Will, 162n
Jozan, Edouard, 165
Jones, Fielder, 14, 257
*June Moon*, 57, 194, 223, 225–27, 234, 273–75, 277, 281, 283
"June Moon" (song), 57, 223
Kahn, Otto, 191
Kalman, C. O., 148–49. LT: 149
Kaufman, George 57, 171n, 197n, 223–26, 270, 275n, 276–77, 280n, 281

Kaufman, Beatrice, 171, 177
Kearns, Jack, 134–36, 236
Keaton, Buster, 277–78
Keeley, James, 103
Kelly, George, 199
Kelly, Robert B. ("Speed"), 7, 32, 34
Keogh, Hugh E. ("H.E.K"), 20, 52–53, 103
Kern, Jerome, 182, 190, 282
Kitchell, Dorothy Atbott, 55, 123–25, 132–34. LT: 124–25, 132–34
Kitchell, Francis R., 124–25, 132–34, 147–48. LT: 124–25, 132–34, 147–48, 227, 229
Kitchell, Howell W., 124–25, 132–34. LT: 124–25, 132–34
Kitchell, Jane Abbott ("Jeannette"), 55, 91, 123–25, 132–34, 147–48, 227, 229–31. LT: 124–25, 132–34, 229–31
Krutch, Joseph Wood, 222
Kryder, Noble, 93
Lacy, George Anne, 63
LaFollette, Robert M., 161
Lajoie, Napoleon, 49
Lannin, Paul, 228, 230
Lardner, Anne (Ring's sister). See Tobin, Anne Lardner.
Lardner, David Ellis (Ring's son), 121, 132, 195n, 196, 205, 227, 234–37, 259, 261, 272–78, 282, 287. LT: 237, 272–78
Lardner, Dora McCarley (Rex's wife), 84, 107
Lardner, Ellis Abbott (Ring's wife), 1–11, 13–17, 19–24, 26–104, 106–08, 112, 114, 128–29, 133, 145, 148, 155–56, 158, 160–61, 164–65, 168, 170, 172, 181–82, 186–87, 191, 194–98, 200, 203–04, 206, 210, 211, 215–16, 220–21, 224, 227, 230–32, 234–37, 240, 242–45, 248, 252, 258, 260–61, 267, 269, 272–73, 276, 278–79, 281, 284, 287. LT: 3, 6–12, 16–17, 19–24, 26–31, 34–37, 39–40, 42–53, 55–57, 59–62, 64–76, 79–93, 100-01, 195–96, 216. LF: 7–8, 11, 13–14, 17, 19, 27–29, 36, 38, 41–42, 44–45, 51–52, 61, 63, 68–69, 73–77, 83, 85–87, 96–98, 101–02, 231–32
Lardner, Harry (Ring's brother), 86
Lardner, Henry (Ring's father), 24, 36, 86, 93, 98
Lardner, James L. (Ring's great-uncle), 124
Lardner, James Phillips (Ring's son), 106–08, 114, 187, 196, 211, 215, 227, 235–37, 243–48, 251, 259, 261, 265–67, 272–78, 280–82, 284, 287. LT: 227, 235–37, 243–48, 251, 266–67, 272–78, 280–81
Lardner, John Abbott (Ring's son), 99, 102, 104, 107–08, 114, 187, 196, 203, 210–11, 215, 224, 227–29, 231–35, 238, 242–44, 248–49, 258–59, 269, 272–78, 282–83, 286–87. LT: 224, 227–29, 231–35, 238, 272–78, 287

Lardner, Lena (Ring's sister), 23, 36, 59, 86, 88, 269. LT: 269
Lardner, Lena Phillips (Ring's mother), 23, 36, 39, 50, 52, 59–60, 70, 86, 88, 90, 93, 96, 98
Lardner, Rex (Ring's brother), 3, 20, 37–39–40, 84n, 86, 92, 97–98, 127, 170, 175, 192, 258, 270–71
Lardner, Ring Jr ("Bill") (Ring's son), 2, 4, 41, 64–65, 82, 108–09, 114, 125, 194n, 196, 199, 207n, 227, 236–37, 240–41, 245, 259, 261, 272–78, 282, 284, 287. LT: 236–37, 240–41, 272–78
Lardner, William (Ring's brother), 86
*Lardners: My Family Remembered, The*, 2, 3, 4, 41, 65, 82, 194, 199
Lawrence, Gertrude, 187
Lawrence, Vincent, 277
Layman, Richard, 1n
Lee, Lila, 183
Leech, Margaret ("Peggy"), 171, 177
LeGallienne, Eva, 181
Lengel, William, 269–70
Leopold, Nathan, 160
Levinson, Edward, 261–62. LT: 262
Lewis, Sinclair ("Red"), 200, 271–72
*Liberty*, 156, 165, 168, 170, 174–75, 179, 182, 192, 225
"Liberty Hall," 217
Lillie, Beatrice, 187
Lincoln, Abraham, 238
Lindbergh baby kidnapping, 256
Lindsay, Ray, 92
Lingle, Jake, 252
Liscomb, Harry F., 173

Literary Guild, 217, 222, 265
*Little Orphan Annie*, 260, 278
"Little Puff of Smoke, Good-Night," 57, 87, 91
Lloyd, Harold, 243, 277–78
Loeb, Richard, 160
Long, Ray, 120, 176–77, 179, 193
Longfellow, Henry Wadsworth (poem "Hiawatha"), 5
Lorimer, George Horace, 104, 120, 131–32, 137, 142, 144, 194, 204, 207, 255, 263. LT: 132, 137, 142, 286. LF: 132
*Lose with a Smile*, 256, 263–64, 271, 285–86
"Love Nest, The," 179–81
*Love Nest, The*, (play), 213, 215
*Love Nest and Other Stories, The*, 175, 184, 186, 192, 200, 217, 265
Lowe, Edmund, 279
Lowell, Amy, 219
Luthy, Mildred, 220, 237–38, 241–42, 244–45, 260–61, 283–84. LT: 221, 237–38, 241–42, 260–61, 283–84
Lynch, Thomas J., 39n
McAdoo, William, 161
McCutcheon, John T., 20
McGee, Ruth, 93
McGeehan, William O., 155, 187, 213n
McGraw, John J., 15n, 257–58. LT: 257–58
McGugin, Dan, 247
McGuire, William Anthony, 228
Mankiewicz, Herman, 181–82, 197n
Manners, J. Hartley, 130
Mansfield, Katherine, 159
Maranville, Walter ("Rabbitt"), 282
Martin, Quinn, 155
*M*A*S*H*, 109
Maurer, James, 261–62

Mayer, Albert, 283
Mayhew, Stella, 56–57
"Maysville Minstrell, The," 26, 218–19
Meighan, Tom, 183, 188, 197, 200
Mencken, Henry L., 4n, 109, 139–40, 147, 156–57, 159, 179–80, 192, 211, 213–14, 231, 265, 267–73, 285–86.
    LT: 139–40, 147, 156–57, 179–80, 192, 211, 213–14, 231, 265, 268–69, 271–72, 286.
    LF: 267, 272
Meredith, George, 80
Metro–Goldwyn–Mayer (MGM), 206
Meyer, Margaret, 93
Micks, Jud, 36
Miller, Marilyn, 146n, 191, 228–30, 235
Mitchell, Fred, 267
Monroe, Harriet, 20
Montague, James J., 156
"Montana Moon" (song), 223
Moore, Julia A., 19, 20n
Morgan, Henry, 194
Morgan, Wallace, 116
Morse, Theodore, 161
*Mourning Becomes Electra*, 249
Mumford, Lewis, 222
Mundin, Herbert, 187
Murphy, Esther, 205
*My Four Weeks in France*, 115, 117, 119, 123n, 166
*My Four Years in Germany*, 117
Nast, Condé, 176–77, 183
Nathan, George Jean, 176–77, 182, 187
Neall, Adelaide W., 255.
    LT: 256
Newberry Library, 207n
Newell, Hugh, 92
*New Klondike, The*, 188, 194, 197, 200

*New Leader*, 261–63.
    LT: 262–63
*New Republic, The*, 211
*Newsweek*, 99
New York *Daily News*, 192, 232–33
New York *Evening Post*, 173, 235
New York *Herald*, 145, 148, 187n, 235
New York *Herald–Tribune*, 114, 222, 243–44, 249, 255, 259, 271, 274, 286–87
New York *Morning World*, 141
New York *Morning Telegraph*, 217, 220
New York *Sun*, 145, 250
New York *Times*, 181n, 182, 200, 222, 270
New York *Tribune*, 186n
New York *World*, 129n, 141n, 145, 181n, 184–85, 201, 203, 205
New York *World–Telegram*, 250–53
*New Yorker, The*, 99, 121, 162, 171n, 227, 248–49, 259, 264
Nicholson, Meredith, 120
"Night Letter from Ring Lardner, A," 232, 238–40
Niles *Daily Star*, 25, 32, 93–94
Nisonger, Grace, 133, 196
*No, No, Nannette*, 182
"Nora," 217
Nordyke, Horace, 92
Nugent, J. C., 188
O'Brien, Edward J., 200
Offenbach, Jacques, 191
Ogden, Paul, 286
"On Meeting Ring Lardner," 196–97
*Orpheus in the Underworld*, 191
Ostrander, Walter, 5–6, 38
*Othello*, 235
"Over the Waves," 162
Overman, Lynne, 215

*Own Your Own Home*, 108, 122–23, 138–39, 166
Parent, Frederick, 14
Parker, Dorothy, 171, 181
Parsons, Louella, 277–78
Patterson, J. M., 192
Perkins, Maxwell Evarts, 150–53, 155–56, 159, 161–63, 165–70, 173–75, 178–80, 182, 184, 186, 192–94, 200–01, 208–09, 212–14, 217, 219, 221–25, 232, 256n, 263–65, 269–71. LT: 151, 153, 155–56, 162–63, 166–68, 173–75, 179, 184, 193–94, 209, 212–14, 219, 222–24, 232, 263–65, 270–71. LF: 150–52, 167, 174, 179–80, 209, 222–23, 264
Pick, Ethel M. Witkowsky, 4, 84, 231
Pinter, Harold, 169
"Poodle," 268–71
Porter, Cole, 264
Preston, James M., 217
Preston, May Wilson, 119, 121, 131, 188, 205
*Prince of Washington Square, The*, 173
"Prohibition Blues," 57
Putnam, Nina Wilcox, 142–44
"Quadroon," 249
Rascoe, Burton, 20, 104, 155, 159, 198–99, 201, 204, 207, 209–10, 216, 219–20, 222, 226, 250–52. LT: 198–99, 204, 207, 210, 216, 219–20, 226, 250–51
Rascoe, Hazel, 159, 198, 201, 204, 210, 216, 220, 251
*Real Dope, The*, 118–21, 123n, 166
*Redbook*, 122
Reinhardt, Max, 191
Rennie, James, 197–200
"Reporter's Diary, A," 115
Reulbach, Ed, 48
Reynolds, Paul, 115
"Rhythm," 193
Rice, Florence ("Floncy"), 200, 210, 245, 279, 283
Rice, Gitz, 241
Rice, Grantland, 106, 114, 160–61, 172–73, 177, 194–95, 197–98, 200–01, 205, 208, 216–17, 221, 232, 241, 245–47, 284, 249–50, 261, 277. LT: 208
Rice, Katherine Hollis ("Kate"), 160–61, 172–73, 177, 186, 194–95, 197–98, 200, 205, 208, 210–11, 216–17, 220, 221, 232, 237, 242, 244–45, 261, 277, 278–79, 283–84, 287. LT: 161, 208, 210–11
Rickard, George L. ("Tex"), 134–37
Rinehart, Mary Roberts, 143
Ring, Blanche, 38, 183
*Ring around Max: The Correspondence of Ring Lardner and Max Perkins*, 150n
*Ring Lardner*, 66n, 175n, 216n, 227n, 238n, 244n, 258n, 261n, 269, 281n
*Ring W. Lardner: A Descriptive Bibliography*, 1n, 57n
"Ring's Side," 220
Rockne, Knute, 248
Rockwell, Bob, 37
Rodgers, Richard, 234
Rogers, Will, 183, 233, 235, 238
*Round Up*, 217–19, 221–23, 226–27, 265
*Ruby Robert*, 201
Runyon, Damon, 135
Russell, Lillian, 20, 44n
Ruth, George Herman ("Babe"), 15, 141, 277
Samuels, Art, 171, 178

Sarre, Gordon, 158, 164
Sarre, Ruth Shepley, 158, 163–65
*Saturday Evening Post*, 11n, 39, 104, 112–13, 115, 117–21, 125, 127, 131–32, 134, 137, 140, 142–44, 156, 160, 194, 204, 207, 244, 255, 263–64, 268–71, 273
*Save Me the Waltz*, 265
*Say It with Oil: A Few Remarks about Wives*, 143
Schulte, Frank, 44, 46, 48–49, 59, 104, 258
Schultz, Adolph ("Germany"), 250
Schwendler, Grace, 36
*Scribner's Magazine*, 271
Scribner's, Charles, Publishing Co., 109, 150, 165–67, 179, 192–94, 208, 216, 222–23, 226, 256n, 264–65
Seavey, Wilma, 286. LT: 286
Seeman, William, 172
*Sentimental Songbook, The*, 19, 20n
Serre, Amy, 234
Sharkey, Jack, 206, 210
Shaw, George Bernard, 278
Shaw, Tom, 275
Sheckard, Jimmy, 106, 120n, 257
Sheehan, John, 234
Sherwood, Robert, 213, 215
Shy, Gus, 234
Siddall, Jean, 239
Siddall, John, 132, 209–10
*Side of Paradise, This*, 167, 170, 175
Skolsky, Sidney, 257
*Smiles*, 228, 235
Smith, Al, 161
Smith, Frank, 14–15, 97–98
Smith College, 1, 10, 13, 15, 24, 29, 31–32, 47

*Some Champions*, 4n, 11n, 137n, 244n
"Some Like Them Cold," 140, 142, 152, 157
Sousa, John Philip, 249
South Bend *Times*, 1, 3
Speare, Dorothy, 277
Spink, Charles, 66, 68, 71, 75, 77–79
*Sporting News, The*, 1n, 66, 75–79, 86
Stagg, Amos Alonzo, 109, 111, 207
Stallings, Laurence, 170, 201
Stephens, Jim, 15
Stevens, Willie, 204
Stewart, Donald Ogden, 168
Stevenson, Robert Louis, 55
Stone, George, 14–15
Stoner, Lucy, 187
*Story of a Wonder Man, The*, 208, 265
Sugrue, Thomas, 274n, 278
Sullivan, Ted, 106
Swain, Tom, 52
*Sweet Singer of Michigan*, 20n
Swift, Jonathan, 279n
Swope, Herbert Bayard, 127, 129, 155, 171, 205, 278
*Symptoms of Being 35*, 132, 166, 169
Taft, William Howard, 31, 34
Tashman, Lilyan, 279
"Taxidea Americana," 169
Taylor, Bert Leston ("B.L.T."), 22n, 52, 114
Taylor, Dean, 92
Taylor, Laurette, 120, 128, 130
*Tender Is the Night*, 223n, 224–25
Tewson, William Orton, 126, 173–74. LT: 173–74
Thackeray, William Makepeace, 172
"There Are Smiles," 218–19
Thomas, Norman, 261–62
"Three Without, Doubled," 112–13
*Time*, 250–53

Tinker, Joe, 50
Tobin, Anne Lardner, 20–21, 23–24, 36, 38, 40, 50–52, 59, 61, 64–65, 71, 73–74, 84–85, 90, 98–99, 102, 186, 242, 274, 283
Tobin, Richard G., 20–21, 23, 36, 38, 40, 51, 56, 64–65, 73, 92, 99, 102
Tobin, Richard Lardner, 55–57, 59, 61, 90, 98, 242–44, 248–50, 255, 259, 272–78, 282. LT: 242–43, 249–50, 255, 272–78, 282–83
*Toro, El*, 146
Torrence, Florence Abbott, 36, 55, 68, 93, 97, 100–01, 107, 123–25, 129, 132–34, 196, 260. LT: 36, 107, 124–25, 132–34
Torrence, Paull, 55, 100–01, 107, 124–25, 129, 132–34. LT: 124–25, 132–34
Treadwell, Sophie, 213
*Treat 'Em Rough*, 117–19, 123n, 166
Trevor, Norman, 192
Tunney, Gene, 203–06, 278
Twain, Mark, 20n, 133n–134n, 165
Tynan, Brandon, 189
Underwood, Oscar W., 163
Van, Billy, 274
Vance, Clarence ("Dazzy"), 275
Van Doren, Carl, 113, 222
*Vanity Fair* (novel), 172
*Vanity Fair* (magazine), 159n, 170, 171n, 172, 177
Van Loan, Charles, 104, 204, 207
Van Loon, Hendrik W., 222, 273
Van Nuys, Rev., 89–90, 93
Veeck, William Sr., 102
Veeck, William Jr., 102n
*Veeck—As in Wreck*, 102n

*Vegetable, The*, 212, 226
Vereen, Lizabeth ("Myrt"), 221, 242, 244–45, 278–80, 284. LT: 278–80
Vidmer, Richards, 274, 278
Waddell, Rube, 14
Walker, June, 171, 177, 213, 215
Walker, Stanley, 255
Walsh, Ed, 15
Waner, Paul, 234
Ward, John, 39n
Weaver, John V.A., 178n, 206
"Weekly Letter, Ring Lardner's," 123, 204, 210
*What of It?*, 166, 169, 173, 226, 265
*What Price Glory*, 170–71
Wheeler, John Neville, 119–20, 122, 179, 192, 212, 217. LT: 119–20, 122
"What Is the American Language," 178n
White, Guy Harris ("Doc"), 15, 57, 66, 89–90, 94
Wiley, Hugh, 146
Willhite, Captain, 68–69, 71, 75, 84, 92
Williams, Bert, 81–82, 102, 141–42. LF: 82–83
Williams, Churchill, 134–36. LT: 134–36. LF: 136
Williams, James, 15
Williams, Henry Lane ("Doc"), 111
Wills, Harry, 206
Wilson, Edmund, 153, 159, 211
Wilson, Harry Leon, 134n
Winchell, Walter, 225
Witkowsky, Ethel. See Pick, Ethel Witkowski.
Wolfe, Thomas, 150
*Woman of the Year*, 109
Women's rights, 72, 86
Women's Suffrage Amendment, 72
Wood, Barry, 246n, 247, 249
Woollcott, Alexander, 155, 199

Woodruff, Harvey T., 155
Wright, Harold Bell, 157
Wylie, Elinor, 222
Wynn, Ed, 148n, 183
Yost, Fielding, 247–48, 259
*You Know Me Al*, 109, 117, 130, 166, 174, 256n
*You Know Me Al* (comic strip), 162, 172
Youmans, Vincent, 182n, 190–91, 228–30, 241
*Young Immigrunts, The*, 125–28, 141, 166, 169, 173

*Young Visiters, The*, 126, 173
Yust, Walter, 178–79.
   LT: 178–79
Ziegfeld, Florenz, 82, 182–83, 190–91, 200, 205, 217, 228–31, 235
Ziegfeld's Follies, 82, 141, 146n, 148n, 149, 160, 172, 176n, 178, 183n, 191n
"Zone of Quiet," 172, 179